FTCE
GENERAL KNOWLEDGE

By: Sharon A. Wynne, M.S.

XAMonline, INC.
Boston

To obtain permission(s) to use the material from this work for any purpose including workshops or seminars, please submit a written request to:

XAMonline, Inc.
21 Orient Avenue
Melrose, MA 02176
Toll Free 1-800-301-4647
Email: info@xamonline.com
Web: www.xamonline.com
Fax: 1-617-583-5552

Library of Congress Cataloging-in-Publication Data

Wynne, Sharon A.
     FTCE General Knowledge / Sharon A. Wynne
     ISBN 978-1-60787-533-8
     1. FTCE General Knowledge
     2. Study Guides
     3. FTCE
     4. Teachers' Certification & Licensure
     5. Careers

Disclaimer:

The opinions expressed in this publication are the sole works of XAMonline and were created independently from the National Education Association, Educational Testing Service, or any State Department of Education, National Evaluation Systems or other testing affiliates.

Between the time of publication and printing, state specific standards as well as testing formats and website information may change and therefore would not be included in part or in whole within this product. Sample test questions are developed by XAMonline and reflect content similar to that on real tests; however, they are not former test questions. XAMonline assembles content that aligns with state standards but makes no claims nor guarantees teacher candidates a passing score. Numerical scores are determined by testing companies such as NES or ETS and then are compared with individual state standards. A passing score varies from state to state.

Printed in the United States of America   œ-1

FTCE General Knowledge
ISBN: 978-1-60787-533-8

Table of Contents

FTCE
GENERAL KNOWLEDGE

DOMAIN II
MATHEMATICS 63

COMPETENCY 4
KNOWLEDGE OF NUMBER SENSE, CONCEPTS, AND OPERATIONS 67

COMPETENCY 5
KNOWLEDGE OF GEOMETRY AND MEASUREMENT 88

COMPETENCY 6
KNOWLEDGE OF ALGEBRAIC THINKING AND THE COORDINATE PLANE 114

COMPETENCY 7
KNOWLEDGE OF PROBABILITY, STATISTICS, AND DATA INTERPRETATION 145

DOMAIN III
READING SKILLS

COMPETENCY 8
KNOWLEDGE OF KEY IDEAS AND DETAILS BASED ON TEXT SELECTIONS

COMPETENCY 9
KNOWLEDGE OF CRAFT AND STRUCTURE BASED ON TEXT SELECTIONS

COMPETENCY 10
KNOWLEDGE OF THE INTEGRATION OF INFORMATION AND IDEAS BASED ON TEXT SELECTIONS

DOMAIN IV

SAMPLE TEST

FTCE
GENERAL KNOWLEDGE

SECTION 1
ABOUT XAMONLINE

XAMonline—A Specialty Teacher Certification Company

Created in 1996, XAMonline was the first company to publish study guides for state-specific teacher certification examinations. Founder Sharon Wynne found it frustrating that materials were not available for teacher certification preparation and decided to create the first single, state-specific guide. XAMonline has grown into a company of over 1,800 contributors and writers and offers over 300 titles for the entire PRAXIS series and every state examination. No matter what state you plan on teaching in, XAMonline has a unique teacher certification study guide just for you.

XAMonline—Value and Innovation

We are committed to providing value and innovation. Our print-on-demand technology allows us to be the first in the market to reflect changes in test standards and user feedback as they occur. Our guides are written by experienced teachers who are experts in their fields. And our content reflects the highest standards of quality. Comprehensive practice tests with varied levels of rigor means that your study experience will closely match the actual in-test experience.

To date, XAMonline has helped nearly 600,000 teachers pass their certification or licensing exams. Our commitment to preparation exceeds simply providing the proper material for study—it extends to helping teachers **gain mastery** of the subject matter, giving them the **tools** to become the most effective classroom leaders possible, and ushering today's students toward a **successful future**.

SECTION 2
ABOUT THIS STUDY GUIDE

Purpose of This Guide

Is there a little voice inside of you saying, "Am I ready?" Our goal is to replace that little voice and remove all doubt with a new voice that says, "I AM READY. **Bring it on!**" by offering the highest quality of teacher certification study guides.

Organization of Content

You can be confident when you buy our guide that it contains the information you need to study for the specific test you are taking. Only XAMonline presents custom content and sample tests along with **focus statements**, the deepest-level details of the skills that are unique to the exam.

Title and field number of test

→Each exam has its own name and number. XAMonline's guides are written to give you the content you need to know for the specific exam you are taking.

Domains

→These are broad subject areas into which the exam is divided. XAMonline's guides provide detailed coverage of all the domains that are included in the exam.

Competencies

→These are the major content areas found on the exam. XAMonline's guides are written to cover all the competencies found in the test frameworks developed for the exam.

Skills

→These are standards that are unique to the exam and represent the subcategories of the competencies. XAMonline's guides are written to address every specific skill required to pass the exam.

Focus statements

→These are examples and interpretations of the skills. You find them in parentheses within the statement of a skill, and they are explained the study guide. They detail the range, type, and level of content that appear in the exam questions. **Only XAMonline's guides drill down to this level.**

How Do We Compare with Our Competitors?

XAMonline—drills down to the focus statement level
CliffsNotes and REA—organized at the skill level
Kaplan—provides only links to content
MoMedia—content not specific to the state test

Each competency is divided into manageable sections that cover the specific skill areas. Explanations are easy to understand and thorough. You'll find that every test answer contains a rationale so if you need a refresher or further review after taking the test, you'll know exactly to which section you must return.

How to Use This Book

Our informal polls show that most people begin studying up to eight weeks prior to the test date, so start early. Then ask yourself some questions: How much do you really know? Are you coming to the test straight from your teacher-education program or are you having to review subjects you haven't considered in ten years? Either way, take a **diagnostic or assessment test** first. Also, spend time on sample tests so that you become accustomed to the way the actual test will appear.

This guide comes with an online diagnostic test of 30 questions found online at *www.XAMonline.com*. It is a little boot camp to get you up for the task and reveal things about your compendium of knowledge in general. Although this guide is structured to follow the order of the test, you are not required to study in that order. By finding a time-management and study plan that fits your life you will be more effective. The results of your diagnostic or self-assessment test can be a guide for how to manage your time and point you toward an area that needs more attention.

After taking the diagnostic exam, fill out the **Personalized Study Plan** page at the beginning of each chapter. Review the competencies and skills covered in that chapter and check the boxes that apply to your study needs. If there are sections you already know you can skip, check the "skip it" box. Taking this step will give you a study plan for each chapter.

Week	Activity
8 weeks prior to test	Take a diagnostic test found at www.XAMonline.com
7 weeks prior to test	Build your Personalized Study Plan for each chapter. Check the "skip it" box for sections you feel you are already strong in. ✗ SKIP IT ☐
6-3 weeks prior to test	For each of these four weeks, choose a content area to study. You don't have to go in the order of the book. It may be that you start with the content that needs the most review. Alternately, you may want to ease yourself into plan by starting with the most familiar material.
2 weeks prior to test	Take the sample test, score it, and create a review plan for the final week before the test.
1 week prior to test	Following your plan (which will likely be aligned with the areas that need the most review) go back and study the sections that align with the questions you may have gotten wrong. Then go back and study the sections related to the questions you answered correctly. If need be, create flashcards and drill yourself on any area that you makes you anxious.

SECTION 3
ABOUT THE FTCE GENERAL KNOWLEDGE EXAM

What Is the FTCE General Knowledge Exam?

The FTCE General Knowledge exam is meant to assess mastery of the basic skills required to teach in Florida public schools. It covers the general areas of reading, writing, and mathematics and is administered by Pearson Education on behalf of the Florida Department of Education.

Often **your own state's requirements** determine whether or not you should take any particular test. The most reliable source of information regarding this is your state's Department of Education. This resource should have a complete list of testing centers and dates. Test dates vary by subject area and not all test dates necessarily include your particular test, so be sure to check carefully.

If you are in a teacher-education program, check with the Education Department or the Certification Officer for specific information for testing and testing time-lines. The Certification Office should have most of the information you need.

If you choose an alternative route to certification you can either rely on our website at *www.XAMonline.com* or on the resources provided by an alternative certi-fication program. Many states now have specific agencies devoted to alternative certification and there are some national organizations as well, for example:

National Association for Alternative Certification
http://www.alt-teachercert.org/index.asp

Interpreting Test Results

Contrary to what you may have heard, the results of the FTCE General Knowledge test are not based on time. More accurately, you will be scored on the raw number of points you earn in relation to the raw number of points available. Each question is worth one raw point. It is likely to your benefit to complete as many questions in the time allotted, but it will not necessarily work to your advantage if you hurry through the test.

Follow the guidelines provided by Pearson for interpreting your score. The website offers a sample test score sheet and clearly explains how/whether the scores are scaled and what to expect if you have an essay portion on your test.

Scores are available approximately 6 weeks after the test date and scores will be sent to you and your chosen institution(s).

What's on the Test?

The FTCE General Knowledge exam consists of four subtests, each of which can be taken as separate exams or all at once. Each subtest consists of multiple-choice questions and there is also 1 essay. The breakdown of the questions is as follows:

Domain	Approximate Number of Questions	Approximate Percentage of the test	Testing Time
I: English Language Skills	40 multiple choice	32%	40 minutes
II: Mathematics	45 multiple choice	36%	1 hour, 40 minutes
III: Reading	40 multiple choice	32%	40 minutes
IV: Essay	1 essay	–	50 minutes

Question Types

You're probably thinking, enough already, I want to study! Indulge us a little longer while we explain that there is actually more than one type of multiple-choice question. You can thank us later after you realize how well prepared you are for your exam.

1. **Complete the Statement.** The name says it all. In this question type you'll be asked to choose the correct completion of a given statement. For example:

    > The Dolch Basic Sight Words consist of a relatively short list of words that children should be able to:
    >
    > A. Sound out
    >
    > B. Know the meaning of
    >
    > C. Recognize on sight
    >
    > D. Use in a sentence

    The correct answer is C. In order to check your answer, test out the statement by adding the choices to the end of it.

2. **Which of the Following.** One way to test your answer choice for this type of question is to replace the phrase "which of the following" with your selection. Use this example:

> **Which of the following words is one of the twelve most frequently used in children's reading texts?**
>
> A. There
>
> B. This
>
> C. The
>
> D. An

Don't look! Test your answer. _____ is one of the twelve most frequently used in children's reading texts. Did you guess C? Then you guessed correctly.

3. **Roman Numeral Choices.** This question type is used when there is more than one possible correct answer. For example:

> **Which of the following two arguments accurately supports the use of cooperative learning as an effective method of instruction?**
> I.   Cooperative learning groups facilitate healthy competition between individuals in the group.
> II. Cooperative learning groups allow academic achievers to carry or cover for academic underachievers.
> III. Cooperative learning groups make each student in the group accountable for the success of the group.
> IV. Cooperative learning groups make it possible for students to reward other group members for achieving.
>
> A. I and II
>
> B. II and III
>
> C. I and III
>
> D. III and IV

Notice that the question states there are **two** possible answers. It's best to read all the possibilities first before looking at the answer choices. In this case, the correct answer is D.

4. **Negative Questions.** This type of question contains words such as "not," "least," and "except." Each correct answer will be the statement that does **not** fit the situation described in the question. Such as:

> **Multicultural education is not**
>
> A. An idea or concept
>
> B. A "tack-on" to the school curriculum
>
> C. An educational reform movement
>
> D. A process

Think to yourself that the statement could be anything but the correct answer. This question form is more open to interpretation than other types, so read carefully and don't forget that you're answering a negative statement.

5. **Questions That Include Graphs, Tables, or Reading Passages.** As always, read the question carefully. It likely asks for a very specific answer and not a broad interpretation of the visual. Here is a simple (though not statistically accurate) example of a graph question:

> **In the following graph, in how many years did more men take the FTCE exam than women?**
>
>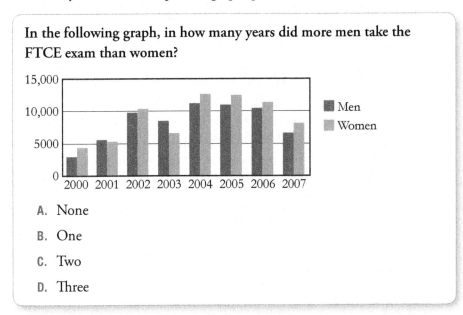
>
> A. None
>
> B. One
>
> C. Two
>
> D. Three

It may help you to simply circle the two years that answer the question. Make sure you've read the question thoroughly and once you've made your determination, double check your work. The correct answer is C.

SECTION 4
HELPFUL HINTS

Study Tips

1. **You are what you eat.** Certain foods aid the learning process by releasing natural memory enhancers called CCKs (cholecystokinin) composed of tryptophan, choline, and phenylalanine. All of these chemicals enhance the neurotransmitters associated with memory and certain foods release memory enhancing chemicals. A light meal or snacks of one of the following foods fall into this category:

   - Milk
   - Rice
   - Eggs
   - Fish
   - Nuts and seeds
   - Oats
   - Turkey

   The better the connections, the more you comprehend!

2. **See the forest for the trees.** In other words, get the concept before you look at the details. One way to do this is to take notes as you read, paraphrasing or summarizing in your own words. Putting the concept in terms that are comfortable and familiar may increase retention.

3. **Question authority.** Ask why, why, why? Pull apart written material paragraph by paragraph and don't forget the captions under the illustrations. For example, if a heading reads *Stream Erosion* put it in the form of a question (Why do streams erode? What is stream erosion?) then find the answer within the material. If you train your mind to think in this manner you will learn more and prepare yourself for answering test questions.

4. **Play mind games.** Using your brain for reading or puzzles keeps it flexible. Even with a limited amount of time your brain can take in data (much like a computer) and store it for later use. In ten minutes you can: read two paragraphs (at least), quiz yourself with flash cards, or review notes. Even if you don't fully understand something on the first pass, your mind stores it for recall, which is why frequent reading or review increases chances of retention and comprehension.

5. **Get pointed in the right direction.** Use arrows to point to important passages or pieces of information. It's easier to read than a page full of yellow highlights. Highlighting can be used sparingly, but add an arrow to the margin to call attention to it.

6. **The pen is mightier than the sword.** Learn to take great notes. A by-product of our modern culture is that we have grown accustomed to getting our information in short doses. We've subconsciously trained ourselves to assimilate information into neat little packages. Messy notes fragment the flow of information. Your notes can be much clearer with proper formatting. *The Cornell Method* is one such format. This method was popularized in *How to Study in College*, Ninth Edition, by Walter Pauk. You can benefit from the method without purchasing an additional book by simply looking up the method online. Below is a sample of how *The Cornell Method* can be adapted for use with this guide.

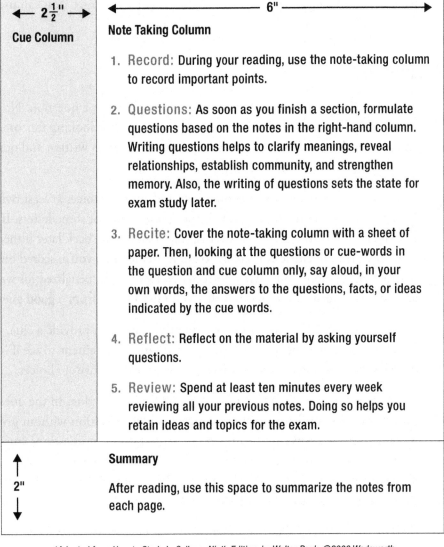

← 2½" →

Cue Column

←————————— 6" —————————→

Note Taking Column

1. Record: During your reading, use the note-taking column to record important points.

2. Questions: As soon as you finish a section, formulate questions based on the notes in the right-hand column. Writing questions helps to clarify meanings, reveal relationships, establish community, and strengthen memory. Also, the writing of questions sets the state for exam study later.

3. Recite: Cover the note-taking column with a sheet of paper. Then, looking at the questions or cue-words in the question and cue column only, say aloud, in your own words, the answers to the questions, facts, or ideas indicated by the cue words.

4. Reflect: Reflect on the material by asking yourself questions.

5. Review: Spend at least ten minutes every week reviewing all your previous notes. Doing so helps you retain ideas and topics for the exam.

↑
2"
↓

Summary

After reading, use this space to summarize the notes from each page.

*Adapted from How to Study in College, Ninth Edition, by Walter Pauk, ©2008 Wadsworth

7. **Place yourself in exile and set the mood.** Set aside a particular place and time to study that best suits your personal needs and biorhythms. If you're a night person, burn the midnight oil. If you're a morning person set yourself up with some coffee and get to it. Make your study time and place as free from distraction as possible and surround yourself with what you need, be it silence or music. Studies have shown that music can aid in concentration, absorption, and retrieval of information. Not all music, though. Classical music is said to work best

The proctor will write the start time where it can be seen and then, later, provide the time remaining, typically fifteen minutes before the end of the test.

8. **Check your budget.** You should at least review all the content material before your test, but allocate the most amount of time to the areas that need the most refreshing. It sounds obvious, but it's easy to forget. You can use the study rubric above to balance your study budget.

Testing Tips

1. **Get smart, play dumb.** Sometimes a question is just a question. No one is out to trick you, so don't assume that the test writer is looking for something other than what was asked. Stick to the question as written and don't overanalyze.

2. **Do a double take.** Read test questions and answer choices at least twice because it's easy to miss something, to transpose a word or some letters. If you have no idea what the correct answer is, skip it and come back later if there's time. If you're still clueless, it's okay to guess. Remember, you're scored on the number of questions you answer correctly and you're not penalized for wrong answers. The worst case scenario is that you miss a point from a good guess.

3. **Turn it on its ear.** The syntax of a question can often provide a clue, so make things interesting and turn the question into a statement to see if it changes the meaning or relates better (or worse) to the answer choices.

4. **Get out your magnifying glass.** Look for hidden clues in the questions because it's difficult to write a multiple-choice question without giving away part of the answer in the options presented. In most questions you can readily eliminate one or two potential answers, increasing your chances of answering correctly to 50/50, which will help out if you've skipped a question and gone back to it (see tip #2).

5. **Call it intuition.** Often your first instinct is correct. If you've been studying the content you've likely absorbed something and have subconsciously retained the knowledge. On questions you're not sure about trust your instincts because a first impression is usually correct.

6. **Graffiti.** Sometimes it's a good idea to mark your answers directly on the test booklet and go back to fill in the optical scan sheet later. You don't get extra points for perfectly blackened ovals. If you choose to manage your test this way, be sure not to mismark your answers when you transcribe to the scan sheet.

7. **Become a clock-watcher.** You have a set amount of time to answer the questions. Don't get bogged down laboring over a question you're not sure about when there are ten others you could answer more readily. If you choose to follow the advice of tip #6, be sure you leave time near the end to go back and fill in the scan sheet.

Do the Drill

No matter how prepared you feel it's sometimes a good idea to apply Murphy's Law. So the following tips might seem silly, mundane, or obvious, but we're including them anyway.

1. **Remember, you are what you eat, so bring a snack.** Choose from the list of energizing foods that appear earlier in the introduction.

2. **You're not too sexy for your test.** Wear comfortable clothes. You'll be distracted if your belt is too tight or if you're too cold or too hot.

3. **Lie to yourself.** Even if you think you're a prompt person, pretend you're not and leave plenty of time to get to the testing center. Map it out ahead of time and do a dry run if you have to. There's no need to add road rage to your list of anxieties.

4. **Bring sharp number 2 pencils.** It may seem impossible to forget this need from your school days, but you might. And make sure the erasers are intact, too.

5. **No ticket, no test.** Bring your admission ticket as well as **two** forms of identification, including one with a picture and signature. You will not be admitted to the test without these things.

6. **You can't take it with you.** Leave any study aids, dictionaries, note-books, computers, and the like at home. Certain tests **do** allow a scientific or four-function calculator, so check ahead of time to see if your test does.

7. **Prepare for the desert.** Any time spent on a bathroom break **cannot** be made up later, so use your judgment on the amount you eat or drink.

8. **Quiet, Please!** Keeping your own time is a good idea, but not with a timepiece that has a loud ticker. If you use a watch, take it off and place it nearby but not so that it distracts you. And **silence your cell phone**.

To the best of our ability, we have compiled the content you need to know in this book and in the accompanying online resources. The rest is up to you. You can use the study and testing tips or you can follow your own methods. Either way, you can be confident that there aren't any missing pieces of information and there shouldn't be any surprises in the content on the test.

If you have questions about test fees, registration, electronic testing, or other content verification issues please visit *www.fl.nesinc.org*.

Good luck!

Sharon Wynne
Founder, XAMonline

DOMAIN I
ENGLISH LANGUAGE SKILLS

PERSONALIZED STUDY PLAN

COMPETENCY 1
KNOWLEDGE OF LANGUAGE STRUCTURE

Evaluate correct placement of modifiers.

Phrases that are not placed near the word they modify often result in misplaced modifiers. Phrases that do not relate to the subject being modified result in dangling modifiers.

Error:	*Weighing the options carefully, a decision was made regarding the punishment of the convicted murderer.*
Problem:	Who is weighing the options? No one capable of weighing is named in the sentence; thus, the participle phrase *weighing the options carefully* dangles. This problem can be corrected by adding a subject to the sentence who is capable of doing the action.
Correction:	*Weighing the options carefully, the judge made a decision regarding the punishment of the convicted murderer.*
Error:	*Returning to my favorite watering hole brought back many fond memories.*
Problem:	The person who returned is never indicated, and the participle phrase dangles. This problem can be corrected by creating a dependent clause from the modifying phrase.
Correction:	*When I returned to my favorite watering hole, many fond memories came back to me.*
Error:	*One damaged house stood only to remind townspeople of the hurricane.*
Problem:	The placement of the modifier *only* suggests that the sole reason the house remained was to serve as a reminder. The misplaced modifier creates ambiguity. This problem can be corrected by moving the modifier.
Correction:	*Only one damaged house stood, reminding townspeople of the hurricane.*

Phrases that are not placed near the word they modify often result in misplaced modifiers. Phrases that do not relate to the subject being modified result in dangling modifiers.

Error:	*Recovered from the five-mile hike, the obstacle course was a piece of cake for the Boy Scout troop.*
Problem:	The obstacle course is not recovered from the five-mile hike, so the modifying phrase must be placed closer to the word that it modifies, troop.
Correction:	*The obstacle course was a piece of cake for the Boy Scout troop, which had just recovered from a five-mile hike.*

Practice Exercise: Misplaced and Dangling Modifiers

Choose the sentence that expresses the thought most clearly and effectively and that has no error in structure.

1. A. Attempting to remove the dog from the well, the paramedic tripped and fell in also.

    B. As the paramedic attempted to remove the dog from the well, he tripped and fell in also.

    C. The paramedic tripped and fell in also attempting to remove the dog from the well.

2. A. To save the wounded child, a powerful explosion ripped through the operating room as the doctors worked.

    B. In the operating room, as the wounded child was being saved, a powerful explosion ripped through.

    C. To save the wounded child, the doctors worked as an explosion ripped through the operating room.

3. A. One hot July morning, a herd of giraffes screamed wildly in the jungle next to the wildlife habitat.

    B. One hot July morning, a herd of giraffes screamed in the jungle wildly next to the wildlife habitat.

    C. One hot July morning, a herd of giraffes screamed in the jungle next to the wildlife habitat, wildly.

4. A. Looking through the file cabinets in the office, the photographs of the crime scene revealed a new suspect in the investigation.

    B. Looking through the file cabinets in the office, the detective discovered photographs of the crime scene that revealed a new suspect in the investigation.

    C. A new suspect in the investigation was revealed in photographs of the crime scene that were discovered while looking through the file cabinets in the office.

5. A. In the grand ballroom, the tables and chairs were moved off to the side to make room for the dancers.

    B. To make room for the dancers, the tables and chairs were moved off to the side in the grand ballroom.

    C. To make room for the dancers, we moved the tables and chairs off to the side in the grand ballroom.

Answer Key: Misplaced and Dangling Modifiers

1. B

   Option B corrects the dangling participle *attempting to remove the dog from the well* by creating a dependent clause introducing the main clause. In Option A, the introductory participle phrase *Attempting . . . well* does not refer to a paramedic, the subject of the main clause. The word *also* in Option C incorrectly implies that the paramedic was doing something besides trying to remove the dog.

2. C

   Option C corrects the dangling modifier *to save the wounded child by* adding the concrete clause *doctors worked*. Option A infers that an explosion was working to save the wounded child. Option B never tells who was trying to save the wounded child.

3. A

   Option A places the adverb *wildly* closest to the verb *screamed*, which it modifies. Both Options B and C incorrectly place the modifier away from the verb.

4. B

   Option B corrects the modifier *looking* through the file cabinets in the *office* by placing it next to the detective who is doing the looking. Option A sounds as though the photographs were looking; Option C has no one doing the looking.

5. C

   Option C corrects the dangling modifier *to make room for the dancers* by adding the concrete subject *we moved the tables and chairs off to the side*. In Option A, the modifier *to make room for the dancers* has no word to refer to in the sentence. Option B puts the modifier *to make room* at the beginning of the sentence, but it still has no referent.

SKILL 1.2 **Apply knowledge of parallelism, including parallel expressions for parallel ideas.**

Faulty Parallelism

Two or more elements stated in a single clause should be expressed with the same (or parallel) structure. For example, the elements could all be adjectives, verb forms, or nouns. When the elements are verbs, the tense should be consistent.

> *Two or more elements stated in a single clause should be expressed with the same (or parallel) structure.*

Error: *She needed to be beautiful, successful, and have fame.*

Problem: The phrase *to be* is followed by two different structures: *beautiful* and *successful* are adjectives, and *have fame* is a verb phrase.

Correction: *She needed to be <u>beautiful</u>, <u>successful</u>, and <u>famous</u>.*
        (adjective) (adjective)   (adjective)

   -OR-
   She needed <u>beauty</u>, <u>success</u>, and <u>fame</u>.
        (noun) (noun)   (noun)

Error: *I plan either to sell my car during the spring or during the summer.*

Problem: Paired conjunctions (also called *correlative conjunctions,* such as *either-or, both-and, neither-nor,* and *not only-but also*) need to be followed with similar structures. In the sentence above, *either* is followed by *to sell my car during the spring*, while *or* is followed only by the phrase *during the summer*.

Correction: *I plan to sell my car during either the spring or the summer.*

Error: *The president pledged to lower taxes and that he would cut spending to lower the national debt.*

Problem: Since the phrase *to lower taxes* follows the verb *pledged*, a similar structure of *to* is needed with the phrase *cut spending*.

Correction: *The president pledged to lower taxes and to cut spending to lower the national debt.*
   -OR-
   The president pledged that he would lower taxes and cut spending to lower the national debt.

Practice Exercise: Parallelism

Choose the sentence that expresses the thought most clearly and effectively and that has no error in structure.

1. A. Andy found the family tree, researches the Irish descendents, and he was compiling a book for everyone to read.

   B. Andy found the family tree, researched the Irish descendents, and compiled a book for everyone to read.

   C. Andy finds the family tree, researched the Irish descendents, and compiled a book for everyone to read.

2. A. In the last ten years, computer technology has advanced so quickly that workers have had difficulty keeping up with the new equipment and the increased number of functions.

   B. Computer technology has advanced so quickly in the last ten years that workers have had difficulty to keep up with the new equipment and by increasing number of functions.

   C. In the last ten years, computer technology has advanced so quickly that workers have had difficulty keeping up with the new equipment, and the number of functions are increasing.

3. A. The State History Museum contains exhibits honoring famous residents, a video presentation about the state's history, an art gallery featuring paintings and sculptures, and they even display a replica of the State House.

   B. The State History Museum contains exhibits honoring famous residents, a video presentation about the state's history, an art gallery featuring paintings and sculptures, and even a replica of the State House.

   C. The State History Museum contains exhibits honoring famous residents, a video presentation about the state's history, an art gallery featuring paintings and sculptures, and there is even a replica of the State House.

4. A. Either the criminal justice students had too much practical experience and limited academic preparation or too much academic preparation and little practical experience.

   B. The criminal justice students either had too much practical experience and limited academic preparation or too much academic preparation and little practical experience.

   C. The criminal justice students either had too much practical experience and limited academic preparation or had too much academic preparation and limited practical experience.

5. A. Filmmaking is an arduous process in which the producer hires the cast and crew, chooses locations for filming, supervises the actual production, and guides the editing.

   B. Because it is an arduous process, filmmaking requires the producer to hire a cast and crew and choose locations, supervise the actual production, and guides the editing.

   C. Filmmaking is an arduous process in which the producer hires the cast and crew, chooses locations for filming, supervises the actual production, and guided the editing.

Answer Key: Parallelism

1. B

    Option B uses parallelism by presenting a series of past tense verbs: *found, researched, and compiled*. Option A interrupts the parallel structure of past tense verbs: found, researches, and *he was compiling*. Option C uses present tense verbs and then shifts to past tense: *finds, researched, and compiled.*

2. A

    Option A uses parallel structure at the end of the sentence: *the new equipment and the increased number of functions*. Option B creates a faulty structure with *to keep up with the new equipment and by increasing number of functions*. Option C creates faulty parallelism with *the number of functions are increasing* (and uses a plural verb for a singular noun).

3. B

    Option B uses parallelism by presenting a series of noun phrases acting as objects of the verb *contains*. Option A interrupts that parallelism by inserting *they even display*, and Option C interrupts the parallelism with the addition of *there is*.

4. C

    In the either-or parallel construction, look for a balance on both sides. Option C creates that balanced parallel structure: *either had ... or had*. Options A and B do not create the balance. In Option A, the structure is *Either the criminal justice students ... or too much*. In Option B, the structure is *either had ... or too much.*

5. A

    Option A uses parallelism by presenting a series of verbs with objects: *hires the cast and crew, chooses locations for filming, supervises the actual production, and guides the editing*. The structure of Option B incorrectly suggests that filmmaking chooses locations, supervises the actual production, and guides the editing. Option C interrupts the series of present tense verbs by inserting the participle *guided* instead of the present tense *guides.*

SKILL 1.3 **Apply knowledge of a variety of effective structures** *(e.g., recognizing fragments, comma splices, run-on sentences, syntax errors)*.

Fragments occur when word groups standing alone are missing either a subject or a verb, or when word groups containing a subject and verb and standing alone are made dependent through the use of subordinating conjunctions or relative pronouns.

Error: *The teacher waiting for the class to complete the assignment.*

Problem: This sentence is not complete because an *-ing* word alone does not function as a verb. When a helping verb is added (for example, *was waiting*), the fragment becomes a sentence.

Correction: *The teacher was waiting for the class to complete the assignment.*

Error: *Until the last toy was removed from the floor.*

Problem: Words such as *until, because, although, when,* and *if* make a clause dependent and thus incapable of standing alone. An independent clause must be added to make the sentence complete.

Correction: *Until the last toy was removed from the floor, the kids could not go outside to play.*

Error: *The city will close the public library. Because of a shortage of funds.*

Problem: The problem is the same as above. The dependent clause must be joined to the independent clause.

Correction: *The city will close the public library because of a shortage of funds.*

Error: *Anyone planning to go on the trip should bring the necessary items. Such as a backpack, boots, a canteen, and bug spray.*

Problem: The second word group is a phrase and cannot stand alone because there is neither a subject nor a verb. The fragment can be corrected by adding the phrase to the sentence.

Correction: *Anyone planning to go on the trip should bring the necessary items, such as a backpack, boots, a canteen, and bug spray.*

Practice Exercise: Fragments

Choose the option that corrects an error in the underlined portion(s). If no error exists, choose "No change is necessary."

1. Despite the lack of funds in the <u>budget it</u> was necessary to rebuild the roads that were damaged from the recent floods.

   A. budget: it

   B. budget, it

   C. budget; it

   D. No change is necessary

2. After determining that the fire was caused by faulty <u>wiring, the</u> building inspector said the construction company should be fined.

   A. wiring. The

   B. wiring the

   C. wiring; the

   D. No change is necessary

3. Many years after buying a grand <u>piano Henry</u> decided he'd rather play the violin instead.

   A. piano: Henry

   B. piano, Henry

   C. piano; Henry

   D. No change is necessary

4. Computers are being used more and more <u>frequently. because</u> of their capacity to store information.

   A. frequently because

   B. frequently, because

   C. frequently; because

   D. No change is necessary

5. Doug washed the floors <u>every day. to</u> keep them clean for the guests.

   A. every day to

   B. every day, to

   C. every day; to

   D. No change is necessary

Answer Key: Fragments

1. B

   The clause that begins with *despite* is introductory and must be separated from the clause that follows by a comma. Option A is incorrect because a colon is used to set off a list or to emphasize what follows. In Option B, a comma incorrectly suggests that the two clauses are dependent.

2. D

   A comma correctly separates the dependent clause *After...wiring* at the beginning of the sentence from the independent clause that follows. Option A incorrectly breaks the two clauses into separate sentences, Option B omits the comma, and Option C incorrectly suggests that the phrase is an independent clause.

3. B

   The phrase *Henry decided... instead* must be joined to the independent clause. Option A incorrectly puts a colon before *Henry decided*, and Option C incorrectly separates the phrase as if it were an independent clause.

4. A

   The second clause *because... information* is dependent and must be joined to the first independent clause. Option B is incorrect because, as the dependent clause comes at the end of the sentence rather than at the beginning, a comma is not necessary. In Option C, a semicolon incorrectly suggests that the two clauses are independent.

5. A

   The second clause to *keep...guests* is dependent and must be joined to the first independent clause. Option B is incorrect because, as the dependent clause comes at the end of the sentence rather than at the beginning, a comma is not necessary. In Option C, a semicolon incorrectly suggests that the two clauses are independent.

Comma splices appear when a comma joins two sentences. Fused sentences appear when two sentences are run together with no punctuation at all.

Comma splices appear when a comma joins two sentences. **Fused sentences** appear when two sentences are run together with no punctuation at all.

Error: *Dr. Sanders is a brilliant scientist, his research on genetic disorders won him a Nobel Prize.*

Problem: A comma alone cannot join two independent clauses (complete sentences). The two clauses can be joined by a semicolon, joined by a conjunction and a comma, or separated into two sentences by a period.

Correction: *Dr. Sanders is a brilliant scientist; his research on genetic disorders won him a Nobel Prize.*
-OR-
Dr. Sanders is a brilliant scientist. His research on genetic disorders won him a Nobel Prize.
-OR-
Dr. Sanders is a brilliant scientist, and his research on genetic disorders won him a Nobel Prize.

Error: *Paradise Island is noted for its beaches they are long, sandy, and beautiful.*

Problem: The first independent clause ends with the word *beaches*, and the second independent clause is fused to the first. The fused sentence error can be corrected in several ways:

1. One clause may be made dependent on another by inserting a subordinating conjunction or a relative pronoun.

2. A semicolon may be used to combine two equally important ideas.

3. The two independent clauses may be separated by a period.

4. The independent clauses may be joined by a conjunction and a comma.

Correction: *Paradise Island is noted for its beaches, which are long, sandy, and beautiful.*
-OR-
Paradise Island is noted for its beaches; they are long, sandy, and beautiful.
-OR -
Paradise Island is noted for its beaches. They are long, sandy, and beautiful.

-OR-

Paradise Island is noted for its beaches, for they are long, sandy, and beautiful.

Error: *The number of hotels has increased, however, the number of visitors has grown also.*

Problem: The first sentence ends with the word *increased,* and a comma is not strong enough to connect it to the second sentence. The adverbial transition *however* does not function in the same way as a coordinating conjunction and cannot be used with commas to link two sentences. Several different corrections are available.

Correction: *The number of hotels has increased; however, the number of visitors has grown also.*

[Two separate but closely related sentences are created with the use of the semicolon.]

-OR-

The number of hotels has increased. However, the number of visitors has grown also.

[Two separate sentences are created.]

-OR-

Although the number of hotels has increased, the number of visitors has grown also.

[One idea is made subordinate to the other and separated with a comma.]

-OR-

The number of hotels has increased, but the number of visitors has grown also.

[The comma before the coordinating conjunction *but* is appropriate. The adverbial transition *however* does not function in the same way as the coordinating conjunction *but.*]

Practice Exercise: Fused Sentences and Comma Splices

Choose the option that corrects an error in the underlined portion(s). If no error exists, choose "No change is necessary."

1. Scientists are excited at the ability to clone a sheep: however, it is not yet known if the same can be done to humans.

   A. sheep, however,
   B. sheep. However,
   C. sheep, however;
   D. No change is necessary

2. Because of the rising cost of college tuition the federal government now offers special financial assistance, such as loans, to students.

   A. tuition, the
   B. tuition; the
   C. such as loans
   D. No change is necessary

3. As the number of homeless people continues to rise, the major cities such as New York and Chicago, are now investing millions of dollars in low-income housing.

   A. rise. The major cities
   B. rise; the major cities
   C. New York and Chicago
   D. No change is necessary

4. Unlike in the 1950s, in most households the husband and wife work full-time to make ends meet in many different career fields.

   A. the 1950s; in most
   B. the 1950s in most
   C. ends meet, in many
   D. No change is necessary

Answer Key: Fused Sentences and Comma Splices

1. B

   Option B correctly separates two independent clauses. The comma in Option A after the word *sheep* creates a run-on sentence. The semicolon in Option C does not separate the two clauses because it occurs at an inappropriate point.

2. A

   The comma in Option A correctly separates the independent clause and the dependent clause. The semicolon in Option B is incorrect because one of the clauses is independent. Option C requires a comma to prevent a run-on sentence.

3. C

   Option C is correct because a comma creates a run-on sentence. Option A is incorrect because the first clause is dependent. The semicolon in Option B incorrectly separates the dependent clause from the independent clause.

4. D

   Option D correctly separates the two clauses with a comma. Option A incorrectly uses a semicolon to separate the clauses. The lack of a comma in Option B creates a run-on sentence. Option C puts a comma in an inappropriate place.

Determine patterns of organization in a written passage *(i.e., modes of rhetoric).*

The **organization** of written work includes two main elements: the **order** in which writers choose to present the different parts of the discussion or argument, and the **relationships** they construct between these parts.

There are many different ways to order a series of ideas, but all aim to lead readers along desired paths to writers' main ideas. These are some of the ways in which paragraphs may be effectively organized:

> *Written ideas must be presented in a **logical order** so that readers can follow the information easily and quickly.*

- **Sequence of events:** In this type of organization, the details are presented in the order in which they have occurred. Paragraphs that describe a process or procedure, give directions, or outline a given period of time (such as a day or a month) are often arranged as a sequence of events, or CHRONOLOGICALLY.

> **CHRONOLOGICALLY:** organized as a sequence of events

- **Statement support:** In this type of organization, the main idea is stated and the rest of the paragraph explains or proves this idea. This type of organization is also referred to as **relative importance**. There are four ways in which statement support can be organized: most-to-least, least-to-most, most-least-most, and least-most-least.

- **Comparison-contrast:** The compare-contrast pattern is used to present the differences between or similarities among two or more ideas, actions, events, or things. Usually the topic sentence describes the basic relationship between the ideas or items and the rest of the paragraph explains this relationship.

- **Classification:** In this type of organization, the paragraph presents grouped information about a topic. The topic sentence usually states the general category, and the rest of the sentences show how various elements of the category have (or to what extent they deviate from) a common base.

- **Cause and effect:** This pattern describes how two or more events are connected. The main sentence usually states the primary cause(s), the primary effect(s), and the general way in which they are connected. The rest of the sentences explain the connection in more detail.

- **Spatial/place:** In this type of organization, descriptions are organized according to the location of items in relation to each other and to the larger context. The orderly arrangement guides readers' eyes as they mentally envision the scene or place being described.

TRANSITIONS: words that signal relationships between ideas

Even if the sentences that make up a given paragraph or passage are arranged in logical order, the document as a whole can still seem choppy and the various ideas disconnected. TRANSITIONS, words that signal relationships between ideas, can improve the flow of a document.

Transitions build each sentence on the ideas in the last, and link clearly to the preceding one.

Transitions can help achieve a clear and effective presentation of information by establishing connections between sentences, paragraphs, and whole sections of a document. By signaling how to organize, interpret, and react to information, transitions allow writers to effectively and elegantly explain their ideas.

COMMON TRANSITIONS	
Similarity	also, in the same way, just as … so too, likewise, similarly
Exception/Contrast	but, however, in spite of, on the one hand … on the other hand, nevertheless, nonetheless, notwithstanding, in contrast, on the contrary, still, yet, although
Sequence/Order	first, second, third, … next, then, finally, until
Time	after, afterward, at last, before, currently, during, earlier, immediately, later, meanwhile, now, presently, recently, simultaneously, since, subsequently, then
Example	for example, for instance, namely, specifically, to illustrate
Emphasis	even, indeed, in fact, of course, truly
Place/Position	above, adjacent, below, beyond, here, in front, in back, nearby, there
Cause and Effect	accordingly, consequently, hence, so, therefore, thus, as a result, because, consequently, hence, if … then, in short
Additional Support or Evidence	additionally, again, also, and, as well, besides, equally important, further, furthermore, in addition, moreover, then
Conclusion/ Summary	finally, in a word, in brief, in conclusion, in the end, in the final analysis, on the whole, thus, to conclude, to summarize, in sum, in summary
Statement Support	most important, more significant, primarily, most essential
Addition	again, also, and, besides, equally important, finally, furthermore, in addition, last, likewise, moreover, too
Clarification	actually, clearly, evidently, in fact, in other words, obviously, of course, indeed

The following example shows good logical order and transitions. The transition words are highlighted in **bold**.

No one really knows how Valentine's Day started. There are several legends, **however**, which are often told. The **first** attributes Valentine's Day to a Christian priest who lived in Rome during the third century under the rule of Emperor Claudius. Rome was at war and, **apparently,** Claudius felt that married men did not fight as well as bachelors. **Consequently**, Claudius banned marriage for the duration of the war. **But** Valentinus, the priest, risked his life to marry couples secretly in violation of Claudius' law. The **second** legend is **even more** romantic. In this story, Valentinus is a prisoner, having been condemned to death for refusing to worship pagan deities. **While** in jail, he fell in love with his jailer's daughter, who happened to be blind. Daily, he prayed for her sight to return and miraculously, it did. On February 14, the day that he was condemned to die, he was allowed to write the young woman a note. **In this farewell letter**, he promised eternal love and signed at the bottom of the page the now famous words, "Your Valentine."

Practice Exercises: Word Choice I

Choose the sentence that expresses the thought most clearly and most effectively and that is structurally correct in grammar and syntax.

1. A. The movie was three hours in length, featuring interesting characters, and moved at a fast pace.

    B. The movie was three hours long, featured interesting characters, and moved at a fast pace.

    C. Moving at a fast pace, the movie was three hours long and featured interesting characters.

2. A. We were so offended by the waiter's demeanor that we left the restaurant without paying the check.

    B. The waiter's demeanor offended us so much that without paying the check, we left the restaurant.

    C. We left the restaurant without paying the check because we were offended by the waiter's demeanor.

3. A. In today's society, information about our lives is provided to us by computers.

    B. We rely on computers in today's society to provide us information about our lives.

    C. In today's society, we rely on computers to provide us with information about our lives.

4. A. Folding the sides of the tent carefully, Jack made sure to be quiet so none of the other campers would be woken up.

    B. So none of the other campers would be woken up, Jack made sure to be quiet by folding the sides of the tent carefully.

    C. Folding the sides of the tent carefully, so none of the other campers would wake up, Jack made sure to be quiet.

Answer Key: Word Choice I

1. B
2. A

3. C
4. A

Practice Exercises: Word Choice II

Choose the most effective word or phrase within the context suggested by the sentence(s).

1. The six hundred employees of General Electric were _____ by the company due to budgetary cutbacks.

    A. released

    B. terminated

    C. downsized

2. The force of the tornado _____ the many residents of the town of Russell, Kansas.

    A. intimidated

    B. repulsed

    C. frightened

3. Even though his new car was easy to drive, Fred _____ to walk to work every day because he liked the exercise.

    A. needed

    B. preferred

    C. considered

4. June's parents were very upset over the school board's decision to suspend her from Adams High for a week. Before they filed a lawsuit against the board, they _____ with a lawyer to help them make a decision.

    A. consulted

    B. debated

    C. conversed

5. The race car driver's _____ in handling the automobile was a key factor in his victory.

    A. patience

    B. precision

    C. determination

6. After impressing the judges with her talent and charm, the beauty contestant _____ more popularity by singing an aria from *La Bohème*.

    A. captured

    B. scored

    C. gained

7. The stained-glass window was _____ when a large brick flew through it during the riot.

    A. damaged

    B. cracked

    C. shattered

8. The class didn't know what happened to the professor until the principal _____ why the professor quit his job.

    A. informed

    B. discovered

    C. explained

Practice Exercises: Word Choice II

Choose the most effective word or phrase within the context suggested by the sentence(s).

9. The giant penthouse at the top of the building enables the billionaire industrialist _____ the citizens on the street.

    A. to view from above

    B. the chance to see

    C. to glance at

10. Sally's parents _____ her to attend the dance after she promised to return by midnight.

    A. prohibited

    B. permitted

    C. asked

Answer Key: Word Choice II

1.	C	5.	B	9.	C
2.	C	6.	C	10.	B
3.	B	7.	C		
4.	A	8.	C		

COMPETENCY 2
KNOWLEDGE OF VOCABULARY APPLICATION

> **SKILL 2.1** **Determine the meaning of unknown words, multiple-meaning words, and phrases in context.**

Practice Exercise: Word Choice III

Choose the most effective word or phrase within the context suggested by the sentences.

1. The defendant was accused of _____ money from his employer.

   A. stealing

   B. borrowing

   C. robbing

2. Many tourists are attracted to the Paradise Island because of its _____ climate.

   A. friendly

   B. peaceful

   C. balmy

3. The woman was angry because the tomato juice left an _____ stain on her brand new carpet.

   A. unsightly

   B. ugly

   C. unpleasant

4. After disobeying orders, the army private was _____ by his superior officer.

   A. degraded

   B. attacked

   C. reprimanded

5. Sharon's critical evaluation of the student's book report left the student feeling _____, which caused him to want to quit school.

   A. surprised

   B. depressed

   C. discouraged

Practice Exercise: Word Choice III (cont.)

Choose the most effective word or phrase within the context suggested by the sentences.

6. The life-saving medication created by the scientist had a _____ impact on further developments in the treatment of cancer.

   A. beneficial

   B. fortunate

   C. miraculous

7. *The Phantom of the Opera* is one of Andrew Lloyd Webber's most successful musicals, largely because of its _____ themes.

   A. romantic

   B. melodramatic

   C. imaginary

8. The massive Fourth of July fireworks display _____ the partygoers with lots of colored lights and sound.

   A. disgusted

   B. captivated

   C. captured

9. Many of the residents of Grand Forks, North Dakota, were forced to _____ their homes because of the flood.

   A. escape

   B. evacuate

   C. exit

Answer Key: Word Choice III

1.	A		6.	A
2.	C		7.	A
3.	A		8.	B
4.	C		9.	B
5.	C			

SKILL 2.2 Determine and select the correct use of commonly confused words, misused words, and phrases.

HOMONYM: a word that is spelled and pronounced just like another word but that has a different meaning

Students frequently encounter problems with homonyms. Strictly speaking, a **HOMONYM** is a word that is spelled and pronounced just like another word but that has a different meaning. An example is the word *mean*, which can be a verb—"to intend"; an adjective—"unkind"; or a noun or adjective—"average."

HOMOGRAPHS are words that share the same spelling, regardless of how they are pronounced, and have different meanings. Words that are pronounced the same but may or may not have different spellings are called HOMOPHONES. HETERONYMS (sometimes called heterophones) share the same spelling but have different pronunciations and meanings. For example, the homographs *desert* (abandon) and *desert* (arid region) are heteronyms (pronounced differently), but the homographs *mean* (intend) and *mean* (average) are homophones because they are pronounced the same (they are also homonyms).

CAPITONYMS are words that are spelled the same but have different meanings when capitalized. A capitonym may or may not have different pronunciations; for example, *polish* (to make shiny) and *Polish* (from Poland).

Some of the most troubling homophones are those that are spelled differently but that sound the same. Some examples include its (third person singular neuter pronoun) and *it's* ("it is"); *there* (a location), *their* (third person plural pronoun), and *they're* ("they are"). Another common example is *to*, *too*, and *two*.

Some homonyms/homographs are particularly intriguing. *Fluke*, for instance, refers to a fish, a flatworm, the end parts of an anchor, the fins on a whale's tail, and a stroke of luck.

HOMOGRAPHS: words that share the same spelling, regardless of how they are pronounced, and have different meanings

HOMOPHONES: words that are pronounced the same but may or may not have different spellings

HETERONYMS: (sometimes called heterophones) share the same spelling but have different pronunciations and meanings

CAPITONYMS: words that are spelled the same but have different meanings when capitalized

COMMONLY MISUSED WORDS		
Accept is a verb meaning "to receive or to tolerate"	**Except** is usually a preposition meaning "excluding"	**Except** is also a verb meaning "to exclude"
Advice is a noun meaning "recommendation"	**Advise** is a verb meaning "to recommend"	
Affect is usually a verb meaning "to influence"	**Effect** is usually a noun meaning "result." Effect can also be a verb meaning "to bring about"	
An **allusion** is "an indirect reference"	An **illusion** is "a misconception or false impression"	
Add is a verb meaning "to put together"	**Ad** is a noun that is the abbreviation for the word "advertisement"	
Ain't is a common, nonstandard contraction for the contraction "aren't"		

Continued on next page

Allot is a verb meaning "to distribute"	**A lot** can act as an adverb that means "often," "to a great degree," or "a large quantity" (example: She shops a lot)	
Allowed is used as an adjective that means "permitted"	**Aloud** is an adverb that means "audible"	
Bare is an adjective that means "naked" or "exposed"; it can also indicate a minimum	As a noun, **bear** is a large mammal	As a verb, **bear** means "to carry a heavy burden"
Capital refers to a city; capitol to "a building where lawmakers meet"	**Capital** also refers to "wealth" or "resources"	
A **chord** is a noun that refers to "a group of musical notes"	**Cord** is a noun meaning "rope" or "a long electrical line"	
Compliment is a noun meaning "a praising or flattering remark"	**Complement** is a noun that means "something that completes or makes perfect"	
Climactic is derived from climax, "the point of greatest intensity in a series or progression of events"	**Climatic** is derived from climate; it refers to meteorological conditions	
Discreet is an adjective that means "tactful" or "diplomatic"	**Discrete** is an adjective that means "separate" or "distinct"	
Dye is a noun or verb used to indicate artificial coloring	**Die** is a verb that means "to pass away"	**Die** is also a noun that means "a cube-shaped game piece"
Effect is a noun that means "outcome"	**Affect** is a verb that means "to influence"	
Elicit is a verb meaning "to bring out" or "to evoke"	**Illicit** is an adjective meaning "unlawful"	
Emigrate means "to leave one country or region to settle in another"	**Immigrate** means "to enter another country and reside there"	
Gorilla is a noun meaning "a large great ape"	**Guerrilla** is "a member of a band of irregular soldiers"	
Hoard is a verb that means "to accumulate" or "store up"	A **horde** is "a large group"	

Continued on next page

✗

Lead is a verb that means "to guide" or "to serve as the head of"; it is also a noun that is a type of metal		
Medal is a noun that means "an award that is strung round the neck"	**Meddle** is a verb that means "to involve oneself in a matter without right or invitation"	**Metal** is "an element such as silver or gold"; **mettle** is a noun meaning "toughness" or "courage"
Morning is a noun indicating "the time between midnight and midday"	**Mourning** is a verb or noun pertaining to "the period of grieving after a death"	
Past is a noun meaning "a time before now" (past, present, and future)	**Passed** is the past tense of the verb "to pass"	
Piece is a noun meaning "portion"	**Peace** is a noun meaning "the opposite of war, or serenity"	
Peak is a noun meaning "the tip" or "height to reach the highest point"	**Peek** is a verb that means "to take a brief look"	**Pique** is a verb meaning "to incite or raise interest"
Principal is a noun most commonly meaning "the chief or head"; it also means "a capital sum of money"	**Principle** is a noun meaning "a basic truth or law"	
Rite is a noun meaning "a special ceremony"	**Right** is an adjective meaning "correct" or "the opposite direction of left"	**Write** is a verb meaning "to compose in writing"
Than is a conjunction used in comparisons (that pizza is more *than* I can eat)	**Then** is an adverb denoting time (Tom laughed, and *then* we recognized him)	To remember the correct use of these words, you can use the following: **Than** is used to *compare*; both words have the letter a in them **Then** tells *when*; both words are spelled the same, except for the first letter
There is an adverb specifying place (Sylvia is lying *there* unconscious); it is also an expletive (*there* are two plums left)	**Their** is a possessive pronoun	**They're** is a contraction of "they are": Fred and Jane finally washed *their* car, or *they're* later than usual today.
To is a preposition	**Too** is an adverb	**Two** is a number
Your is a possessive pronoun	**You're** is a contraction of "you are"	

To help students master these difficult distinctions, practice using these words in sentences. Context is useful in understanding differences, and drill is necessary to overcome misuses.

Denotative and Connotative Language

To effectively teach language, it is necessary to understand that as human beings acquire language, they realize that words have denotative and connotative meanings. Generally, denotative words point to things, and connotative words deal with the mental suggestions that the words convey.

*The word **skunk** has a denotative meaning if the speaker intends the word to identify the animal. **Skunk** has connotative meaning depending upon the tone of delivery, the socially acceptable attitudes about the animal, and the speaker's personal feelings about the animal.*

PROBLEM PHRASES	
CORRECT	**INCORRECT**
Supposed to	Suppose to
Used to	Use to
Toward	Towards
Anyway	Anyways
Couldn't care less	Could care less
For all intents and purposes	For all intensive purposes
Come to see me	Come and see me
En route	In route
Regardless	Irregardless
Second, Third	Secondly, Thirdly

Other Confusing Words

Lie is an intransitive verb meaning to recline or rest on a surface. Its principal parts are *lie, lay,* and *lain.* **Lay** is a transitive verb meaning "to put or place." Its principal parts are *lay, laid,* and *laid.*

Birds lay eggs.

I lie down for bed around 10 p.m.

Set is a transitive verb meaning "to put or to place." Its principal parts are *set, set,* and *set.* **Sit** is an intransitive verb meaning "to be seated." Its principal parts are *sit, sat,* and *sat.*

> I set my backpack down near the front door.
>
> They sat in the park until the sun went down.

Among is a preposition to be used with three or more items. **Between** is to be used with two items.

> Between you and me, I cannot tell the difference among those three Johnson sisters.

As is a subordinating conjunction used to introduce a subordinating clause. **Like** is a preposition and is followed by a noun or a noun phrase.

> As I walked to the lab, I realized that the recent experiment findings were much like those we found last year.

Can is a verb that means "to be able." **May** is a verb that means "to have permission." "Can" and "may" are only interchangeable in cases of possibility.

> I can lift 250 pounds.
>
> May I go to Alex's house?

<table><tr><td>SKILL 2.3</td><td>**Determine diction and tone appropriate to a given audience.**</td></tr></table>

Tailoring language for a particular audience is an important skill. Writing intended to be read by a business associate will surely sound different from writing intended to be read by a young child. Not only are the vocabularies different, but the formality of the discourse needs to be adjusted as well.

Determining the appropriate language for a particular audience hinges on two things: word choice and formality/informality.

Determining the appropriate language for a particular audience hinges on two things: word choice and formality/informality. The most formal language does not use contractions or slang. The most informal language will probably feature a more casual use of common sayings and anecdotes. Formal language will use longer sentences and will not sound like a conversation. The most informal language will use shorter sentences—not necessarily simple sentences, but shorter constructions—and may sound like a conversation.

In both formal and informal writing, there exists a TONE—the writer's attitude toward the material and/or reader. The tone may be playful, formal, intimate,

TONE: the author's attitude toward the material and/or the reader

angry, serious, ironic, outraged, baffled, tender, serene, depressed, and so on. Both the subject matter and the audience dictate the overall tone of a piece of writing. Tone is also related to the actual words that make up the document, since we attach affective meanings, called **connotations**, to words. Gaining conscious control over language makes it possible for the writer to use language appropriately in various situations. By evoking the proper responses from readers/listeners, the writer can prompt them to take action.

The following questions are an excellent way to help the writer choose the appropriate audience and tone for a piece of writing.

1. Who is your audience? (friend, teacher, businessperson, etc.)

2. How much does this person know about you and/or your topic?

3. What is your purpose? (to prove an argument, to persuade, to amuse, to register a complaint, to ask for a raise, etc.)

4. What emotions do you have about the topic? (nervousness, happiness, confidence, anger, sadness, no feelings at all)

5. What emotions do you want to register with your audience? (anger, nervousness, happiness, boredom, interest)

6. What persona do you need to create in order to achieve your purpose?

7. What choice of language is best suited to achieving your purpose with your particular subject? (slang, friendly but respectful, formal)

8. What emotional quality do you want to transmit to achieve your purpose? (matter-of-fact, informative, authoritative, inquisitive, sympathetic, or angry) To what degree do you want to express this tone?

COMPETENCY 3
KNOWLEDGE OF STANDARD ENGLISH CONVENTIONS

SKILL 3.1	Determine and select standard verb forms.

Past Tense and Past Participles

Both regular and irregular verbs must appear in their standard forms for each tense.

Note: The -ed or -d ending is added to regular verbs in the past tense and to past participles.

REGULAR VERB FORMS		
Infinitive	Past Tense	Past Participle
bake	baked	baked

IRREGULAR VERB FORMS		
Infinitive	Past Tense	Past Participle
be	was/were	been
become	became	become
break	broke	broken
bring	brought	brought
choose	chose	chosen
come	came	come
do	did	done
draw	drew	drawn

Continued on next page

Infinitive	Past Tense	Past Participle
eat	ate	eaten
fall	fell	fallen
forget	forgot	forgotten
freeze	froze	frozen
give	gave	given
go	went	gone
grow	grew	grown
have/has	had	had
hide	hid	hidden
know	knew	known
lay	laid	laid
lie	lay	lain
ride	rode	ridden
rise	rose	risen
run	ran	run
see	saw	seen
steal	stole	stolen
take	took	taken
tell	told	told
throw	threw	thrown
wear	wore	worn
write	wrote	written

Error: *She should have went to her doctor's appointment at the scheduled time.*

Problem: The past participle of the verb *to go* is *gone. Went* expresses the simple past tense.

Correction: *She should have gone to her doctor's appointment at the scheduled time.*

Error: *My train is suppose to arrive before two o'clock.*

Problem: The verb following *train* is a present tense passive construction, which requires the present tense verb *to be* and the past participle.

Correction: *My train is supposed to arrive before two o'clock.*

Error: *Linda should of known that the car wouldn't start after leaving it out in the cold all night.*

Problem: *Should of* is a nonstandard expression. *Of* is not a verb.

Correction: *Linda should have known that the car wouldn't start after leaving it out in the cold all night.*

Practice Exercise: Standard Verb Forms

Choose the option that corrects an error in the underlined portion(s). If no error exists, choose "No change is necessary."

1. My professor <u>had knew</u> all along that we would pass his course.

   A. know

   B. had known

   C. knowing

   D. No change is necessary

2. Kevin was asked to erase the vulgar words he <u>had wrote</u>.

   A. writes

   B. has write

   C. had written

   D. No change is necessary

Practice Exercise: Standard Verb Forms (cont.)

Choose the option that corrects an error in the underlined portion(s). If no error exists, choose "No change is necessary."

3. Melanie <u>had forget</u> to tell her parents that she left the cat in the closet.

    A. had forgotten
    B. forgot
    C. forget
    D. No change is necessary

4. Craig always <u>leave</u> the house a mess when his parents aren't there.

    A. left
    B. leaves
    C. leaving
    D. No change is necessary

5. The store manager accused Kathy of <u>having stole</u> more than five hundred dollars from the safe.

    A. has stolen
    B. having stolen
    C. stole
    D. No change is necessary

Answer Key: Standard Verb Forms

1. B

    Option B is correct because the past participle needs the helping verb *had*. Option A is incorrect because *it* is in the infinitive tense. Option C incorrectly uses the present participle.

2. C

    Option C is correct because the past participle follows the helping verb *had*. Option A uses the verb in the present tense. Option B is an incorrect use of the verb.

3. A

    Option A is correct because the past participle uses the helping verb *had*. Option B uses the wrong form of the verb. Option C uses the wrong form of the verb.

4. B

    Option B correctly uses the present tense of the verb. Option A uses the verb in an incorrect way. Option C uses the verb without a helping verb such as *is*.

5. B

    Option B is correct because it is the past participle. Options A and C use the verb incorrectly.

SKILL 3.2 Determine and select inappropriate shifts in verb tense.

Unless a change in time is required, verb tenses within a sentence must consistently refer to the same time period.

Error: *Despite the increased number of students attending school this year, overall attendance is higher last year at the sporting events.*

Problem: The verb *is* represents an inconsistent shift to the present tense when the action refers to a past occurrence.

Correction: *Despite the increased number of students attending school this year, overall attendance was higher last year at sporting events.*

Error: *My friend Lou, who just competed in the marathon, ran since he was twelve years old.*

Problem: Because Lou continues to run, the present perfect tense is needed.

Correction: *My friend Lou, who just competed in the marathon, has run since he was twelve years old.*

Error: *The mayor congratulated Wallace Mangham, who renovates the city hall last year.*

Problem: Although the speaker is talking in the present, the action of renovating the city hall was in the past.

Correction: *The mayor congratulated Wallace Mangham, who renovated the city hall last year.*

Practice Exercise: Shifts in Tense

Choose the option that corrects an error in the underlined portion(s). If no error exists, choose "No change is necessary."

1. After we <u>washed</u> the fruit that had <u>growing</u> in the garden, we knew there <u>was</u> a store that would buy the fruit.

   A. washing

   B. grown

   C. is

   D. No change is necessary

2. The tourists <u>used</u> to visit the Atlantic City boardwalk whenever they <u>vacationed</u> during the summer. Unfortunately, their numbers have <u>diminished</u> every year.

   A. use

   B. vacation

   C. diminish

   D. No change is necessary

3. When the temperature <u>drops</u> to below thirty-two degrees Fahrenheit, the water on the lake <u>freezes</u>, which <u>allowed</u> children to skate across it.

   A. dropped

   B. froze

   C. allows

   D. No change is necessary

4. The artists were <u>hired</u> to <u>create</u> a monument that would pay tribute to the men who were <u>killed</u> in World War II.

   A. hiring

   B. created

   C. killing

   D. No change is necessary

5. Emergency medical personnel rushed to the scene of the shooting, where many injured people <u>waiting</u> for treatment.

   A. wait

   B. waited

   C. waits

   D. No change is necessary

Answer Key: Shifts in Tense

1. **B**

   The past participle *grown* is needed instead of *growing*, which is the progressive tense. Option A is incorrect because the past participle *washed* takes the *-ed*. Option C incorrectly replaces the past participle *was* with the present tense *is*.

2. **D**

   Option A is incorrect because *use* is the present tense. Option B incorrectly uses the present tense of the verb *vacation*. Option C incorrectly uses the present tense *diminish* instead of the past tense *diminished*.

3. **C**

   The present tense *allows* is necessary in the context of the sentence. Option A is incorrect because *dropped* is a past participle. Option B is incorrect because *froze* is also a past participle.

4. **D**

   Option A is incorrect because *hiring* is the present tense. Option B is incorrect because *created* is a past participle. In Option C, *killing* does not fit into the context of the sentence.

5. **B**

   In Option B, *waited* corresponds with the past tense *rushed*. In Option A, *wait* is incorrect because it is present tense. In Option C, *waits* is incorrect because the noun *people* is plural and requires the singular form of the verb.

SKILL 3.3 Determine and select agreement between subject and verb.

A verb must correspond in the singular or plural form with the simple subject; interfering elements do not affect it.

> **Note:** A simple subject is never found in a prepositional phrase (that is, a phrase beginning with a word such as *of, by, over, through, until*).

PRESENT TENSE VERB FORM		
	Singular	**Plural**
1st person (talking about oneself)	I do	We do
2nd person (talking to another)	You do	You do
3rd person (talking about someone or something)	He does She does It does	They do

Error:	*Sally, as well as her sister, plan to go into nursing.*
Problem:	The subject of the sentence is *Sally* and does not include the word *sister*. Therefore, the verb must be singular.
Correction:	*Sally, as well as her sister, plans to go into nursing.*

Error:	*There has been many car accidents lately on that street.*
Problem:	The subject *accidents* in this sentence is plural; the verb must be plural also, even though it comes before the subject.
Correction:	*There have been many car accidents lately on that street.*

Error:	*Every one of us have a reason to attend the school musical.*
Problem:	The simple subject is the phrase *every one*, not the *us* in the prepositional phrase. Therefore, the verb must be singular also.
Correction:	*Every one of us has a reason to attend the school musical.*

Error:	*Either the police captain or his officers is going to the convention.*
Problem:	In either/or and neither/nor constructions, the verb agrees with the subject closer to it.
Correction:	*Either the police captain or his officers are going to the convention.*

Practice Exercise: Subject-Verb Agreement

Choose the option that corrects an error in the underlined portion(s). If no error exists, choose "No change is necessary."

1. Every year, the store <u>stays</u> open late while shoppers desperately <u>try</u> to purchase Christmas presents as they <u>prepare</u> for the holiday.

   A. stay

   B. tries

   C. prepared

   D. No change is necessary

2. Paul McCartney, together with George Harrison and Ringo Starr, <u>sing</u> classic Beatles songs on a special greatest-hits CD.

   A. singing

   B. sings

   C. sung

   D. No change is necessary

Practice Exercise: Subject-Verb Agreement (cont.)

Choose the option that corrects an error in the underlined portion(s). If no error exists, choose "No change is necessary."

3. My friend's cocker spaniel, while <u>chasing</u> cats across the street, always <u>manages</u> to <u>knock</u> over the trash cans.

   A. chased

   B. manage

   C. knocks

   D. No change is necessary

4. Some of the ice on the driveway <u>have melted</u>.

   A. having melted

   B. has melted

   C. has melt

   D. No change is necessary

5. Neither the criminal forensics expert nor the DNA blood evidence <u>provide</u> enough support for that verdict.

   A. provides

   B. were providing

   C. are providing

   D. No change is necessary

Answer Key: Subject-Verb Agreement

1. D

   Option D is correct because *store* is third person singular and requires the third person singular verb *stays*. Option B is incorrect because the plural noun *shoppers* requires a plural verb *try*. In Option C, there is no reason to shift to the past tense *prepared*.

2. B

   Option B is correct because the subject, Paul McCartney, is singular and requires the singular verb *sings*. Option A is incorrect because the present participle *singing* does not stand alone as a verb. Option C is incorrect because the past participle *sung* cannot function as the verb in this sentence.

3. D

   Option D is the correct answer because the subject *cocker spaniel* is singular and requires the singular verb *manages*. Options A, B, and C do not work structurally with the sentence.

4. B

   The subject of the sentence is *some*, which requires a third-person, singular verb: *has melted*. Option A incorrectly uses the present participle *having*, which does not act as a helping verb. Option C does not work structurally with the sentence.

5. A

   In Option A, the singular subject *evidence* is closer to the verb and thus requires the singular in the neither/nor construction. Both Options B and C are plural forms with the helping verb and the present participle.

SKILL 3.4 Determine and select agreement between pronoun and antecedent.

A pronoun must correspond to its antecedent in number (singular or plural), person (first, second, or third person), and gender (male, female, or neutral).

PRONOUN SHIFT: a grammatical error in which the author starts a sentence, paragraph, or section of a paper using one particular type of pronoun and then suddenly shifts to another

A pronoun must correspond to its antecedent in number (singular or plural), person (first, second, or third person), and gender (male, female, or neutral). A pronoun must refer clearly to a single word, not to a complete idea.

A **PRONOUN SHIFT** is a grammatical error in which the author starts a sentence, paragraph, or section of a paper using one particular type of pronoun and then suddenly shifts to another. This often confuses the reader.

Error: *A teacher should treat all their students fairly.*

Problem: Because *teacher* is singular, the pronoun referring to it must also be singular. Otherwise, the noun has to be made plural.

Correction: *Teachers should treat all their students fairly.*

Error: *When an actor is rehearsing for a play, it often helps if you can memorize the lines in advance.*

Problem: *Actor* is a third-person word; that is, the writer is talking about the subject. The pronoun *you* is in the second person, which means the writer is talking to the subject.

Correction: *When actors are rehearsing for plays, it helps if they can memorize the lines in advance.*

Error: *The workers in the factory were upset when his or her paychecks didn't arrive on time.*

Problem: *Workers* is a plural form, while *his or her* refers to one person.

Correction: *The workers in the factory were upset when their paychecks didn't arrive on time.*

Error: *The charity auction was highly successful, which pleased everyone.*

Problem: In this sentence, the pronoun *which* refers to the idea of the auction's success. In fact, *which* has no antecedent in the sentence; the word *success* is not stated.

Correction: *Everyone was pleased at the success of the auction.*

Error: *Lana told Melanie that she would like aerobics.*

Problem: The person that *she* refers to is unclear; *she* could be either Lana or Melanie.

Correction: *Lana said that Melanie would like aerobics.*
      -OR-
     Lana told Melanie that she, Melanie, would like aerobics.

Error: *I dislike accounting even though my brother is one.*

Problem: A person's occupation is not the same as a field, and the pronoun *one* is thus incorrect. Note that the word *accountant* is not used in the sentence, so *one* has no antecedent.

Correction: *I dislike accounting even though my brother is an accountant.*

Practice Exercise: Pronoun/Antecedent Agreement

Choose the option that corrects an error in the underlined portion(s). If no error exists, choose "No change is necessary."

1. <u>You</u> can get to Martha's Vineyard by driving from Boston to Woods Hole. Once there, you can travel on a ship, but <u>you</u> may find traveling by <u>airplane</u> to be an exciting experience.

  A. They

  B. visitors

  C. it

  D. No change is necessary

2. Both the city leader and the <u>journalist</u> are worried about the new interstate; <u>she fears the new roadway</u> will destroy precious farmland.

  A. journalist herself

  B. they fear

  C. it

  D. No change is necessary

3. When <u>hunters</u> are looking for deer in <u>the woods</u>, <u>you</u> must remain quiet for long periods of time.

  A. you

  B. it

  C. they

  D. No change is necessary

Practice Exercise: Pronoun/Antecedent Agreement (cont.)

Choose the option that corrects an error in the underlined portion(s). If no error exists, choose "No change is necessary."

4. The strong economy is based on the importance of the citrus industry. **Producing orange juice for most of the country.**

   A. They produce

   B. Who produce

   C. Farmers there produce

   D. No change is necessary

5. Dr. Kennedy told Paul Elliot, <u>his</u> assistant, that <u>he</u> would have to finish grading the tests before going home, no matter how long <u>it</u> took.

   A. their

   B. he, Paul,

   C. they

   D. No change is necessary

Answer Key: Pronoun/Antecedent Agreement

1. D

   Pronouns must be consistent. As *you* is used throughout the sentence, the shift to *visitors* is incorrect. Option A, *They*, is vague and unclear. Option C, *it*, is also unclear.

2. B

   The plural pronoun *they* is necessary to agree with the two nouns *leader* and *journalist*. There is no need for the reflexive pronoun *herself* in Option A. In Option C, *it* is vague.

3. C

   The shift to *you* is unnecessary. The plural pronoun *they* is necessary to agree with the noun *hunters*. The word *it* in Option B is vague; the reader does not know to what the word *it* refers. *It* has no antecedent.

4. C

   The noun *farmers* is needed for clarification because *producing* alone creates a fragment. Option A is incorrect because *they produce* is vague. Option B is incorrect because *who* has no antecedent and creates a fragment.

5. B

   The repetition of the name *Paul* is necessary to clarify who the pronoun *he* refers to. (*He* could be Dr. Kennedy.) Option A is incorrect because the singular pronoun *his* is needed, not the plural pronoun *their*. Option C is incorrect because the pronoun *it* refers to the grading of the tests, not the tests themselves.

SKILL 3.5 Determine and select inappropriate pronoun shifts.

See Skill 3.4

SKILL 3.6 Determine and select clear pronoun references.

Rules for Clearly Identifying Pronoun Reference

Make sure that the antecedent reference is clear and cannot refer to something else

A "distant relative" is a relative pronoun or a relative clause that has been placed too far away from the antecedent to which it refers. It is a common error to place a verb between the relative pronoun and its antecedent.

Error: *Return the books to the library that are overdue.*

Problem: The relative clause *that are overdue* refers to the books and should be placed immediately after the antecedent.

Correction: *Return the books that are overdue to the library.*
-OR-
Return the overdue books to the library.

A pronoun should not refer to adjectives or possessive nouns

Adjectives, nouns, or possessive pronouns should not be used as antecedents. This will create ambiguity in sentences.

Error: *In Todd's letter, he told his mom he'd broken the priceless vase.*

Problem: In this sentence, the pronoun *he* seems to refer to the noun phrase *Todd's letter*, though it is probably meant to refer to the possessive noun *Todd's*.

Correction: *In his letter, Todd told his mom that he had broken the priceless vase.*

A pronoun should not refer to an implied idea

A pronoun must refer to a specific antecedent rather than an implied antecedent. When an antecedent is not stated specifically, the reader has to guess or assume the meaning of a sentence. Pronouns that do not have antecedents are called **EXPLETIVES**. "It" and "there" are the most common expletives, though other pronouns can become expletives as well.

> **EXPLETIVE:** a pronoun that does not have an antecedent

> In informal conversation, expletives allow for casual presentation of ideas without supporting evidence. However, in more formal writing, it is best to be more precise.

Error:	*She said that it is important to floss every day.*
Problem:	The pronoun *it* refers to an implied idea.
Correction:	*She said that flossing every day is important.*

Error:	*Milt and Bette returned the books because they had missing pages.*
Problem:	The pronoun *they* does not refer to the antecedent.
Correction:	*The customers returned the books with missing pages.*

Using Who, That, and Which

Who, whom, and *whose* refer to human beings and can introduce either essential or nonessential clauses. *That* refers to things other than humans and is used to introduce essential clauses. *Which* refers to things other than humans and is used to introduce nonessential clauses.

Error:	*The doctor that performed the surgery said the patient would recover fully.*
Problem:	Since the relative pronoun is referring to a human, *who* should be used.
Correction:	*The doctor who performed the surgery said the patient would recover fully.*

Error:	*That ice cream cone that you just ate looked delicious.*
Problem:	*That* has already been used, so you must use *which* to introduce the next clause, whether it is essential or nonessential.
Correction:	*That ice cream cone, which you just ate, looked delicious.*

SKILL 3.7 Determine and select pronoun case forms (e.g., subjective, objective, possessive).

Pronouns must be in the subjective, objective, or possessive form, according to their function in the sentence.

Pronouns, unlike nouns, change case forms.

PERSONAL PRONOUNS						
	SUBJECTIVE (NOMINATIVE)		POSSESSIVE		OBJECTIVE	
	Singular	Plural	Singular	Plural	Singular	Plural
1st person	I	We	My	Our Ours	Me	Us
2nd person	You	You	Your Yours	Your Yours	You	You
3rd person	He She It	They	His Her/ Hers Its	Their Theirs	Him Her It	Them

RELATIVE PRONOUNS	
Who	Subjective/Nominative
Whom	Objective
Whose	Possessive

Error: *Tom and me have reserved seats for next week's baseball game.*

Problem: The pronoun *me* is the subject of the verb *have reserved* and should be in the subjective form.

Correction: *Tom and I have reserved seats for next week's baseball game.*

Error: *Mr. Green showed all of we students how to make paper hats.*

Problem: The pronoun *we* is the object of the preposition *of*. It should be in the objective form, us.

Correction: *Mr. Green showed all of us students how to make paper hats.*

Error: *Who's coat is this?*

Problem: The interrogative possessive pronoun is *whose*; *who's* is the contraction for *who is*.

Correction: *Whose coat is this?*

Practice Exercise: Pronoun Case

Choose the option that corrects an error in the underlined portion(s). If no error exists, choose "No change is necessary."

1. Even though Sheila and <u>he</u> had planned to be alone at the diner, <u>they</u> were joined by three friends of <u>their's</u> instead.

   A. him

   B. him and her

   C. theirs

   D. No change is necessary

2. Uncle Walter promised to give his car to <u>whomever</u> would guarantee to drive it safely.

   A. whom

   B. whoever

   C. them

   D. No change is necessary

3. Eddie and <u>him</u> gently laid <u>the body</u> on the ground next to <u>the sign</u>.

   A. he

   B. them

   C. it

   D. No change is necessary

4. Mary, <u>who</u> is competing in the chess tournament, is a better player than <u>me</u>.

   A. whose

   B. whom

   C. I

   D. No change is necessary

5. <u>We ourselves</u> have decided not to buy property in that development; however, our friends have already bought <u>themselves</u> some land.

   A. We, ourself,

   B. their selves

   C. their self

   D. No change is necessary

Answer Key: Pronoun Case

1. **C**

   The possessive pronoun *theirs* does not need an apostrophe. Option A is incorrect because the subjective pronoun *he* is needed in this sentence. Option B is incorrect because the subjective pronoun *they*, not the objective pronouns *him* and *her*, is needed.

2. **B**

   The subjective case *whoever*—not the objective case *whomever*—is the subject of the relative clause *whoever would guarantee to drive it safely*. Option A is incorrect because *whom* is an objective pronoun. Option C is incorrect because *car* is singular and takes the pronoun *it*.

3. **A**

   The subjective pronoun *he* is needed as the subject of the verb *laid*. Option B is incorrect because *them* is vague; the noun *body* is needed to clarify *it*. Option C is incorrect because *it* is vague, and the noun *sign* is necessary for clarification.

4. **C**

   The subjective pronoun *I* is needed because the comparison is understood. Option A incorrectly uses the possessive *whose*. Option B is incorrect because the subjective pronoun *who*, and not the objective *whom*, is needed.

5. **D**

   The reflexive pronoun *themselves* refers to the plural *friends*. Option A is incorrect because the plural we requires the reflexive *ourselves*. Option C is incorrect because the possessive pronoun *their* is never joined with either *self* or *selves*.

SKILL 3.8   Evaluate the correct use of adjectives and adverbs.

ADJECTIVES are words that modify or describe nouns or pronouns. Adjectives usually precede the words they modify but not always; for example, an adjective may occur after a linking verb.

ADVERBS are words that modify verbs, adjectives, or other adverbs. They cannot modify nouns. Adverbs answer such questions as how, why, when, where, how much, or how often. Many adverbs are formed by adding *-ly*.

> **ADJECTIVES:** words that modify or describe nouns or pronouns

> **ADVERBS:** words that modify verbs, adjectives, or other adverbs

Many adverbs are formed by adding the suffix –ly to the end of adjectives.

Error: *The birthday cake tasted sweetly.*

Problem: *Tasted* is a linking verb; the modifier that follows should be an adjective, not an adverb.

Correction: *The birthday cake tasted sweet.*

Error: *You have done good with this project.*

Problem: *Good* is an adjective and cannot be used to modify a verb phrase such as *have done.*

Correction: *You have done well with this project.*

Error: *The coach was positive happy about the team's chance of winning.*

Problem: The adjective positive cannot be used to modify another adjective, *happy.* An adverb is needed instead.

Correction: *The coach was positively happy about the team's chance of winning.*

Error: *The fireman acted quick and brave to save the child from the burning building.*

Problem: *Quick* and *brave* are adjectives and cannot be used to describe a verb. Adverbs are needed instead.

Correction: *The fireman acted quickly and bravely to save the child from the burning building.*

Practice Exercise: Adjectives and Adverbs

Choose the option that corrects an error in the underlined portion(s). If no error exists, choose "No change is necessary."

1. Moving <u>quick</u> throughout the house, the burglar <u>removed</u> several priceless antiques before <u>carelessly</u> dropping his wallet.

   A. quickly

   B. remove

   C. careless

   D. No change is necessary

2. The car <u>crashed</u> <u>loudly</u> into the retaining wall before spinning <u>wildly</u> on the sidewalk.

   A. crashes

   B. loudly

   C. wild

   D. No change is necessary

Practice Exercise: Adjectives and Adverbs (cont.)

Choose the option that corrects an error in the underlined portion(s). If no error exists, choose "No change is necessary."

3. The airplane <u>landed</u> safe on the runway after <u>nearly</u> colliding with a helicopter.

   A. land

   B. safely

   C. near

   D. No change is necessary

4. The <u>horribly bad</u> special effects in the movie disappointed us <u>great</u>.

   A. horrible

   B. badly

   C. greatly

   D. No change is necessary

5. The man promised to obey <u>faithfully</u> the rules of the social club.

   A. faithful

   B. faithfulness

   C. faith

   D. No change is necessary

Answer Key: Adjectives and Adverbs

1. A

   The adverb *quickly* is needed to modify *moving*. Option B is incorrect because it uses the wrong form of the verb. Option C is incorrect because the adverb *carelessly*, not the adjective *careless*, is needed before the verb *dropping*.

2. D

   The sentence is correct as it is written. The adverbs *loudly* and *wildly* are needed to modify *crashed* and *spinning*. Option A incorrectly uses the verb *crashes* instead of the participle *crashing*, which acts as an adjective.

3. B

   The adverb *safely* is needed to modify the verb *landed*. Option A is incorrect because *land* is a noun. Option C is incorrect because *near* is an adjective, not an adverb.

4. C

   The adverb *greatly* is needed to modify the verb *disappointed*. Option A is incorrect because *horrible* is an adjective, not an adverb. Option B is incorrect because the adverb *horribly* needs to modify the adjective *bad*.

5. D

   The adverb *faithfully* is the correct modifier of the verb *promised*. Option A is an adjective used to modify nouns. Neither Option B nor Option C, both of which are nouns, is a modifier.

SKILL 3.9 Determine and select appropriate comparative and superlative degree forms.

Comparative and Superlative Forms

COMPARATIVE FORM: used to compare two items

SUPERLATIVE FORM: used to compare more than two items

When comparisons are made, the correct form of the adjective or adverb must be used. The **COMPARATIVE FORM** is used for two items. The **SUPERLATIVE FORM** is used for more than two items.

	Comparative	Superlative
slow	slower	slowest
young	younger	youngest
tall	taller	tallest

With some words, *more* and *most* are used to make comparisons instead of *-er* and *-est*.

	Comparative	Superlative
energetic	more energetic	most energetic
quick	more quickly	most quickly

Comparisons must be made between similar structures or items. In the sentence "My house is similar in color to Steve's," one house is being compared to another house, as understood by the use of the possessive *Steve's*.

On the other hand, if the sentence reads "My house is similar in color to Steve," the comparison would be faulty because it would be comparing the house to Steve, not to Steve's house.

Error: *Last year's rides at the carnival were bigger than this year.*

Problem: In the sentence as it is worded, the rides at the carnival are being compared to this year, not to this year's rides.

Correction: *Last year's rides at the carnival were bigger than this year's.*

Practice Exercise: Logical Comparisons

Choose the sentence that logically and correctly expresses the comparison.

1.   A. This year's standards are higher than last year.

     B. This year's standards are more high than last year.

     C. This year's standards are higher than last year's.

2.   A. Tom's attitudes are very different from his father's.

     B. Toms attitudes are very different from his father.

     C. Tom's attitudes are very different from his father.

3.   A. John is the stronger member of the gymnastics team.

     B. John is the strongest member of the gymnastics team.

     C. John is the most strong member of the gymnastics team.

4.   A. Tracy's book report was longer than Tony's.

     B. Tracy's book report was more long than Tony's.

     C. Tracy's book report was longer than Tony.

5.   A. Becoming a lawyer is as difficult as, if not more difficult than, becoming a doctor.

     B. Becoming a lawyer is as difficult, if not more difficult than, becoming a doctor.

     C. Becoming a lawyer is difficult, if not more difficult than, becoming a doctor.

6.   A. Better than any movie of the modern era, *Schindler's List* portrays the destructiveness of hate.

     B. More better than any movie of the modern era, *Schindler's List* portrays the destructiveness of hate.

     C. Better than any other movie of the modern era, *Schindler's List* portrays the destructiveness of hate.

Answer Key: Logical Comparisons

1. C

Option C is correct because the comparison is between this year's standards and last year's (*standards* is understood). Option A compares the standards to last year. In Option B, the faulty comparative *more high* should be *higher*.

2. A

Option A is correct because Tom's attitudes are compared to his father's (*attitudes* is understood). Option B deletes the apostrophe that is necessary to show possession (*Tom's*), and the comparison is faulty because *attitudes* is compared to *father*. While Option C uses the correct possessive, it retains the faulty comparison shown in Option B.

3. B

In Option B, John is correctly the strongest member of a team that consists of more than two people. Option A uses the comparative *stronger* (comparison of two items) rather than the superlative *strongest* (comparison of more than two items). Option C uses a faulty superlative, *most strong*.

4. A

Option A is correct because the comparison is between Tracy's book report and Tony's (book report). Option B uses the faulty comparative *more long* instead of *longer*. Option C wrongly compares Tracy's book report to Tony.

5. A

In Option A, the dual comparison is correctly stated: *as difficult as, if not more difficult than*. Remember to test the dual comparison by taking out the intervening comparison. Option B deletes the necessary *as* after the first *difficult*. Option C deletes the *as* before and after the first *difficult*.

6. C

Option C includes the necessary word *other* in the comparison *better than any other movie*. The comparison in Option A is not complete, and Option B uses the faulty comparative *more better*.

Demonstrate command of standard spelling conventions.

Spelling correctly is not always easy because English not only utilizes an often inconsistent spelling system, but also uses many words derived from other languages.

Good spelling is important because incorrect spelling damages the physical appearance of writing and can puzzle readers.

Common Misspellings

The following is a list of the most often misspelled words in the English language:

COMMONLY MISSPELLED WORDS			
commitment	patience	height	guarantee
succeed	obstinate	leisurely	tropical
necessary	achievement	shield	misfortune
connected	responsibility	foreign	particular
opportunity	prejudice	innovative	yield
embarrassed	familiar	similar	possession
occasionally	hindrance	proceed	accumulate
receive	controversial	contemporary	hospitality
their	publicity	beneficial	judgment
accelerate	prescription	attachment	conscious

Spelling Plurals and Possessives

Most plurals of nouns that end in hard consonants or in hard consonant sounds followed by a silent *e* are made by adding *-s*. Plurals of some words ending in vowels are formed by adding only *-s*.

fingers, numerals, banks, bugs, riots, homes, gates, radios, bananas

Spelling errors resulting from the multiplicity and complexity of spelling rules based on phonics, letter doubling, and exceptions can be avoided by consulting a good dictionary. Learning to use a dictionary and thesaurus effectively is more efficient than attempting to master the bewildering forest of rules.

For nouns that end in soft consonant sounds—*s, j, x, z, ch,* and *sh*—the plurals are formed by adding *-es*. Plurals of some nouns ending in *o* are formed by adding *-es*.

> *dresses, waxes, churches, brushes, tomatoes*

For nouns ending in *y* preceded by a vowel, just add *-s*.

> *boys, alleys*

For nouns ending in *y* preceded by a consonant, change the *y* to *i* and add *-es*.

> *babies, corollaries, frugalities, poppies*

Irregular plurals

Some nouns' plurals are formed irregularly or remain the same.

> *sheep, deer, children, leaves, oxen*

Some nouns derived from foreign words, especially Latin words, are made plural in two different ways. Sometimes the meanings are the same; other times the two plural forms are used in slightly different contexts. It is always wise to consult the dictionary.

> *appendices, appendixes*   *criterion, criteria*
> *indexes, indices*   *crisis, crises*

Make the plurals of closed (solid) compound words in the usual way.

> *timelines, hairpins*
> *cupfuls, handfuls*

Make the plurals of open or hyphenated compounds by adding the change in inflection to the word that changes in number.

> *fathers-in-law, courts-martial, masters of art, doctors of medicine*

Make the plurals of letters, numbers, and abbreviations by adding *-s*.

> *fives and tens, IBMs, 1990s,* **ps** *and* **qs** *(note that letters are italicized.)*

I BEFORE E	
i before e	grieve, fiend, niece, friend
except after c	receive, conceive, receipt
or when sounded like "a"	as in reindeer, weight, and reign
Exceptions:	weird, foreign, seize, leisure

Practice Exercise: EI/IE WORDS

Circle the correct spelling of the word in each parenthesis.

1. The (sheild, shield) protected the gladiator from serious injury.

2. Tony (received, recieved) an award for his science project.

3. Our (neighbors, nieghbors), the Thomsons, are in the Witness Protection Program.

4. Janet's (friend, freind), Olivia, broke her leg while running the marathon.

5. She was unable to (conceive, concieve) a child after her miscarriage.

6. "Rudolph the Red-Nosed (Riendeer, Reindeer)" is my favorite Christmas song.

7. The farmer spent all day plowing his (feild, field).

8. Kat's (wieght, weight) loss plan failed, and she gained twenty pounds!

9. They couldn't (beleive, believe) how many people showed up for the concert.

10. Ruby's (niece, neice) was disappointed when the movie was sold out.

Answer Key: EI/IE WORDS

1. shield
2. received
3. neighbors
4. friend
5. conceive
6. reindeer
7. field
8. weight
9. believe
10. niece

Demonstrate command of standard punctuation.

Commas

> **COMMA:** used to indicate a brief pause

COMMAS are used to indicate a brief pause. They are used to set off dependent clauses and long introductory word groups, to separate words in a series, to set off unimportant material that interrupts the flow of the sentence, and to separate independent clauses joined by conjunctions.

Error: *After I finish my master's thesis I plan to work in Chicago.*

Problem: A comma is needed after an introductory dependent word group containing a subject and verb.

Correction: *After I finish my master's thesis, I plan to work in Chicago.*

Error: *I washed waxed and vacuumed my car today.*

Problem: Commas should separate nouns, phrases, or clauses in a list, as well as two or more coordinate adjectives that modify one word. Although the word *and* is sometimes considered optional, it is often necessary to clarify the meaning.

Correction: *I washed, waxed, and vacuumed my car today.*

Error: *She was a talented dancer but she is mostly remembered for her singing ability.*

Problem: A comma is needed before a conjunction that joins two independent clauses (complete sentences).

Correction: *She was a talented dancer, but she is mostly remembered for her singing ability.*

Error: *This incident is I think typical of what can happen when the community remains so divided.*

Problem: Commas are needed between nonessential words or words that interrupt the main clause.

Correction: *This incident is, I think, typical of what can happen when the community remains so divided.*

Semicolons and Colons

SEMICOLONS are needed to separate two or more closely related independent clauses when a transitional adverb introduces the second clause. (These clauses may also be written as separate sentences, preferably by placing the adverb within the second sentence.)

SEMICOLONS: used to separate two or more closely related independent clauses when a transitional adverb introduces the second clause

Error: *I climbed to the top of the mountain, it took me three hours.*

Problem: A comma alone cannot separate two independent clauses. Instead, a semicolon is needed to separate two related sentences.

Correction: *I climbed to the top of the mountain; it took me three hours.*

Error: *In the movie, asteroids destroyed Dallas, Texas, Kansas City, Missouri, and Boston, Massachusetts.*

Problem: Semicolons are needed to separate items in a series that already contain internal punctuation.

Correction: *In the movie, asteroids destroyed Dallas, Texas; Kansas City, Missouri; and Boston, Massachusetts.*

COLONS are used to introduce lists and to emphasize what follows.

COLONS: used to introduce lists and to emphasize the text that follows

Error: *Essays will receive the following grades, A for excellent, B for good, C for average, and D for unsatisfactory.*

Problem: A colon is needed to emphasize the information or list that follows.

Correction: *Essays will receive the following grades: A for excellent, B for good, C for average, and D for unsatisfactory.*

Error: *The school carnival included: amusement rides, clowns, food booths, and a variety of games.*

Problem: The material preceding the colon and the list that follows are not complete sentences. Do not separate a verb (or preposition) from the object.

Correction: *The school carnival included amusement rides, clowns, food booths, and a variety of games.*

Apostrophes

APOSTROPHES: used to show contractions or possession

APOSTROPHES are used to show contractions or possession.

Error: *She shouldnt be permitted to smoke cigarettes in the building.*

Problem: An apostrophe is needed in a contraction in place of the missing letter.

Correction: *She shouldn't be permitted to smoke cigarettes in the building.*

Error: *My cousins motorcycle was stolen from his driveway.*

Problem: An apostrophe is needed to show possession.

Correction: *My cousin's motorcycle was stolen from his driveway. (Note: The use of the apostrophe before the letter "s" means that there is just one cousin. The plural form would read as follows: My cousins' motorcycle was stolen from their driveway.)*

Error: *The childrens new kindergarten teacher was also a singer.*

Problem: An apostrophe is needed to show possession.

Correction: *The children's new kindergarten teacher was also a singer.*

Error: *Children screams could be heard for miles.*

Problem: An apostrophe and the letter *s* are needed in the sentence to show who is screaming.

Correction: *Children's screams could he heard for miles. (Note: Because the word children is already plural, the apostrophe and -s must be added afterward to show ownership.)*

Quotation Marks

In a quoted statement that is either declarative or imperative, place the period inside the closing quotation marks.

"The airplane crashed on the runway during takeoff."

If other words in the sentence follow the quotation, place a comma inside the closing quotations marks and a period at the end of the sentence.

> *"The airplane crashed on the runway during takeoff," said the announcer.*

Usually, when a quoted title or expression occurs at the end of a sentence, the period is placed before the single or double quotation marks.

> *"The middle school readers were unprepared to understand Bryant's poem 'Thanatopsis.'"*
>
> *Early book-length adventure stories such as* **Don Quixote** *and* **The Three Musketeers** *were known as "picaresque novels."*

The final quotation mark precedes the period if the content of the sentence is about a speech or quote.

> *The first thing out of his mouth was "Hi, I'm home."*
>
> *-BUT-*
>
> *The first line of his speech began: "I arrived home to an empty house".*

In interrogatory or exclamatory sentences, the question mark or exclamation point should be positioned outside the closing quotation marks if the quote itself is a statement, command, or cited title.

> *Who decided to lead us in the recitation of the "Pledge of Allegiance"?*
>
> *Why was Tillie shaking as she began her recitation, "Once upon a midnight dreary. . ."?*
>
> *I was embarrassed when Mrs. White said, "Your slip is showing"!*

In declarative sentences, where the quotation is a question or an exclamation, place the question mark or exclamation point inside the quotation marks.

> *The hall monitor yelled, "Fire! Fire!"*
>
> *"Fire! Fire!" yelled the hall monitor.*
>
> *Cory shrieked, "Is there a mouse in the room?" (In this instance, the question supersedes the exclamation.)*

Quotations—whether words, phrases, or clauses—should be punctuated according to the rules of the grammatical function they serve in the sentence.

> *The works of Shakespeare, "the Bard of Avon," have been contested as originating with other authors.*
>
> *"You'll get my money," the old man warned, "when 'hell freezes over'."*
>
> *Sheila cited the passage that began "Four score and seven years ago . . . ." (Note the ellipsis followed by an enclosed period.)*
>
> *"Old Ironsides" inspired the preservation of the U.S.S. Constitution.*

Use quotation marks to enclose the titles of shorter works: songs, short poems, short stories, essays, and chapters of books. (See "Dashes and Italics" for rules on punctuating longer titles.)

> *"The Tell-Tale Heart" "Casey at the Bat" "America the Beautiful"*

Dashes and Italics

Place **EM DASHES** to denote sudden breaks in thought.

> *Some periods in literature—the Romantic Age, for example—spanned different periods in different countries.*

EM DASHES: used to denote sudden breaks in thought or if commas are already used in the sentence for amplification or explanation

Use dashes instead of commas if commas are already used elsewhere in the sentence for amplification or explanation.

> *The Fireside Poets included three Brahmans—James Russell Lowell, Henry David Wadsworth, and Oliver Wendell Holmes.*

ITALICS: used to punctuate the titles of long works of literature, names of periodical publications, musical scores, works of art, and motion picture, television, and radio programs

Use **ITALICS** to punctuate the titles of long works of literature, names of periodical publications, musical scores, works of art, and motion picture, television, and radio programs. (If italic type is unavailable, students should be instructed to use underlining where italics would be appropriate.)

The Idylls of the King	*Hiawatha*	*The Sound and the Fury*
Mary Poppins	*Newsweek*	*The Nutcracker Suite*

SKILL 3.12 Demonstrate command of standard capitalization.

Capitalize all proper names of persons (including specific organizations or agencies of government), places (countries, states, cities, parks, and specific geographical areas), things (political parties, structures, historical and cultural terms, and calendar and time designations), and religious terms (deities, revered persons or groups, and sacred writings).

> *Percy Bysshe Shelley, Argentina, Mount Rainier National Park, Grand Canyon, League of Nations, the Sears Tower, Birmingham, Lyric Theater, Americans, Midwesterners, Democrats, Renaissance, Boy Scouts of America, Easter, God, Bible, Dead Sea Scrolls, Koran*

Capitalize proper adjectives and titles used with proper names.

> *California gold rush, President John Adams, French fries, Homeric epic, Romanesque architecture, Senator John Glenn*

Note: Some words that represent titles and offices are not capitalized unless used with a proper name.

> *Capitalize all main words in titles of works of literature, art, and music.*

Capitalized	Not Capitalized
Congressman McKay	*the congressman from Hawaii*
Commander Alger	*the commander of the Pacific Fleet*
Queen Elizabeth	*the queen of England*

Error: *Emma went to Dr. Peters for treatment because her own Doctor was on vacation.*

Problem: The use of capital letters with *Emma* and *Dr. Peters* is correct because they are specific (proper) names; the title *Dr.* is also capitalized. However, the word *doctor* is not a specific name and should not be capitalized.

Correction: *Emma went to Dr. Peters for treatment because her own doctor was on vacation.*

Error: *Our Winter break does not start until next wednesday.*

Problem: Days of the week are capitalized, but seasons are not capitalized.

Correction: *Our winter break does not start until next Wednesday.*

Error: *The exchange student from Israel, who came to study biochemistry, spoke spanish very well.*

Problem: Languages and the names of countries are always capitalized. Courses are capitalized when one is referring to a specific course; courses in general are not capitalized.

Correction: *The exchange student from Israel, who came to study biochemistry, spoke Spanish very well.*

Practice Exercise: Capitalization and Punctualization

Choose the option that corrects an error in the underlined portion(s). If no error exists, choose "No change is necessary."

1. <u>Greenpeace</u> is an <u>Organization</u> that works to preserve the <u>world's</u> environment.

   A. greenpeace

   B. organization

   C. worlds

   D. No change is necessary

2. When our class travels to <u>France</u> next <u>year, we</u> will see the <u>country's</u> many famous landmarks.

   A. france

   B. year; we

   C. countries

   D. No change is necessary

3. <u>New York City</u>, the most heavily populated city <u>in America has</u> more than eight million people living there <u>every day</u>.

   A. new york city

   B. in America, has

   C. Everyday

   D. No change is necessary

4. The <u>television</u> show *Lost* gained a huge <u>following because</u> it focused on paranormal phenomena, time travel, and the frailties of <u>human existence</u>.

   A. Television

   B. following, because

   C. Human existence

   D. No change is necessary

5. Being a <u>Policeman</u> requires having many <u>qualities</u>: physical <u>agility</u>, good reflexes, and the ability to make quick decisions.

   A. policeman

   B. qualities;

   C. agility:

   D. No change is necessary

6. "Tis <u>better to have loved and lost, than never to have loved at all</u>," wrote <u>Tennyson</u>, the poet <u>who</u> demonstrates the value of love in a <u>mans</u> life.

   A. Better to have loved and lost than never to have loved at all

   B. Tennyson who

   C. man's

   D. No change is necessary

7. The <u>Boston Americans</u> won the first <u>world series</u> championship by defeating the Pittsburgh Pirates in <u>October 1903</u>.

   A. Boston americans

   B. World Series

   C. October, 1903

   D. No change is necessary

Answer Key: Capitalization and Punctualization

1. B

   In the sentence, the word *organization* does not need to be capitalized because it is a general noun. In Option A, the name of the organization should be capitalized. In Option C, an apostrophe is needed to show that one world is being protected, not more than one.

2. D

   In Option A, *France* must be capitalized because it is the name of a country. In Option B, a comma, not a semicolon, should separate the dependent clause from the main clause. In Option C, an apostrophe and an -s are needed to indicate that only one country is being visited.

3. B

   In Option A, New York City must be capitalized because it is the name of a place. In Option B, a comma is needed to separate the adjective clause ending with *America* from the verb **has**. In Option C, *every day* needs no capitalization and should not be joined as a compound word. (The word *everyday* is an adjective meaning *routine.*)

4. D

   In Option A, *television* does not need to be capitalized because it is a common noun. In Option B, a comma is only necessary to separate an independent clause from the main clause. In Option C, *human existence* is a general term that does not need capitalization.

5. A

   In Option A, *policeman* does not need capitalization because it is a common noun. In Option B, a colon, not a semicolon, is needed because the rest of the sentence is related to the main clause. In Option C, a comma, not a colon, is needed to separate the adjectives.

6. C

   In Option A, a comma is needed to break the quote into distinct parts that give it greater clarity. In Option B, a comma is needed to separate the subject of the sentence from the relative clause. In Option C, an apostrophe is needed to show possession.

7. B

   In Option A, *Americans* must be capitalized because it is the name of a team. In Option B, *World Series* is capitalized because it is the title of a sporting event. In Option C, no comma is needed because month and year need no distinction; they are general terms.

DOMAIN II
MATHEMATICS

PERSONALIZED STUDY PLAN

KNOWN MATERIAL/ SKIP IT

PAGE	COMPETENCY AND SKILL	
67	**4: Knowledge of number sense, concepts, and operations**	☐
	4.1: Compare real numbers and identify their location on a number line	☐
	4.2: Solve real-world problems involving the four operations with rational numbers	☐
	4.3: Evaluate expressions involving order of operations	☐
82	**5: Knowledge of geometry and measurement**	☐
	5.1: Identify and classify simple two- and three-dimensional figures according to their mathematical properties	☐
	5.2: Solve problems involving ratio and proportion *(e.g., scaled drawings, models, real-world scenarios)*	☐
	5.3: Determine an appropriate measurement unit and form *(e.g., scientific notation)* for real-world problems involving length, area, volume, or mass	☐
	5.4: Solve real-world measurement problems including fundamental units *(e.g., length, mass, time)*, derived units *(e.g., miles per hour, dollars per gallon)*, and unit conversions	☐
105	**6: Knowledge of algebraic thinking and the coordinate plane**	☐
	6.1: Determine whether two algebraic expressions are equivalent by applying properties of operations or equality	☐
	6.2: Identify an algebraic expression, equation, or inequality that models a real-world situation	☐
	6.3: Solve equations and inequalities *(e.g., linear, quadratic)* graphically or algebraically	☐
	6.4: Determine and solve equations or inequalities, graphically or algebraically, in real-world problems	☐
	6.5: Graph and interpret a linear equation in real-world problems *(e.g., use data to plot points, explain slope and y-intercept, determine additional solutions)*	☐
	6.6: Identify relations that satisfy the definition of a function	☐
	6.7: Compare the slopes of two linear functions represented algebraically and graphically	☐

PERSONALIZED STUDY PLAN

KNOWN MATERIAL/ SKIP IT

PAGE	COMPETENCY AND SKILL	
123	**7: Knowledge of probability, statistics, and data interpretation**	☐
	7.1: Analyze data presented in various forms *(e.g., histograms, bar graphs, circle graphs, pictographs, line plots, tables)* to solve problems	☐
	7.2: Analyze and evaluate how the presentation of data can lead to different or inappropriate interpretations in the context of a real-world situation	☐
	7.3: Calculate range, mean, median, and mode of data sets	☐
	7.4: Interpret the meaning of measures of central tendency *(i.e., mean, median, mode)* and dispersion *(i.e., range, standard deviation)* in the context of a real-world situation	☐
	7.5: Analyze and evaluate how the selection of statistics *(e.g., mean, median, mode)* can lead to different or inappropriate interpretations in the context of a real-world situation	☐
	7.6: Solve and interpret real-world problems involving probability using counting procedures, tables, and tree diagrams	☐
	7.7: Infer and analyze conclusions from sample surveys, experiments, and observational studies	☐

COMPETENCY 4
KNOWLEDGE OF NUMBER SENSE, CONCEPTS, AND OPERATIONS

> **SKILL** **Compare real numbers and identify their location on a number line.**
> **4.1**

Real Numbers

Real numbers include rational numbers and irrational numbers. All real numbers can be represented as points along an infinite number line.

RATIONAL NUMBERS can be expressed as the ratio of two integers, $\frac{a}{b}$, where $b \neq 0$. For example, $\frac{2}{3}$, $-\frac{4}{5}$, $5 = \frac{5}{1}$ are all rational numbers.

Rational numbers include integers, fractions, mixed numbers, and terminating and repeating decimals.

IRRATIONAL NUMBERS are real numbers that cannot be written as the ratio of two integers. They are infinite, non-repeating decimals.

For example, π and $\sqrt{5}$ are irrational numbers.

> **INTEGERS:** the positive and negative whole numbers and zero

> **IRRATIONAL NUMBERS:** real numbers that cannot be written as the ratio of two integers

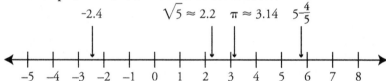

The following chart shows the relationships among the subsets of the real numbers.

Real Numbers

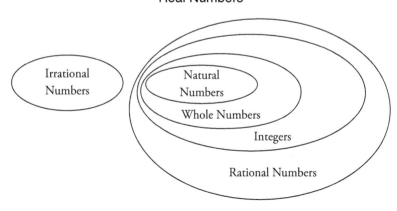

INTEGERS are the positive and negative whole numbers and zero.

...-6, -5, -4, -3, -2, -1, 0, 1, 2, 3, 4, 5, 6,...

WHOLE NUMBERS are the natural numbers and zero.

0, 1, 2, 3, 4, 5, 6...

NATURAL NUMBERS are the counting numbers.

1, 2, 3, 4, 5, 6...

A PRIME NUMBER is a natural number n that is divisible by two numbers only: 1 and n. The number 1 does not qualify as a prime number because it is divisible by only one number, itself, whereas a prime is divisible by exactly two numbers.

Example:

91 is divisible by 7 and 13 in addition to being divisible by 91 and 1, so 91 **is not** a prime number.

93 is divisible only by 93 and 1, so 93 **is** a prime number.

ABSOLUTE VALUE is the distance a number is from zero, and is always positive.

Examples:

$|-4| = 4$

$|3| = 3$

$|x - 6| = 2$; *both $x = 8$ and 4 work!*

A FRACTION is an expression of numbers in the form of $\frac{x}{y}$, where x is the numerator and y is the denominator, which cannot be zero.

$\frac{3}{7}$ 3 is the numerator; 7 is the denominator

If the fraction has common factors for the numerator and denominator, divide both by the common factor to reduce the fraction to its lowest form.

$\frac{13}{39} = \frac{1 \cdot 13}{3 \cdot 13} = \frac{1}{3}$ Divide by the common factor 13.

A MIXED NUMBER has an integer part and a fractional part.

$2\frac{1}{4}, -5\frac{1}{6}, 7\frac{1}{3}$

PERCENT means hundredths (written with the symbol %).

$10\% = \frac{10}{100} = \frac{1}{10}$

DECIMALS are fractions expressed in tenths and fractional powers of ten such as hundredths or thousandths. To convert a fraction to a decimal, divide the numerator by the denominator:

$\frac{7}{10} = 0.7$

WHOLE NUMBERS: the natural numbers and zero

NATURAL NUMBERS: the counting numbers

PRIME NUMBER: a natural number n that is divisible by two numbers only: 1 and n.

FRACTION: an expression of numbers in the form of $\frac{x}{y}$ where x is the numerator and y is the denominator

MIXED NUMBER: a number that has an integer part and a fractional part

PERCENT: means "per 100;" ten percent is 10 parts out of 100

DECIMAL: a number written with a whole-number part, a decimal point, and a decimal part

The **EXPONENT FORM** is a shortcut method to write repeated multiplication. The basic form is b^n, where b is called the **BASE** and n is the **EXPONENT**. The expression b^n implies that n factors of b have been multiplied together.

Examples:

$$3^4 = 3 \cdot 3 \cdot 3 \cdot 3 = 81$$
$$2^3 = 2 \cdot 2 \cdot 2 = 8$$
$$(-2)^4 = (-2) \cdot (-2) \cdot (-2) \cdot (-2) = 16$$
$$-2^4 = -(2 \cdot 2 \cdot 2 \cdot 2) = -16$$

Caution: The exponent does not affect the sign unless the negative sign is inside the parentheses and the exponent is outside the parentheses.

$(-2)^4$ implies that -2 is multiplied by itself 4 times.

-2^4 implies that 2 is multiplied by itself 4 times, and then the answer becomes. negative.

Some useful properties of exponents

FOR 'a' AND 'b' NONZERO, AND 'n' AND 'm' REAL NUMBERS	
Product Rule	$a^m \cdot a^n = a^{(m+n)}$
Quotient Rule	$\dfrac{a^m}{a^n} = a^{(m-n)}$
Rule of Negative Exponents	$a^{-m} = \dfrac{1}{a^m}$
	$\dfrac{a^{-m}}{b^{-n}} = \dfrac{b^n}{a^m}$
Zero as an Exponent	$a^0 = 1$

Examples:

Product Rule

> Be careful! Note that this is true only when the base is the same (3, in this example).
>
> $$3^2 \cdot 3^4 = 3^{(2+4)} = 3^6 = 729$$
> $$(3 \cdot 3) \cdot (3 \cdot 3 \cdot 3 \cdot 3) = 9 \cdot 81 = 729$$
>
> *A common mistake is to try to use the product rule when the bases are not the same. For example, $6^2 \cdot 5^2$ cannot be simplified using the product rule.*
> $$6^2 \cdot 5^2 = 6 \cdot 6 \cdot 5 \cdot 5 = 900$$

EXPONENT FORM: a shorthand way of writing repeated multiplication

BASE: the number to be multiplied as many times as indicated by the exponent

EXPONENT: tells how many times the base is multiplied by itself

Quotient Rule

As with the Product Rule, this is true only when the base is the same in the numerator and denominator (4, in this example).

$$\frac{4^5}{4^3} = 4^{(5-3)} = 4^2 = 16$$

$$\frac{4^5}{4^3} = \frac{4 \cdot 4 \cdot 4 \cdot 4 \cdot 4}{4 \cdot 4 \cdot 4} = 4 \cdot 4 = 16$$

Rule of Negative Exponents

To make a negative exponent positive, move it to the other side of the fraction bar.

$$2^{-5} = \frac{1}{2^5}$$

$$\frac{1}{3^{-4}} = 3^4$$

Using this rule twice in the same fraction,

$$\frac{4^{-2}}{5^{-6}} = \frac{5^6}{4^2}$$

Zero as an Exponent

Any number raised to the zero power =1 (except zero! Remember the base must be nonzero).

$$7^0 = 1$$
$$(-5)^0 = 1$$

When 10 is raised to any power, the exponent tells the numbers of zeros in the product.

Example:

$$10^7 = 10,000,000$$

Scientific Notation

SCIENTIFIC NOTATION is a convenient method for writing very large and very small numbers. It employs two factors. The first factor is a number between 1 and 10. The second factor is a power of 10. This notation is considered "shorthand" for expressing very large numbers (such as the weight of 100 elephants) or very small numbers (such as the weight of an atom in pounds).

Recall that:

10^n	=	Ten multiplied by itself n times
10^0	=	Any nonzero number raised to the zero power is 1
10^1	=	10
10^2	=	$10 \times 10 = 100$
10^3	=	$10 \times 10 \times 10 = 1000$
10^{-1}	=	$\frac{1}{10}$ (deci)
10^{-2}	=	$\frac{1}{100}$ (centi)
10^{-3}	=	$\frac{1}{1000}$ (milli)
10^{-6}	=	$\frac{1}{1,000,000}$ (micro)

Example: Write 46,368,000 in scientific notation.

1. Introduce a decimal point and decimal places.
   $46,368,000 = 46,368,000.0000$

2. Make a mark between the two digits that give a number between
   -9.9 and 9.9.
   $4 \wedge 6,368,000.0000$

3. Count the number of digit places between the decimal point and the $\wedge$ mark when moving left from the decimal point. This number is the *nth* power of ten.
   So, $46,368,000 = 4.6368 \times 10^7$.

Example: Write 0.00397 in scientific notation.

1. Decimal place is already in place.

2. Make a mark between 3 and 9 to obtain a number between -9.9 and. 9.9.

3. Between the decimal point and the mark
   there are three digits: $0.003 \wedge 97$
   Motion is to the right, so n in 10^n is negative.
   Therefore, $0.00397 = 3.97 \times 10^{-3}$.

Although the use of '$\times$' in multiplication is discouraged in math after the elementary levels, scientific notation is expressed as m $\times$ 10^n. On scientific calculators, the '$\times$' is often replaced by 'E'.

We can use scientific notation along with exponent rules.

Example:

Find $(3.7 \times 10^5)(5.1 \times 10^{-2})$

Multiply the parts that don't have exponents, and then use the exponent rules on the numbers with a common base (10).

$(3.7)(5.1)(10^5)(10^{-2})$ Combine $10^5 \cdot 10^{-2}$ to get 10^3 using the Product Rule.

$= (18.87) \cdot 10^{(5-2)}$

$= 18.87 \cdot 10^3$

$= 18,870$

Example:

Evaluate $\frac{6.4 \times 10^8}{3.2 \times 10^5}$

Divide the parts that don't have exponents ($\frac{6.4}{3.2}$), then use the quotient rule on the base 10 terms.

$\frac{(6.4)(10^8)}{(3.2)(10^5)} = 2.0 \cdot 10^{(8-5)} = 2.0 \cdot 10^3 = 2000$

Square Roots

The square root of a number is the value that, when multiplied by itself, gives that number. For example, $\sqrt{9} = 3$, since 3^2 *or* $3 \cdot 3 = 9$. While $(-3)(-3)$ also equals 9, when a radical sign ($\sqrt{}$) is used, we are only interested in the positive number (3 in this example).

Since only a 4 function calculator is available for the FTCE, you will likely be given square roots that are easily found.

Some Perfect Squares

$0^2 = 0 \rightarrow \sqrt{0} = 0$

$1^2 = 1 \rightarrow \sqrt{1} = 1$

$2^2 = 4 \rightarrow \sqrt{4} = 2$

$3^2 = 9 \rightarrow \sqrt{9} = 3$

$4^2 = 16 \rightarrow \sqrt{16} = 4$

$5^2 = 25 \rightarrow \sqrt{25} = 5$

$6^2 = 36 \rightarrow \sqrt{36} = 6$

$7^2 = 49 \rightarrow \sqrt{49} = 7$

$8^2 = 64 \rightarrow \sqrt{64} = 8$

$9^2 = 81 \rightarrow \sqrt{81} = 9$

$10^2 = 100 \rightarrow \sqrt{100} = 10$

Note that we can sometimes simplify a root, for example by factoring within the root. A root is a type of exponent and follows the same rules.

Example:
$$\sqrt{50} = \sqrt{(25 \cdot 2)} = \sqrt{25} \cdot \sqrt{2} = 5\sqrt{2}$$

Example:
$$\sqrt{2} \cdot \sqrt{10} = \sqrt{20} = \sqrt{(4 \cdot 5)} = \sqrt{4} \cdot \sqrt{5} = 2\sqrt{5}$$

Example:
$$\frac{\sqrt{12}}{\sqrt{6}} = \sqrt{2}$$

Example:
$$2\sqrt{3} - 3\sqrt{7} + 4\sqrt{3} = 6\sqrt{3} - 3\sqrt{7}$$

If you need to estimate a square root because it is not one of the perfect squares, look at the nearest perfect squares. For example, to estimate $\sqrt{3}$, we know that it will be between $\sqrt{1} = 1$ and $\sqrt{4} = 2$. So we can say
$$1 < \sqrt{3} < 2$$

Comparing Numbers

To compare numbers that are not similar, first put them in a form that allows easy comparison. Sometimes it is easiest to put numbers in decimal form. At other times, it is convenient to find a common denominator.

Example:
Put the following in order from smallest to largest:
$$6, -3, -5\frac{1}{2}, \sqrt{5}, 16\%, -0.46, 2\frac{2}{3}$$

Some of these are easy to compare. We know that the negative numbers are smaller than all the positive numbers, for example. To facilitate comparison, it is easiest in this case to convert all the numbers to decimals. In the order they are given in the original problem, these become:

$$6, -3, -5.5, 2.24, 0.16, -0.46, 2.67$$

Putting these in order from smallest to largest,

$$-5.5, -3, -0.46, 0.16, 2.24, 2.67, 6 \rightarrow -5\frac{1}{2}, -3, -0.46, 16\%, \sqrt{5}, 2\frac{2}{3}, 6$$

Example:

Compare 18% and $\frac{5}{8}$ using < or >

Remember that > means greater than and < means less than (put the point toward the smaller quantity). To compare 18% and $\frac{5}{8}$, convert both to decimal form.

18% = 0.18 $\frac{5}{8}$ = 0.625

Therefore,

18% < 5/8

Be careful when comparing negative quantities!

Example:

Compare $\frac{-4}{5}$ and -0.67 using >, <, or =

Begin by converting the fraction to a decimal.

$\frac{-4}{5}$ = -0.8

$\frac{-4}{5}$ < -0.67, since $\frac{-4}{5}$ is the more negative number (more to the left on the number line). If you have trouble deciding, plot the numbers on a number line.

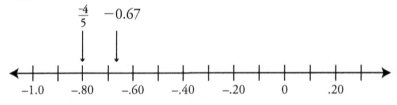

SKILL 4.2 **Solve real-world problems involving the four operations with rational numbers.**

Some examples of basic problems involving addition, subtraction, multiplication and division:

Example: At the end of a day of shopping, a shopper had $24 remaining in his wallet. He spent $45 on various goods. How much money did the shopper have at the beginning of the day?

The total amount of money the shopper started with is the sum of the amount spent and the amount remaining at the end of the day.

$ 24
+ 45
$ 69   The original total was $69.

Example: A race took the winner 1 h 58 min 12 sec on the first half of the race and 2 h 9 min 57 sec on the second. How much time did the entire race take?

1 hr 58 min 12 sec	
+ 2 hr 9 min 57 sec	Add these numbers.
3 hr 67 min 69 sec	
+ 1 min − 60 sec	Change 60 sec to 1 min.
3 hr 68 min 9 sec	
+ 1 hr − 60 min	Change 60 min to 1 hr.
4 hr 8 min 9 sec	Final answer.

Example: At the end of his shift, a cashier has $96 in the cash register. At the beginning of his shift, he had $15. How much money did the cashier collect during his shift?

The total collected is the difference between the ending amount and the starting amount.

$ 96	
−15	
$ 81	The total collected was $81.

Example: A student buys 4 boxes of crayons. Each box contains 16 crayons. How many total crayons does the student have?

The total number of crayons is 16×4.

16	
× 4	
64	The total number of crayons equals 64.

Example: Each box of apples contains 24 apples. How many boxes must a grocer purchase to supply a group of 252 people with one apple each?

The grocer needs 252 apples. Because he must buy apples in groups of 24, we divide 252 by 24 to determine how many boxes he needs to buy.

$$\begin{array}{r} 10 \\ 24{\overline{)252}} \\ -24 \\ \hline 12 \\ -0 \\ \hline 12 \end{array}$$ → The quotient is 10 with a remainder of 12.

Thus, the grocer needs 10 boxes plus 12 more apples. Therefore, the minimum number of boxes the grocer can purchase is 11.

Example: At his job, John gets paid $20 for every hour he works. If John made $940 in a week, how many hours did he work?

This is a division problem. To determine the number of hours John worked, we divide the total amount made ($940) by the hourly rate of pay ($20). Thus, the number of hours worked equals 940 divided by 20.

$$\frac{\$940}{\$20/hour} = 47 \text{ hours}$$

Example: A shopper has 5 one-dollar bills, 6 quarters, 3 nickels, and 4 pennies in his pocket. How much money does he have?

$$5 \times \$1.00 = \$5.00$$

	1 3	1	
	$0.25	$0.05	$0.01
	× 6	× 3	× 4
	$1.50	$0.15	$0.04

Note the placement of the decimals in the multiplication products. Thus, the total amount of money in the shopper's pocket is:

$$\begin{array}{r} \$5.00 \\ 1.50 \\ 0.15 \\ + 0.04 \\ \hline \$6.69 \end{array}$$

Division of Decimals

When dividing decimal numbers, we first remove the decimal in the divisor by moving the decimal in the dividend the same number of spaces to the right. For example, when dividing 1.45 into 5.3, we move the decimal point two spaces to the right to convert 1.45 to a whole number, 145. Then we move the decimal point in 5.3 two spaces to the right as well, which gives us 530. Then we divide.

Example: Find the quotient of 5.3 divided by 1.45.

Convert to 145 and 530.

Divide.

$$\begin{array}{r} 3 \\ 145\overline{)530} \\ -435 \\ \hline 95 \end{array} \qquad \begin{array}{r} 3.65 \\ 145\overline{)530.00} \\ -435 \\ \hline 950 \\ -870 \\ \hline 800 \end{array}$$

Note that we insert the decimal to continue division.

Because one of the numbers divided contained only one decimal place, we round the quotient to one decimal place. Thus, the final quotient is 3.7.

Operating with Percents

To convert decimals to percents, move the decimal point 2 places to the right and add %.

For example:

$0.456 \rightarrow 45.6\%$

$2.698 \rightarrow 269.8\%$

$0.0325 \rightarrow 3.25\%$

If you need to convert a fraction to a decimal, it is sometimes easiest to first convert to a decimal.

Example: Convert $\frac{5}{6}$ to a percent.

$\frac{5}{6} = 0.833 \rightarrow 83.3\%$

Do the opposite to change from a percent to a decimal (move the decimal 2 places to the left).

For example,

$45.6\% \rightarrow 0.456$

$269.8\% \rightarrow 2.698$

$3.25\% \rightarrow 0.0325$

To go from a decimal to a fraction, recall place values after the decimal.

45.7139	
4	tens
5	ones
7	tenths
1	hundredths
3	thousandths
9	ten thousandths

To change from a decimal to a fraction, select the denominator based on the smallest place value of what is after the decimal point, then simplify if possible.

Example:

Write as a fraction

0.7	$\frac{7}{10}$
0.56	$\frac{56}{100} = \frac{14}{25}$
0.431	$\frac{431}{1000}$
2.64	$2\frac{64}{100} = 2\frac{16}{25}$

Example: 5 is what percent of 20?

This is the same as converting $\frac{5}{20}$ to % form.

$\frac{5}{20} = 0.25 \rightarrow 25\%$

Example: There are 64 dogs in the kennel. 48 are collies. What percent are collies?

Restate the problem.   48 is what fraction of 64?

Write an equation. $48 = n \cdot 64$

Solve. $\frac{48}{64} = n$

$n = \frac{3}{4} = 0.75 = 75\%$

75% of the dogs are collies.

Example: The auditorium was filled to 90% capacity. There were 558 seats occupied. What is the capacity of the auditorium?

Restate the problem.   90% of what number is 558?

Write an equation. $0.9n = 558$

Solve. $n = \frac{558}{.9}$

$n = 620$

The capacity of the auditorium is 620 people.

Hint: If at this point you have trouble knowing which numbers to multiply or divide, it may be helpful to remember that in math word sentences, = can be substituted for the word "is", and the multiplication sign can be substituted for the word "of". Substitute words that indicate unknowns, like "what", with a variable. Using the last example,

90% of what number is 558?

90% · n = 558

Example: Joe's rent was $525 a month, but is going up to $575. What is the percent increase?

Percent increase or decrease can be found by dividing the amount of increase or decrease by the **original amount** and converting to a percent.

$$percent\ increase\ or\ decrease = \frac{amount\ of\ increase\ or\ decrease}{\textbf{original amount}} \cdot 100$$

Joe's rent went up $50, so

$$\%\ increase = \frac{\$50}{\$525} = 0.095 \rightarrow 9.5\%$$

The most common mistake in finding percent increase is dividing by the new value, $575 in this example, instead of the original amount, $525.

Example: A car is on sale for $22,450. The original sticker price was $25,450. Find the percent decrease.

$$\%\ decrease = \frac{(\$25,450 - \$22,450)}{\$25,450} = \frac{\$3000}{\$25,450} = 0.12 \rightarrow 12\%$$

Example: A pair of shoes costs $42.00. The sales tax is 6%. What is the total cost of the shoes?

Restate the problem.	What is 42 + 6% of 42?
Write an equation.	$n = 42 + 0.06(42)$
Solve.	$n = \$42 + \$2.52 = \$44.52$

The total cost of the shoes, including sales tax, is $44.52.

Addition and Subtraction of Fractions Review

Key points

1. You need a common denominator in order to add and subtract reduced and improper fractions.

   Example:
   $$\frac{1}{3} + \frac{7}{3} = \frac{1+7}{3} = \frac{8}{3} = 2\frac{2}{3}$$

   Example:
   $$\frac{4}{12} + \frac{6}{12} - \frac{3}{12} = \frac{4+6-3}{12} = \frac{7}{12}$$

2. Adding an integer and a fraction of the same sign results directly in a mixed fraction.

   Example:
   $$2 + \frac{2}{3} = 2\frac{2}{3}$$

Example:

$$-2 - \frac{2}{3} = -2\frac{2}{3}$$

3. Adding an integer and a fraction with different signs involves the following steps.

   • Get a common denominator using the least common multiple (LCM)

   • Add or subtract as needed

   • Change to a mixed fraction if possible

Example:

$$2 - \frac{1}{3} = (\frac{2}{1} \cdot \frac{3}{3}) - \frac{1}{3} = \frac{6}{3} - \frac{1}{3} = \frac{5}{3} = 1\frac{2}{3}$$

Example:

Add $7\frac{3}{8} + 5\frac{2}{7}$

Add the whole numbers, add the fractions, and combine the two results:

$7\frac{3}{8} + 5\frac{2}{7} = (7 + 5) + (\frac{3}{8} + \frac{2}{7})$ Get a common denominator for the fractions. 56 is the LCM of 7 and 8.

$$= 12 + (\frac{3}{8} \cdot \frac{7}{7}) + (\frac{2}{7} \cdot \frac{8}{8})$$

$$= 12 + \frac{3 \cdot 7}{56} + \frac{2 \cdot 8}{56}$$

$$= 12 + \frac{21 + 16}{56} = 12 + \frac{37}{56} = 12\frac{37}{56}$$

Example:

$$-7\frac{1}{4} + 2\frac{7}{8}$$

$$-7\frac{1}{4} + 2\frac{7}{8} = (-7 + 2) + (\frac{-1}{4} + \frac{7}{8})$$

$$= (-5) + \frac{-2 + 7}{8} = (-5) + (\frac{5}{8})$$

$$= (-5) + \frac{5}{8} = \frac{-5 \cdot 8}{1 \cdot 8} + \frac{5}{8} = \frac{-40 + 5}{8}$$

$$= \frac{-35}{8} = -4\frac{3}{8}$$

Divide 35 by 8 to get 4, remainder 3.

Example:

Caution: A common error would be:

$-7\frac{1}{4} + 2\frac{7}{8} = -7\frac{2}{8} + 2\frac{7}{8} = -5\frac{9}{8}$ Wrong.

It is correct to add -7 and 2 to get -5, but adding $\frac{2}{8} + \frac{7}{8} = \frac{9}{8}$ is wrong. It should have been $\frac{-2}{8} + \frac{7}{8} = \frac{5}{8}$. Then, $-5 + \frac{5}{8} = -4\frac{3}{8}$ as before.

Alternatively, we can change the mixed fractions to improper fractions in the first step, then find a common denominator.

$$-7\frac{1}{4} + 2\frac{7}{8} = \frac{-29}{4} + \frac{23}{8} = \frac{-58}{8} + \frac{23}{8} = \frac{-35}{8} = -4\frac{3}{8}$$

Example: John ate $\frac{1}{4}$ of one pizza for lunch. He ate an additional $\frac{1}{3}$ of the pizza before bed. What fraction of the pizza is left?

To find the total fraction of the pizza John has eaten, add 1/4 and 1/3.

$\frac{1}{4} + \frac{1}{3}$

$= \frac{1}{4} \cdot \frac{3}{3} + \frac{1}{3} \cdot \frac{4}{4}$ find a common denominator using the LCM

$= \frac{3}{12} + \frac{4}{12}$

$= \frac{7}{12}$

John has consumed $\frac{7}{12}$ of the pizza. To find how much is left, subtract $\frac{7}{12}$ from 1.

$1 - \frac{7}{12}$

$= \frac{12}{12} - \frac{7}{12}$

$= \frac{5}{12}$

Example: Kate bought $3\frac{3}{8}$ yards of fabric from a remnant bin. She used $2\frac{2}{3}$ yards on a skirt. How much does she have left? If she needs $\frac{2}{3}$ of a yard to make a scarf, does she have enough?

$3\frac{3}{8} - 2\frac{2}{3}$

$= \frac{27}{8} - \frac{8}{3}$ change to improper fractions

$= \frac{27}{8} \cdot \frac{3}{3} - \frac{8}{3} \cdot \frac{8}{8}$ find a common denominator using the LCM

$= \frac{81}{24} - \frac{64}{24}$

$= \frac{17}{24}$

She has $\frac{17}{24}$ of a yard left.

Is this more or less than the $\frac{2}{3}$ of a yard needed to make a scarf?

There are 2 ways to find the answer. We can either convert to a decimal and compare, or find a common denominator and compare.

Converting to decimals:

$\frac{17}{24} \approx 0.71$ and $\frac{2}{3} \approx 0.67$

Finding a common denominator for $\frac{2}{3}$ and $\frac{17}{24}$,

$\frac{2}{3} \cdot \frac{8}{8} = \frac{16}{24}$

Using either method shows us that she has enough material.

Multiplication of Fractions Review

1. Change any mixed fractions to improper fractions.

2. Reduce (cancel) any common factors in the numerator and denominator.

3. Multiply the numerators by each other and the denominators by each other.

4. Reduced to lowest terms.

5. Convert the improper fraction back to a mixed fraction.

Example:

$3\frac{1}{4} \cdot \frac{5}{6}$ Convert the mixed fraction $(3\frac{1}{4})$ to an improper fraction.

$= \frac{13}{4} \cdot \frac{5}{6}$ There are no common factors in the numerator and denominator.

$= \frac{65}{24}$ Multiply the numerators by each other, and the denominators by each other.

$= 2\frac{17}{24}$ Convert to a mixed fraction by dividing the numerator by the denominator.

$$\frac{65}{24} = 24\overline{)65} \qquad = 2\frac{17}{24}$$
$$\underline{48}$$
$$17$$

Summary of Sign Changes for Multiplication

1. $(+) \times (+) = (+)$

2. $(-) \times (+) = (-)$

3. $(+) \times (-) = (-)$

4. $(-) \times (-) = (+)$

Example:

$7\frac{1}{3} \cdot \frac{5}{11}$

$= \frac{22}{3} \cdot \frac{5}{11}$ Reduce by cancelling the common factor 11

$= \frac{2}{3} \cdot \frac{5}{1}$ Multiply the numerators by each other, and the denominators by each other.

$= \frac{10}{3}$ Convert to a mixed fraction by dividing the numerator by the denominator.

$= 3\frac{1}{3}$

Example:

$$-6\frac{1}{4} \cdot 2\frac{5}{9}$$

$$= \frac{-25}{4} \cdot \frac{23}{9}$$

$$= \frac{-575}{36}$$

$$= -15\frac{35}{36}$$

Example:

$\frac{-3}{4} \cdot \frac{-2}{9}$ Cancel the common factors 2 and 3.

$= \frac{-1}{2} \cdot \frac{-1}{3}$ Remember that a negative multiplied by a negative equals a positive.

$= \frac{1}{6}$

Division of Fractions Review

1. Change mixed fractions to improper fractions

2. To divide by a fraction, turn the divisor upside down and rewrite the division as a multiplication.

3. Find the sign of the final product

4. Cancel any common factors between the numerator and the denominator

5. Multiply the numerators together and the denominators together

6. Change the improper fraction to a mixed number

Example:

$3\frac{1}{5} \div 2\frac{1}{4}$ Change to an improper fraction.

$= \frac{16}{5} \div \frac{9}{4}$ Change to a multiplication problem by using the reciprocal of the number after the division sign.

$= \frac{16}{5} \cdot \frac{4}{9}$ Multiply the numerators by each other and the denominators by each other.

$= \frac{64}{45}$

$= 1\frac{19}{45}$

Example:

$7\frac{3}{4} \div 11\frac{5}{8}$ Change to an improper fraction.

$= \frac{31}{4} \div \frac{93}{8}$ Change to a multiplication problem by using the reciprocal of the number after the division sign.

$= \frac{31}{4} \cdot \frac{8}{93}$ Cancel the common factors of 31 and 4.

$= \frac{1}{1} \cdot \frac{2}{3}$

$= \frac{2}{3}$

Example:

$-5\frac{3}{8} \div \frac{-7}{16}$ Change to an improper fraction.

$= \frac{-43}{8} \div \frac{-7}{16}$ Change to a multiplication problem by using the reciprocal of the number after the division sign.

$= \frac{-43}{8} \cdot \frac{-16}{7}$ Cancel the common factor 8.

$= \frac{-43}{1} \cdot \frac{-2}{7}$ A negative multiplied by a negative equals a positive.

$= \frac{86}{7}$

$= 12\frac{2}{7}$

Example:

A recipe for a certain cake frosting makes $2\frac{1}{4}$ pounds of frosting. If Josh wanted to put $\frac{2}{3}$ of the frosting on the sides of his cake and $\frac{1}{3}$ of the frosting on top, how much should he use on the sides?

The amount of frosting used on the sides will be $2\frac{1}{4} \cdot \frac{2}{3}$

$= \frac{9}{4} \cdot \frac{2}{3}$ Change the mixed fraction to an improper fraction.

$= \frac{3}{2} \cdot \frac{1}{1}$ Cancel common factors in the numerator and denominator.

$= \frac{3}{2} = 1\frac{1}{2}$ Change to a mixed fraction.

$1\frac{1}{2}$ pounds of frosting should be used on the sides.

Example:

Harry has a $2\frac{1}{2}$ gallon container of gas that he uses to refill a mower he uses for his lawn care business. If the tank on the mower is $\frac{2}{3}$ of a gallon, how many times can he fill the tank on his mower?

To find the answer, divide $2\frac{1}{2}$ by $\frac{2}{3}$.

$$2\frac{1}{2} \div \frac{2}{3}$$
$$= \frac{5}{2} \div \frac{2}{3}$$
$$= \frac{5}{2} \cdot \frac{3}{2}$$
$$= \frac{15}{4}$$
$$= 3\frac{3}{4}$$

He can fill his tank $3\frac{3}{4}$ times.

SKILL 4.3 Evaluate expressions involving order of operations.

PROPERTIES OF OPERATIONS are rules that apply for addition, subtraction, multiplication, or division of real numbers.

> **PROPERTIES OF OPERATIONS:** rules that apply for addition, subtraction, multiplication, or division of real numbers

Commutative Property

You can change the order of the terms or factors as follows.

For addition:	$a + b = b + a$
For multiplication:	$ab = ba$

This rule does not apply for division and subtraction.

Examples: $17 + 23 = 23 + 17 = 40$
$8 \cdot 19 = 19 \cdot 8 = 152$

Associative Property

You can regroup the terms as you like.

For addition:	$a + (b + c) = (a + b) + c$
For multiplication:	$a(bc) = (ab)c$

This rule also does not apply for division and subtraction.

Example: $(-2 + 7) + 5 = -2 + (7 + 5)$
$5 + 5 = -2 + 12 = 10$

Example: $(3 \cdot -7) \cdot 5 = 3 \cdot (-7 \cdot 5)$
$-21 \cdot 5 = 3 \cdot -35 = -105$

Identity Properties

Adding 0 to a number results in that number, with no change (additive identity of 0); multiplying a number by 1 results in that number, with no change (multiplicative identity of 1).

For addition:	$a + 0 = a$	(additive identity of 0)
For multiplication:	$a \cdot 1 = a$	(multiplicative identity of 1)

Example: $17 + 0 = 17$

Example: $-34 \cdot 1 = -34$

Inverse Properties

The additive inverse of a number a is the number that when added to a results in zero. The multiplicative inverse (or reciprocal) of a number a is the number that when multiplied by a results in 1.

For addition: $\quad a + (-a) = 0$

Example: $25 + -25 = 0$

For multiplication: $\quad a \times \dfrac{1}{a} = 1$ (multiplicative identity of 1)

Example: $5 \times \dfrac{1}{5} = 1$

The additive inverse of a is $(-a)$. The reciprocal or multiplicative inverse of a is $\dfrac{1}{a}$.

The sum of any number and its additive inverse is 0. The product of any number and its reciprocal is 1.

Distributive Property of Multiplication over Addition and Subtraction

This property allows us to operate on terms within parentheses without first performing operations within the parentheses. This is especially helpful when terms within the parentheses cannot be combined.

$$a(b + c) = ab + ac$$

Example: $\quad 6 \cdot (-4 + 9) = (6 \cdot -4) + (6 \cdot 9)$
$$6 \cdot 5 = -24 + 54 = 30$$

To multiply a sum by a number, multiply each addend by the number, then add the products.

Summary of the properties of operations

PROPERTY	OF ADDITION	OF MULTIPLICATION
Commutative	$a + b = b + a$	$ab = ba$
Associative	$a + (b + c) = (a + b) + c$	$a(bc) = (ab)c$
Identity	$a + 0 = a$	$a \cdot 1 = a$
Inverse	$a + (-a) = 0$	$a \cdot \frac{1}{a} = 1, a \neq 0$
Distributive property of multiplication over addition and subtraction	$a(b + c) = ab + ac$	$a(b - c) = ab - ac$

Note: the order of operation can be remembered using the acronym "PEMDAS", Parentheses, Exponents, Multiplication, Division, Addition, Subtraction

Example: $3^3 - 5(b + 2)$
$$= 3^3 - 5b - 10$$
$$= 27 - 5b - 10$$
$$= 17 - 5b$$

Example: $2 - 4 \cdot 2^3 - 2(4 - 2 \cdot 3)$
$$= 2 - 4 \cdot 2^3 - 2(4 - 6)$$
$$= 2 - 4 \cdot 2^3 - 2(-2)$$
$$= 2 - 4 \cdot 2^3 + 4$$
$$= 2 - 4 \cdot 8 + 4$$
$$= 2 - 32 + 4$$
$$= 6 - 32$$
$$= -26$$

Example:

Place parentheses as needed in the following so that the statement is true.

$25 \div 9 - 4 + 1 \div 3 = 2$

As written, order of operation dictates that we first divide 25 by 9, then subtract 4, then add $\frac{1}{3}$. This of course does not equal 2.

$\frac{25}{9} - 4 + \frac{1}{3} \neq 2$

However,

$\left[25 \div (9 - 4) + 1\right] \div 3 = 2$

Example:

Place parentheses as needed in the following so that the statement is true.

$-2 \cdot 3^2 + 2 = 38$

As written, order of operation dictates that we first apply the exponent, then multiply by -2, then add 2. This of course does not equal 38.

$-2 \cdot 9 + 2 = -18 + 2 \neq 38$

However,

$(-2 \cdot 3)^2 + 2 = (-6)^2 + 2 = 36 + 2 = 38$

COMPETENCY 5
KNOWLEDGE OF GEOMETRY AND MEASUREMENT

> **SKILL 5.1** Identify and classify simple two- and three-dimensional figures according to their mathematical properties.

Two-Dimensional Figures

Simple two dimensional figures that we will be concerned with include circles and polygons. A polygon is a closed plane figure composed of line segments.

A **CIRCLE** is the locus of all points that are a given distance (called the radius) from a fixed point (called the center). The diameter, *d*, of a circle is the distance across the circle, passing through the center. The radius, *r*, is the distance from the center to the outside of the circle, and is $\frac{1}{2}$ the diameter.

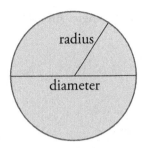

The area of a circle can be found using the formula $A=\pi r^2$. The distance around the circle, the circumference, is found using the formula $C=\pi d$ or $C=2\pi r$. When finding area or circumference, be careful to note whether you have been given radius or diameter.

Example:

Find the area and circumference of a circle with diameter 6.0 cm. Use the approximation $\pi = 3.14$.

To find circumference,

$C = \pi d$

$C = 6\text{cm} \cdot 3.14 = 18.8$ cm

To find area,

$A = \pi r^2$

$A = 3.14 \cdot 3^2 = 28.3$ cm^2 Remember to use the radius (3.0) instead of the diameter.

We name **POLYGONS**—simple, closed, two-dimensional figures composed of line segments—according to the number of sides they have.

Triangles

A **TRIANGLE** is a polygon with three sides. The sum of the interior angles of a triangle is 180°. We can classify triangles by the types of angles or the lengths of their sides.

An **ACUTE TRIANGLE** has exactly three *acute* angles. An **ACUTE ANGLE** is an angle that measures less than 90°.

A **RIGHT TRIANGLE** has one *right* angle. A **RIGHT ANGLE** is an angle that measures 90°.

POLYGON: a simple, closed, two-dimensional figure composed of line segments

TRIANGLE: a polygon with three sides

ACUTE TRIANGLE: a triangle with exactly three *acute* angles

ACUTE ANGLE: an angle that measures less than 90°

RIGHT TRIANGLE: a triangle with one *right* angle

RIGHT ANGLE: an angle that measures 90°

OBTUSE TRIANGLE: a triangle with one *obtuse* angle

OBTUSE ANGLE: an angle that measures more than 90° and less than 180°.

EQUILATERAL TRIANGLE: a triangle in which all sides are the same length

ISOSCELES TRIANGLE: a triangle in which at least two sides are the same length

SCALENE TRIANGLE: a triangle in which no sides are the same length

An **OBTUSE TRIANGLE** has one *obtuse* angle. An **OBTUSE ANGLE** measures more than 90° and less than 180°.

acute　　　　　　　right　　　　　　　obtuse

All three sides of an **EQUILATERAL TRIANGLE** are the same length.

At least two sides of an **ISOSCELES TRIANGLE** are the same length.

None of the sides of a **SCALENE TRIANGLE** are the same length.

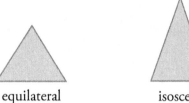

equilateral　　　　　　isosceles　　　　　　scalene

Example: Can a triangle have two right angles?
No. A right angle measures 90°; therefore, the sum of two right angles would be 180°, and there could not be a third angle.

Example: Can a triangle have two obtuse angles?
No. Since an obtuse angle measures more than 90°, the sum of two obtuse angles would be greater than 180°.

Quadrilaterals

A **QUADRILATERAL** is a polygon with four sides.

QUADRILATERAL: a polygon with four sides

The sum of the measures of the interior angles of a quadrilateral is 360°.

A **TRAPEZOID** is a quadrilateral with exactly one pair of parallel sides.

TRAPEZOID: a quadrilateral with exactly *one* pair of parallel sides

In an **ISOSCELES TRAPEZOID**, the nonparallel sides are congruent.

A **PARALLELOGRAM** is a quadrilateral with two pairs of parallel sides.

In a parallelogram:

- The diagonals bisect each other
- Each diagonal divides the parallelogram into two congruent triangles
- Both pairs of opposite sides are congruent
- Both pairs of opposite angles are congruent
- Two adjacent angles are supplementary

Remember that supplementary angles add up to 180°. Complementary angles add up to 90°

A **RECTANGLE** is a parallelogram with a right angle.

A **RHOMBUS** is a parallelogram with all sides equal in length.

A **SQUARE** is a rectangle with all sides equal in length.

Example: True or false?

All squares are rhombuses	True
All parallelograms are rectangles	False—*some* parallelograms are rectangles
All rectangles are parallelograms	True
Some rhombuses are squares	True
Some rectangles are trapezoids	False—trapezoids have only *one* pair of parallel sides
All quadrilaterals are parallelograms	False—some quadrilaterals are parallelograms
Some squares are rectangles	False—all squares are rectangles
Some parallelograms are rhombuses	True

Perimeter and Area

The **PERIMETER** of any polygon is the sum of the lengths of the sides.

> **PERIMETER:** the sum of the lengths of the sides of any polygon

Finding Area for Basic Polygons

	PERIMETER FORMULA	AREA FORMULA	
Triangle	Sum of the lengths of the sides	$A = \frac{1}{2} b \cdot h$	
Rectangle	$P = 2l + 2w$	$A = l \cdot w$	
		Table continued on next page	

Trapezoid	Sum of the lengths of the sides	$A = \frac{1}{2}h(b_1 + b_2)$ Note: b_1 and b_2 are the parallel bases. h is the distance between them.	
Parallelogram	Sum of the lengths of the sides	$A = b \cdot h$	

Example:

Find the perimeter and area of the trapezoid shown.

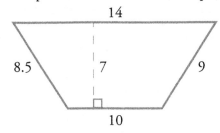

The perimeter is simply the sum of the side lengths.

$P = 14 + 10 + 9 + 8.5 = 41.5$

The area is:

$A = \frac{1}{2}h(b_1 + b_2)$

$A = \frac{1}{2}7(10 + 14) = 84$

Example: Find the area of a parallelogram if its base is 6.5 cm long and the height of the altitude to that base is 3.7 cm.

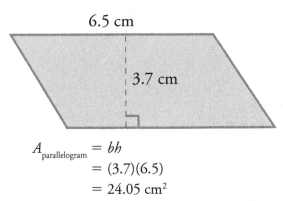

$A_{parallelogram} = bh$

$= (3.7)(6.5)$

$= 24.05 \text{ cm}^2$

Example: Find the area of this triangle.

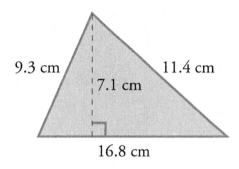

9.3 cm
11.4 cm
7.1 cm
16.8 cm

$A_{\text{triangle}} = \frac{1}{2} bh$
$= 0.5(16.8)(7.1)$
$= 59.64 \text{ cm}^2$

Example: Find the area of this trapezoid.

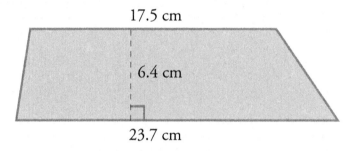

17.5 cm

6.4 cm

23.7 cm

The area of a trapezoid equals one-half the sum of the bases times the altitude.

$A_{\text{trapezoid}} = \frac{1}{2} h(b_1 + b_2)$
$A_{\text{trapezoid}} = 0.5(6.4)(17.5 + 23.7)$
$A_{\text{trapezoid}} = 131.84 \text{ cm}^2$

Example: Find the circumference and area of a circle whose radius is 7 meters.

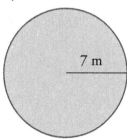

7 m

$C = 2\pi r$
$\approx 2(3.14)(7)$
$\approx 43.96 \text{ m}$

$A = \pi r^2$
$\approx 3.14(7)(7)$
$\approx 153.86 \text{ m}^2$

Three-dimensional figures

A **CYLINDER** is a space figure that has two parallel, congruent circular bases.

A **SPHERE** is a space figure having all its points the same distance from the center.

A **CONE** is a space figure having a circular base and a single vertex.

A **PYRAMID** is a space figure with a polygon base and triangle-shaped sides.

A **TETRAHEDRON** is a four-sided space triangle. Each face is a triangle.

A **PRISM** is a space figure with two congruent, parallel bases that are polygons.

CYLINDER: a space figure that has two parallel, congruent circular bases

SPHERE: a space figure having all its points the same distance from the center

CONE: a space figure having a circular base and a single vertex

PYRAMID: a space figure with a polygon base and triangle-shaped sides

TETRAHEDRON: a four-sided space triangle; each face is a triangle

PRISM: a space figure with two congruent, parallel bases that are polygons

Finding Surface Area and Volume of Common Three-Dimensional Figures

	SURFACE AREA (S.A.)	VOLUME (V)	
Cylinder We present here a right circular cylinder only (one with circular ends, parallel to each other, and a rectangular side).	$S.A. = 2\pi r^2 + 2\pi rh$ Surface area of a cylinder consists of 2 circles and a rectangle of length $2\pi r$ and width h.	$V = \pi r^2 h$ Volume of a cylinder is the area of the base, a circle (πr^2), multiplied by the height, h.	
Prism Prisms have 2 parallel bases and rectangular or parallelogram sides. The bases must be the same, and can be any polygon. Only right prisms (those with rectangular sides) are covered here.	Surface area of a prism is the sum of areas of the rectangular sides and the areas of the bases. The base can be in the shape of any polygon, but is the same for the top and the bottom bases.	$V = Bh$ B is the area of the base, and depends on the shape of the base.	
Cone The formulas in this table are based on a right cone with a circular base.	$S.A. = \pi r^2 + \pi rh$	$V = \frac{1}{3}\pi r^2 h$	
Sphere	$S.A. = 4\pi r^2$	$V = \frac{4}{3}\pi r^3$	
Pyramid	Surface area of a pyramid is the sum of areas of the triangular sides and the area of the base. Be sure to use s, called the slant height, when finding the area of the side triangles – not h, the height of the pyramid. The base can be in the shape of any polygon.	$V = \frac{1}{3}Bh$ B is the area of the base, and depends on the shape of the base.	

A few notes:

Surface area is the sum of the areas of each surface that makes up a three-dimensional figure.

Volume for figures with parallel bases (prisms, cylinders) is the area of the base multiplied by the distance between the bases (the height, h). Although there are cylinders and prisms that are not *right* (the bases are not lined up directly over each other), they will not be on the FTCE and are not covered here.

Note that volume of pyramids and cones (figures that come to a point instead of having 2 bases) are $\frac{1}{3}$ the volume of the corresponding cylinder or prism.

Example:

Find the volume and surface area of a cylinder with a radius of 5cm and a height of 12 cm.

$$S.A.=2\pi r^2+2\pi rh$$
$$S.A.=2\pi(5)^2+2\pi(5)(12)$$
$$S.A.=50\pi+120\pi=170\pi=534 \text{ cm}^2$$

You may be asked to leave your answer in terms of π (170π in this case), or to use $\pi=3.14$ or $\pi=\frac{22}{7}$ and provide an approximate number (534). Remember that area has units of length squared (cm^2 in this case).

Example:

Find the volume and surface area of a prism with a rectangular base, with length 20ft., width of 5 ft., and height 6 ft.

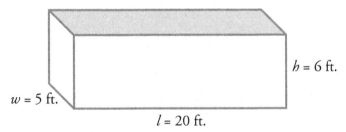

h = 6 ft.

w = 5 ft.

l = 20 ft.

To find the volume, first find the area of the base. For this example, note that there is more than one choice for a base, since there are more than one pair of parallel polygons. Choosing the 20 ft. $\times$ 5ft. surface as the base, the base area is:

$$B = 20 \text{ ft} \cdot 5 \text{ ft} = 100 \text{ ft}^2$$

and volume:

$V = Bh = 100 \text{ ft}^2 \cdot 6 \text{ ft}^2 = 600 \text{ ft}^3$

Or, for a rectangular prism, $V = l \cdot w \cdot h$

To find surface area, add the areas of each surface. There are 2 rectangles that measure 5 ft. by 6 ft. (the right and left ends), 2 rectangles that measure 20 ft. by 6 ft. (front and back), and 2 rectangles that measure 20 ft. by 5 ft. (top and bottom).

S.A. = 2(5 ft)(6 ft) + 2(20 ft)(6 ft) + 2(20 ft)(5 ft)

= 60 ft² + 240 ft²+ 200 ft²

= 500 ft²

The volume is 600 ft³ and the surface area is 500 ft².

SKILL 5.2 **Solve problems involving ratio and proportion** *(e.g., scaled drawings, models, real-world scenarios).*

Ratios

RATIO: a comparison of two numbers

A **RATIO** is a comparison of two numbers. If a class has 11 boys and 14 girls, we can write the ratio of boys to girls in 3 ways:

- 11:14
- 11 to 14
- $\frac{11}{14}$

The ratio of girls to boys is:

- 14:11
- 14 to 11
- $\frac{14}{11}$

Read ratio questions carefully. Given a group of 6 adults and 5 children, the ratio of children to adults is 5:6, but the ratio of children to the entire group is 5:11.

We should reduce ratios when possible. A ratio of 12 cats to 18 dogs reduces to 2:3, 2 to 3, or $\frac{2}{3}$.

Proportions

PROPORTION: an equation in which one fraction is set equal to another

A **PROPORTION** is an equation in which one fraction is set equal to another. To solve the proportion, multiply each numerator by the other fraction's denominator. Set these two products equal to each other and solve the resulting equation. This is called **cross-multiplying** the proportion.

Example: $\frac{4}{15} = \frac{x}{60}$ *is a proportion.*

To solve, cross-multiply.

$(4)(60) = (15)(x)$

$240 = 15x$

$16 = x$

Example: $\frac{x+3}{3x+4} = \frac{2}{5}$ *is a proportion.*

To solve, cross-multiply.

$5(x + 3) = 2(3x + 4)$

$5x + 15 = 6x + 8$

$7 = x$

Proportions can be used to solve word problems whenever relationships are compared. Some situations include scale drawings and maps, similar polygons, speed, time and distance, cost, and comparison shopping.

Example: Which is the better buy, 6 items for $1.29 or 8 items for $1.69?

Find the unit price.

$\frac{6}{1.29} = \frac{1}{x}$ $\qquad\qquad\qquad$ $\frac{8}{1.69} = \frac{1}{x}$

$\quad 6x = 1.29$ $\qquad\qquad\qquad\quad$ $8x = 1.69$

$\quad\;\; x = 0.215$ $\qquad\qquad\qquad\;\;\; x = 0.21125$

Thus, 8 items for $1.69 is the better buy.

Example: A car travels 125 miles in 2.5 hours. How far will it go in 6 hours?

Write a proportion comparing the distances and times.

Let x represent distance in miles. Then,

$\frac{miles}{hours} \qquad\quad \frac{125}{2.5} = \frac{x}{6}$

$\qquad\qquad\qquad 2.5x = 750$

$\qquad\qquad\qquad\;\;\; x = 300$

Thus, the car can travel 300 miles in 6 hours.

Example: The scale on a map is $\frac{3}{4}$ inch = 6 miles. What is the actual distance between two cities if they are $1\frac{1}{2}$ inches apart on the map?

Write a proportion comparing the scale to the actual distance.

	Scale		Actual
	$\dfrac{\frac{3}{4}}{1\frac{1}{2}}$	=	$\dfrac{6}{x}$
	$\frac{3}{4}x$	=	$1\frac{1}{2} \times 6$
	$\frac{3}{4}x$	=	9
	x	=	12

Thus, the actual distance between the cities is 12 miles.

Congruence

CONGRUENT FIGURES have the same size and shape. If one is placed atop the other, it will fit exactly. Congruent lines have the same length. Congruent angles have equal measures.

The symbol for congruence is $\cong$.

Polygons (pentagons) *ABCDE* and *VWXYZ* are congruent. They are exactly the same size and shape.

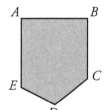 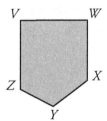

$$ABCDE \cong VWXYZ$$

The corresponding parts are these congruent angles and congruent sides:

Corresponding angles	Corresponding sides
$\angle A \leftrightarrow \angle V$	$AB \leftrightarrow VW$
$\angle B \leftrightarrow \angle W$	$BC \leftrightarrow WX$
$\angle C \leftrightarrow \angle X$	$CD \leftrightarrow XY$
$\angle D \leftrightarrow \angle Y$	$DE \leftrightarrow YZ$
$\angle E \leftrightarrow \angle Z$	$AE \leftrightarrow VZ$

When writing a congruence statement, such as ABCDE $\cong$ VWXYZ, the order of the letters is important. The corresponding letters tell which points correspond. In this example, point A corresponds to point V, point B to point W, point C to point X, D to Y, and E to Z. Note that sometimes figures are not shown in the same orientation, so take care to list corresponding points in the correct order. Here, ABCDE $\cong$ FGHIJ.

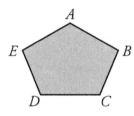 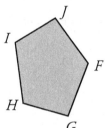

Similarity

Two figures that have the same shape are **SIMILAR**. Polygons are similar if and only if corresponding angles are congruent and corresponding sides are in proportion. Corresponding parts of similar polygons are proportional.

> **SIMILAR:** two figures that have the same shape but not necessarily the same size.

Example: Given the rectangles below, compare the sides and perimeter.

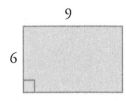 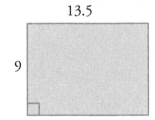

$$\frac{L_1}{L_2} = \frac{9}{13.5} = \frac{2}{3}$$ 1. Write formula.

$$\frac{W_1}{W_2} = \frac{6}{9} = \frac{2}{3}$$ 2. Substitute known values.

3. Compute.

$$P = 2(L + W)$$ 1. Write formula.

$$\frac{P_1}{P_2} = \frac{2(6 + 9)}{2(9 + 13.5)}$$ 2. Substitute known values.

$$= \frac{30}{45} = \frac{2}{3}$$ 3. Compute.

The perimeters are related to each other in the following manner:

Ratio of sides $\frac{9}{13.5} = \frac{2}{3}$

Multiply the perimeter of the first by the reciprocal of the ratio $\left(\frac{3}{2}\right)$ to get the perimeter of the second.

$$30 \times \frac{3}{2} = 45$$

Example: Given two similar quadrilaterals, find the lengths of sides x, y, and z.

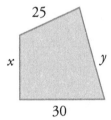 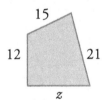

Use the corresponding sides of 15 and 25 to find the ratio of the 2 figures:

$$\frac{15}{25} = \frac{3}{5}$$

So the ratio of the figures is $\frac{3}{5}$. This ratio can be used to find the unknown sides by setting up proportions as follows:

$$\frac{12}{x} = \frac{3}{5} \qquad \frac{21}{y} = \frac{3}{5} \qquad \frac{z}{30} = \frac{3}{5}$$
$$3x = 60 \qquad\quad 3y = 105 \qquad 5z = 90$$
$$x = 20 \qquad\quad\; y = 35 \qquad\;\; z = 18$$

Example: Given ABC ~ ADE, AB = 4, BC = 3, AE = 15 and AD = 12, find DE and AC.

Begin by using the known corresponding sides to find the ratio of the sides.

$\frac{AB}{AD} = \frac{4}{12} = \frac{1}{3}$

This tells us the ratio of the side lengths of the 2 triangles.

So, $\frac{BC}{DE} = \frac{1}{3} \to \frac{3}{DE} = \frac{1}{3}$

Solving the proportion, DE = 9

To find AC,

$\frac{AC}{AE} = \frac{1}{3} \to \frac{AC}{15} = \frac{1}{3}$

Solving the proportion, AC = $\frac{15}{3}$ = 5

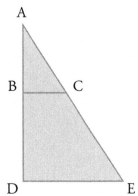

Example: Tommy draws and cuts out two triangles for a school project. One of them has sides of 3, 6, and 9 inches. The other triangle has sides of 2, 4, and 6 inches. Is there a relationship between the two triangles?

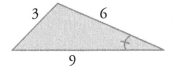
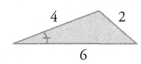

Take the proportion of the corresponding sides.

$\frac{2}{3}$ $\qquad\qquad$ $\frac{4}{6} = \frac{2}{3}$ $\qquad\qquad$ $\frac{6}{9} = \frac{2}{3}$

The smaller triangle has sides that are $\frac{2}{3}$ the size of the large triangle.

The Pythagorean Theorem

Given any right triangle ΔABC the square of the hypotenuse is equal to the sum of the squares of the other two sides.

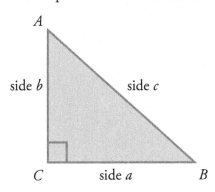

Hypotenuse (side opposite the 90° angle)

This theorem says that $(AB)^2 = (BC)^2 + (AC)^2$ or $c^2 = a^2 + b^2$.

Example: Find the area and perimeter of a rectangle if its length is 12 inches and its diagonal is 15 inches.

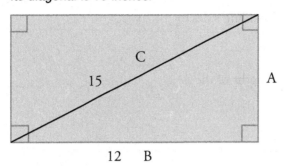

1. Draw and label sketch.
2. Since the height is still needed, use Pythagorean formula to find missing leg of the triangle.

$A^2 + B^2 = C^2$
$A^2 + 12^2 = 15^2$
$A^2 = 15^2 - 12^2$
$A^2 = 81$
$A = 9$

Now use this information to find the area and perimeter.

A = LW	P = 2(L + W)	1. Write formula.
A = (12)(9)	P = 2(12 + 9)	2. Substitute.
A = 108 in²	P = 42 inches	3. Solve.

Example: Two old cars leave a road intersection at the same time. One car traveled due north at 55 mph while the other car traveled due east. After 3 hours, the cars were 180 miles apart. Find the speed of the second car.

Using a right triangle to represent the problem we get the figure:

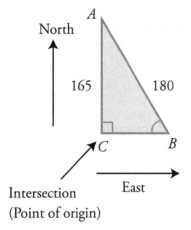

Traveling at 55 mph for 3 hours, the northbound car has driven (55)(3) = 165 miles. This is the side *AC*. The cars are 180 miles apart. This is side *AB*.

Since $\triangle ABC$ is a right triangle, then, by the Pythagorean theorem, we get:

$(AB)^2 = (BC)^2 + (AC)^2$ or
$(BC)^2 = (AB)^2 - (AC)^2$

$(BC)^2 = 180^2 - 165^2$
$(BC)^2 = 32400 - 27225$
$(BC)^2 = 5175$

Take the square root of both sides to get:

$$\sqrt{(BC)^2} = \sqrt{5175} \approx 71.93 \text{ miles}$$

Since the east bound car has traveled 71.93 miles in 3 hours, then the average speed is:

$\frac{71.93}{3} \approx 23.98$ mph

SKILL 5.3 **Determine an appropriate measurement unit and form** *(e.g., scientific notation)* **for real-world problems involving length, area, volume, or mass.**

To determine an appropriate measurement unit and form for real world problems, we will first review some common units of measure.

LENGTH	
The coastline of Florida	miles or kilometers
The width of a ribbon	inches or millimeters
The thickness of a book	inches or centimeters
The length of a football field	yards or meters
The depth of water in a pool	feet or meters

WEIGHT OR MASS	
A bag of sugar	pounds or grams
A school bus	tons or kilograms
A dime	ounces or grams

CAPACITY OR VOLUME	
Paint to paint a bedroom	gallons or liters
Glass of milk	cups or liters
Bottle of soda	quarts or liters
Medicine for child	ounces or milliliters

It is necessary to be familiar with the metric and customary system in order to estimate measurements.

Some common equivalents include:

ITEM	APPROXIMATELY EQUAL TO	
	METRIC	CUSTOMARY
Large paper clip	1 gram	0.1 ounce
Average sized adult	75 kilograms	170 pounds
Length of an office desk	1 meter	1 yard
Length of dollar bill	15 centimeters	6 inches
Area of football field		6,400 sq. yd
Temperature of boiling water	100°C	212°F
Temperature of ice	0°C	32°F
1 cup of liquid	240 mL	8 fl oz
1 teaspoon	5 ml	

Example: Estimate the measurement of the following items:
The length of dollar bill = ____6____ inches
Weight of a baseball = ____1____ pound
Distance from New York to Florida = ____1100____ km
Volume of water to fill a medicine dropper = ____1____ milliliter
Length of a desk = ____2____ meters
Temperature of water in a swimming pool = ____80°____ F

Example:

Identify an Appropriate Unit.

Area of a building site $= 60$ acres

Weight of a Blue Whale $= 3 \times 10^8$ pounds

Weight of a carbon atom $= 1.99 \times 10^{-23}$ grams

Volume of a coffee cup $= 0.23$ liters

Depending on the degree of accuracy needed, we can measure an object with different units. For example, a pencil may be 6 inches when measured to the nearest inch or $6\frac{3}{8}$ inches when measured to the nearest eighth of an inch.

Using the metric system, the pencil might be 15 cm when measured to the nearest cm or 154 mm when measured to the nearest mm.

Rounding Measurements

When rounding to a given place value, it is necessary to look at the number in the place smaller than the place to which the number will be rounded, that is, the number to its right. If this number is 5 or more, increase the number in the place above and change all numbers to its right to zero. If the number is less than 5, leave the number in the place above as it is and change all numbers to its right to zero.

Given a set of objects and their measurements, rounding procedures are helpful when attempting to round to the nearest given unit.

Rounding measurements can require an additional step. When the measurement to be rounded is not in decimal form, convert the measurement to a decimal number before applying the rules of rounding.

Example: Round the measurements to the given units.

MEASUREMENT	ROUND TO NEAREST	ANSWER
1 foot 7 inches	foot	2 ft
5 pound 6 ounces	pound	5 pounds
$5\frac{9}{16}$ inches	inch	6 inches

Convert each measurement to a decimal number. Then apply the rules for rounding.

$\quad$ 1 foot 7 inches $= 1\frac{7}{12}$ ft $= 1.58333$ ft, round up to 2 ft.

$\quad$ 5 pounds 6 ounces $= 5\frac{6}{16}$ pounds $= 5.375$ pound, round to 5 pounds.

$\quad$ $5\frac{9}{16}$ inches $= 5.5625$ inches, round up to 6 inches.

Rounding numbers is a form of estimation that is useful in many mathematical operations. For example, when estimating the sum of two three-digit numbers it is helpful to round the two numbers to the nearest hundred prior to addition.

Rounding Whole Numbers

To round whole numbers, first find the place value you want to round to (the rounding digit). Look at the digit directly to the right. If the digit is less than 5, do not change the rounding digit and replace all numbers after the rounding digit with zeros. If the digit is greater than or equal to 5, increase the rounding digit by 1, and replace all numbers after the rounding digit with zeros.

Example: Round 517 to the nearest ten.

1 is the rounding digit because it occupies the tens place. 517 rounded to the nearest ten = 520; because 7 > 5, we add 1 to the rounding digit.

Example: Round 15,449 to the nearest hundred.

The first 4 is the rounding digit because it occupies the hundreds place. 15,449 rounded to the nearest hundred = 15,400; because 4 < 5, we do not add to the rounding digit.

Rounding Decimals

Rounding decimals is identical to rounding whole numbers except that you simply drop all the digits to the right of the rounding digit.

Example: Round 417.3621 to the nearest tenth.

3 is the rounding digit because it occupies the tenths place. 417.3621 rounded to the nearest tenth = 417.4; because 6 > 5, we add 1 to the rounding digit.

Common Conversions and Units of Measure

ENGLISH SYSTEM	METRIC SYSTEM*	PURPOSE
1 yard = 3 feet = 36 inches	1 meter = 100 centimeters = 1000 millimeters	Length
1 mile = 5,280 feet = 1760 yards	1 kilometer = 1000 meters	Distance
1 acre = 43,560 square feet		Area
Table continued on next page		

1 hour = 60 minutes		Time
1 minute = 60 seconds		Time
1 cup = 8 fluid ounces		Volume
1 pint = 2 cups		Volume
1 quart = 2 pints		Volume
1 gallon = 4 quarts	1 liter = 1000 milliliters = 1000 cubic centimeters	Volume
1 pound = 16 ounces	1 kilogram = 1000 grams 1 gram = 1000 milligrams	Weight
1 ton = 2000 pounds		Weight

*Note: Metric numbers with 4 digits are presented without a comma (e.g., 5469 kilometers). For metric numbers greater than 4 digits, a space is often used instead of a comma (e.g., 13 638 liters).

Square Units

Square units can be derived with knowledge of basic units of length by squaring the equivalent measurements.

Example:

14 sq. yd. = _____ sq. ft.

$$14\text{yd}^2 \cdot \left(\frac{3\text{ ft}}{1\text{ yd}}\right)^2 = 14\text{ yd}^2 \cdot \frac{9\text{ ft}^2}{1\text{ yd}^2} = 126\text{ ft}^2$$

> 1 square foot (sq. ft.) = 144 sq. in.
>
> 1 sq. yd. = 9 sq. ft.
>
> 1 sq. yd. = 1296 sq. in.

Example: A farmer has a piece of land shaped as shown below. He wishes to fence this land at an estimated cost of $25 per linear foot. What is the total cost of fencing this property to the nearest foot?

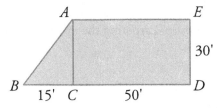

From the right triangle ABC, $AC = 30$ and $BC = 15$.

Since $(AB)^2 = (AC)^2 + (BC)^2$

$(AB)^2 = (30)^2 + (15)^2$

$\sqrt{(AB)^2} = AB = \sqrt{1125} = 33.5410$ feet

To the nearest foot, $AB = 34$ feet.

Perimeter of the piece of land is $= AB + BC + CD + DE + EA$

$= 34 + 15 + 50 + 30 + 50 = 179$ feet

Cost of fencing $= \$25 \times 179 = \$4,475.00$

Example: What will be the cost of carpeting a rectangular office that measures 12 feet by 15 feet if the carpet costs \$12.50 per square yard?

12 ft

15 ft

First determine the area of the office. The area of a rectangle is *length* $\times$ *width* $=$ *A*.

Substitute the given values in the equation $A = lw$.

$A = (12 \text{ ft.})(15 \text{ ft.})$

$A = 180 \text{ ft.}^2$

Since we are given the cost of the carpet per square yard, convert 180 ft.² into yards².

1 yd $= 3$ ft.

$(1 \text{ yd})(1 \text{ yd.}) = (3 \text{ ft.})(3 \text{ ft.})$

$1 \text{ yd}^2 = 9 \text{ ft}^2$

$180 \text{ft}^2 \cdot \frac{1 \text{ yd}^2}{9 \text{ ft}^2} = 20 \text{ yd}^2$

The carpet costs \$12.50 per square yard; thus the cost of carpeting the office described is $\$12.50 \times 20 = \$250.00$.

> **SKILL 5.4** **Solve real-world measurement problems including fundamental units** *(e.g., length, mass, time)*, **derived units** *(e.g., miles per hour, dollars per gallon)*, **and unit conversions.**

Example: Kathy has a bag of potatoes that weighs 5 lbs., 10 oz. She uses one third of the bag to make mashed potatoes. How much does the bag weigh now?

1 lb. = 16 oz.

5(16 oz.) + 10 oz.

= 80 oz + 10 oz = 90 oz.

$90 - (\frac{1}{3})90$ oz

= 90 oz − 30 oz

= 60 oz

60 ÷ 16 = 3.75 lb

.75 = 75%

$75\% = \frac{75}{100} = \frac{3}{4}$

$\frac{3}{4} \times 16$ oz = 12 oz

The bag now weighs 3 lb, 12 oz.

Example: The weight limit of a playground merry-go-round is 1000 pounds. There are 11 children on the merry-go-round. 3 children weigh 100 pounds. 6 children weigh 75 pounds. 2 children weigh 60 pounds. George weighs 80 pounds. Can he get on the merry-go-round?

3(100) + 6(75) + 2(60)

= 300 + 450 + 120

= 870

1000 − 870

= 130

George weighs less than 130, so he can get on the merry-go-round.

Example: A water company is trying to decide whether to use traditional cylindrical paper cups or to offer conical paper cups, since both cost the same. The traditional cups are 8 cm wide and 14 cm high. The conical cups are 12 cm wide and 19 cm high. The company will use the cup that holds the most water. Draw and label a sketch of each.

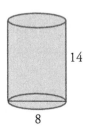

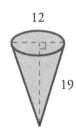

$V = \pi r^2 h$ $V = \frac{\pi r^2 h}{3}$ 1. Write a formula.

$V = \pi(4)^2(14)$ $V = \frac{1}{3}\pi(6)^2(19)$ 2. Substitute.

$V = 703.717$ cm^3 $V = 716.283$ cm^3 3. Solve.

The choice should be the conical cup since its volume is greater.

Example: How much material is needed to make a basketball that has a diameter of 15 inches? How much air is needed to fill the basketball?

Draw and label a sketch:

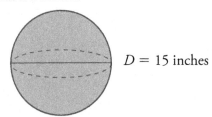

$D = 15$ inches

Total surface area   Volume

$S.A. = 4\pi r^2$ $V = \frac{4}{3}\pi r^3$ 1. Write a formula.

$= 4\pi(7.5)^2$ $= \frac{4}{3}\pi(7.5)^3$ 2. Substitute.

≈ 706.858 in^2 ≈ 1767.1459 in^3 3. Solve.

Example:

Josh has finished the annual maintenance on the swimming pool where he works and must now fill it with water. The pool is 164 feet long, 82 feet wide, and 6 feet deep. How much water does it take to fill the pool? Assume are 7.48 gallons in 1 cubic foot of water. Express your answer in scientific notation.

First find the volume of water in the pool. Since we are given fixed length, width and depth, assume a rectangular prism.

$V = Bh = lwh = (164 \text{ ft})(82 \text{ ft})(6 \text{ ft}) = 80{,}688 \text{ ft}^3$

To find the gallons of water,

$80688 \text{ ft}^3 \cdot \frac{7.48 \text{ gallons}}{1 \text{ ft}^3} = 603546.24 \text{ gallons} \rightarrow 6.0354624 \cdot 10^5 \text{ gallons}$

Example:

If a car is travelling 60 miles per hour, how many feet will it travel in 2.5 hours?

Begin by finding the distance travelled by the car using the distance formula $d = rt$, where d = distance, r = rate, and t = time.

$d = (60 \frac{\text{miles}}{\text{hour}})(2.5 \text{ hours})$

$d = 150$ miles

Now convert miles to feet, knowing 5,280 feet = 1 mile. Don't worry if you can't remember all the conversion factors. They are given to you on the exam. (150 miles)($\frac{5280 \text{ feet}}{1 \text{ mile}}$) = 792,000 feet or $7.92 \cdot 10^5$ feet

You can also use a proportion to do unit conversions.

$\frac{150 \text{ miles}}{x \text{ feet}} = \frac{1 \text{ mile}}{5280 \text{ feet}} \rightarrow x = 792{,}000$ feet

Example:

Julie has a bank savings account that earns 3% simple interest. If she begins with $1,546, what will be the balance after four years?

Simple interest is calculated using the formula

$I = prt$

where I = interest, p = principle, and t = time. Don't forget to convert the rate, given in percent, to a decimal.

Substituting known values,

$I = \$1546(0.03)(4) = \$185.52$

She will earn $185.52 in interest. To find her new balance, add this to the starting balance.

$\$1{,}546.00 + \$185.52 = \$1{,}731.52$

Note: Read the problem carefully to know if the interest earned is asked for or the new balance. Also note if the problem is simple interest or any form of compounded interest. Recall that compound interest is calculated at intervals, and the interest added to the original before a new amount is calculated.

Example:

Kendall borrowed $3,000 from his bank at an annual rate of 4%. If he doesn't make any payments, how much does he owe after 3 years?

YEAR	INTEREST	BALANCE
0 (start of the loan)	$0	$3,000
1	$3000(0.04)(1) = $120	$3,120
2	$3120(0.04)(1) = $124.80	$3,244.80
3	$3244.80(0.04) = $129.79	**$3,374.59**

COMPETENCY 6
KNOWLEDGE OF ALGEBRAIC THINKING AND THE COORDINATE PLANE

> **SKILL 6.1** Determine whether two algebraic expressions are equivalent by applying properties of operations or equality.

Equations and inequalities

Both equations and inequalities relate two quantities which may be expressed as any combination of constants, variables, and functions. In an equation, the two quantities are stated to be equal. In an inequality, one quantity is or may be greater than the other.

Equations

An **equation** consists of two expressions linked by an equal sign (statement H1) = (statement H2)

Left Hand Side (LHS) = Right Hand Side (RHS).

If substituting a value for the variable results in LHS = RHS, or a true statement, then the value is a solution for that equation.

Example: $2x = 6$
                (LHS)   (RHS)

If we substitute 3 for x, we get $2 \cdot 3 = 6$ (True).
Therefore, 3 is a solution for the equation.

Example: Is 2 a solution of $2x - 6 = 6x + 1$?

Substituting 2 for x, we get

$$2(2) - 6 = 6(2) + 1$$
$$4 - 6 = 12 + 1$$
$$-2 = 13 \text{ (False)}$$

Therefore, 2 is not a solution.

Inequalities

An **inequality** has the same form as an equation, but the equals sign is replaced by one of the following inequality signs:

$<$ (less than)

$>$ (greater than)

$\leq$ (less than or equal to)

$\geq$ (greater than or equal to)

The solution to an inequality is not a single value but a set of values that satisfy the inequality.

Example: $x + 2 < 7$

The solution is $x < 5$, meaning that any number less than 5 is a solution of the inequality.

Important facts about inequalities

1. **Sense of an inequality:** This is the direction of the inequality. The larger number is always facing the open side.

   Example: $25 > 3$ (greater than)

   Example: $3 < 25$ (less than)

2. **Notation:**

   $\geq \equiv$ "Greater than *or* equal to".

   $\leq \equiv$ "Less than *or* equal to".

   These relations are satisfied if either half of the relation is satisfied.

   Example: $25 \geq 3$ is true if $25 > 3$ is true or if $25 = 3$ is true. Since $25 > 3$ is true, $25 \geq 3$ is true, even though $25 = 3$ is false.

   Example: $0 \leq 0$ is true if $0 < 0$ is true or $0 = 0$ is true. Since $0 = 0$ is true, $0 \leq 0$ is true, even though $0 < 0$ is false.

3. Multiplying or dividing by a negative number changes the direction of the inequality.

   Example: $-3x > 6$

   Dividing both sides by -3, we get

   $x < -2$ (note the change in direction)

Properties of equations and inequalities

1. We can add any real number to, or subtract any real number from, both sides of the equation (or inequality).

Example: $3 = 3 \rightarrow 3 + 2 = 3 + 2 \rightarrow 5 = 5$ (still true)
Example: $9 = 9 \rightarrow 9 - 3 = 9 - 3 \rightarrow 6 = 6$ (still true)
Example: $x + 3 = 6 \rightarrow x + 3 - 3 = 6 - 3 \rightarrow x = 3$

2. We can multiply or divide both sides of an equation or an inequality by any real number except 0.

> ***Recall:*** When multiplying or dividing by a negative number we change the direction of the inequality.

Example: $3 = 3 \rightarrow 3 \times 2 = 3 \times 2 \rightarrow 6 = 6$ (still true)

Example: $8 = 8 \rightarrow \dfrac{8}{2} = \dfrac{8}{2} \rightarrow 4 = 4$ (still true)

Example: $-2x = 6 \rightarrow \dfrac{-2x}{-2} = \dfrac{6}{-2} \rightarrow x = -3$

Example: $6 > 2 \rightarrow 6 \times 2 > 2 \times 2 \rightarrow 12 > 4$ (still true)

Example: $-2 < 6 \rightarrow \dfrac{-2}{-2} > \dfrac{6}{-2} \rightarrow 1 > -3$ (still true, but with reversed inequality)

Example: $-3x \geq 5 \rightarrow \dfrac{-3x}{-3} \leq \dfrac{5}{-3} \rightarrow x \leq -\dfrac{5}{3}$ (note reversed inequality)

SKILL 6.2 Identify an algebraic expression, equation, or inequality that models a real-world situation.

An algebraic expression is a combination of constants and variables.

Examples of algebraic expressions

fourteen times a number	$14h$
nine less than a number	$x - 9$
one third of a number	$\dfrac{1}{3} \cdot n$
6 more than 5 times a number	$5y + 6$

An equation has algebraic expressions on two sides that have an equals sign or inequality sign between the two sides. When translating real-world problems into algebraic expressions, equations or inequalities, be on the lookout for words that can be translated to mathematical symbols

is	equals (=)
of, times	multiplied by (·)
more than, less than	≤, ≥, > or <
which, what, how much, how far	variable

It is also sometimes helpful to draw or map out information, especially if geometric figures are involved.

Example:

George has a plumbing business. He spends $50 a day on gas, and earns $110 per hour. Write an equation to show how much he makes in a day.

First look for quantities that can change. The two quantities that can change in this example are the number of hours worked and the amount earned. George spends a fixed amount of $50 each day on gas, so his daily income is decreased by this amount.

Let h = number of hours worked and I = daily income.
$I = 110h - 50$

Example:

A farmer wants to fence a rectangular field. He would like to make the length twice the width. If fencing is $2.25/ft, and he has only $3,000 to spend, write an inequality that he can use to find the biggest field he can fence in. Solve to the nearest foot.

Call the length of the field l and the width w. Recall the perimeter, the sum of the lengths of the sides, is $P = 2l+2w$ for a rectangle.
Length is twice the width → $l = 2w$

Substituting this relationship into the perimeter equation,
$P = 2(2w)+2w$
$P = 6w$

Knowing that fencing costs $2.25/ft, cost of the fencing will be $2.25 \cdot 6w$. To keep the cost below $3,000,

$2.25 \cdot 6w \leq \$3,000$
$13.5w \leq \$3,000$
Solving,
$w \leq 222.2$
To the nearest foot, the field can be as much as 222 feet wide and 444 feet long.

Example:

Al worked a summer job and put $2450 in his bank account. He would like to withdraw $30 a week for spending money. Write an inequality to express how many weeks he can do so if he wants to keep at least $350 in the account. Solve.

Assign variables to the quantities that can vary. In this case, only the number of weeks is of interest.

Let w = number of weeks

Relate the variables with the given information: starting bank balance minus $30 per week must be greater than or equal to $350.

$$\$2450 - \$30w \geq \$350$$

Solving,

$$\$2100 \geq 30w$$

$$w \leq 70$$

He can withdraw $30 per week for 70 or fewer weeks.

Example: Mark and Mike are twins. Three times Mark's age, plus 4, equals 4 times Mike's age minus 14. How old are the boys?

Because the boys are twins, their ages are the same. Let x = their age.

$$3x + 4 = 4x - 14$$

$$18 = x$$

The boys are each 18 years old.

SKILL 6.3 Solve equations and inequalities *(e.g., linear, quadratic)* graphically or algebraically.

Linear equations

A **linear equation** is one in which no variable has a higher power than 1.

Solving linear equations

1. Expand to eliminate all parentheses.

2. If there are fractions, multiply each term by the LCD to eliminate all denominators.

3. Combine terms on each side when possible.

4. Perform operations on both sides of the equation to isolate all variables on one side and all constants on the other side.

Example: Solve for x: 3(x + 3) = −2x + 4

$3x + 9 = -2x + 4$ Expand parentheses.

$3x = -2x - 5$ Subtract 9 from both sides.

$5x = -5$ Add $2x$ to both sides.

$x = -1$ Divide both sides by 5.

Example: Solve for x: 2x + 9 − 3x + 10 = 3x + x − 6

$-x + 19 = 4x - 6$ Combine similar terms on each side.

$-x = 4x - 25$ Subtract 19 from both sides.

$-5x = -25$ Subtract $4x$ from both sides.

$x = 5$ Divide both sides by -5.

Example: Solve for x: $3x - \dfrac{2}{3} = \dfrac{5x}{2} + 2$

$18x - 4 = 15x + 12$ Multiply each term by 6, the LCD of 2 and 3.

$18x = 15x + 16$ Add 4 to each side.

$3x = 16$ Subtract $15x$ from each side.

$x = \dfrac{16}{3}$ Divide each side by 3.

Linear inequalities

Linear inequalities are inequalities in which no variable has a higher power than one.

Solving linear inequalities

We use the same procedure used for solving linear equations, but the answer is represented in graphical form on the number line or in interval form.

Example: Solve the inequality, show its solution using interval form, and graph the solution on the number line.

$$\frac{5x}{8} + 3 \geq 2x - 5$$

$5x + 24 \geq 16x - 40$ Multiply each term by 8 to clear denominator.

$5x \geq 16x - 64$ Subtract 24 from each side.

$-11x \geq -64$ Subtract $16x$ from each side.

$x \leq 5\dfrac{9}{11}$ Divide each side by -11; reverse inequality sign.

Solution in interval form: $(-\infty, 5\frac{9}{11}]$ (Note that "[" means $5\frac{9}{11}$ is included in the solution.)

Graph of solution:

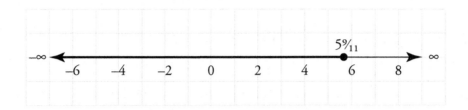

Interval and graph notation for inequalities

1. [and   ] mean that the lower and upper limit, respectively, are included as solutions. In graphing, a *closed dot* (•) indicates the same thing. Inclusive limits are specified with "greater than or equal to" or "less than or equal to" inequalities.

2. (and   ) mean that the lower and upper limit, respectively, are excluded as solutions. In graphing, *an open* dot (○) indicates the same thing. Exclusive limits are specified with "greater than" or "less than" inequalities.

Example: **Solve the following inequality and express your answer in both interval and graphical form.**

$3x - 8 < 2(3x - 1)$
$3x - 8 < 6x - 2$ Distributive property.
$3x < 6x + 6$ Add 8 to each side.
$-3x < 6$ Subtract $6x$ from each side.
$x > -2$ Divide each side by -3; reverse inequality.

In graphical form:

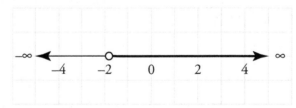

Interval form: $(-2, \infty)$ (Note that the "(" means that -2 is NOT included as a solution.)

Example: Is − 2 one of the solutions of the following inequality?

$$2x - 6 \leq x + 4$$

Substituting -2 for x, we get

$$2(-2) - 6 \leq -2 + 4$$
$$-10 \leq 2$$

This is a true statement; therefore, -2 is a solution of the inequality.

Example: Is 3 one of the solutions of the following inequality?

$$3x \leq 3 + 2$$

Substituting 3 for x, we get

$$3(3) \leq 3 + 2$$
$$9 \leq 5$$

This statement is false; therefore, 3 is not a solution of the inequality.

Note: a. A linear equation has one solution, no solution, or an infinite number of solutions.

   b. A linear inequality can have any number of solutions.

Representing Algebraic Equations Graphically

A first-degree equation has an equation of the form $ax + by = c$. To find the slope of a line, solve the equation for y. This gets the equation into **slope-intercept form**, $y = mx + b$. In this equation, m is the line's slope.

> *Slope-intercept form is*
> $y = mx + b$

The y-intercept is the coordinate of the point where a line crosses the y-axis. To find the y-intercept, substitute 0 for x and solve for y. This is the y-intercept. In slope-intercept form, $y = mx + b$, b is the y-intercept.

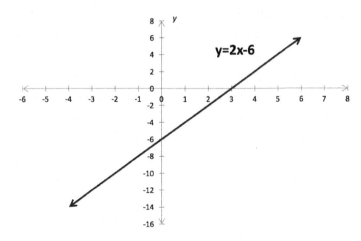

To find the x-intercept, substitute 0 for y and solve for x. This is the x-intercept.

Example:

In the graph above, showing the line $y = 2x - 6$, the line is in slope intercept form and we can see that the y-intercept is -6. To find the x-intercept, substitute 0 for y into the equation and solve for x.

$$y = 2x - 6$$
$$0 = 2x - 6$$
$$2x = 6$$
$$x = 3$$

So the x-intercept is (3,0).

Sometimes we are given the equation of a line in Standard Form, $Ax + By = C$. In the previous example, the equation would look like this:

$$2x - y = 6$$

To put the equation into slope-intercept form, solve for y.

$$2x - y = 6 \qquad \text{subtract } 2x \text{ from both sides}$$
$$-y = -2x + 6 \qquad \text{multiply both sides of the equation by } -1$$
$$y = 2x - 6$$

Sometimes it is easier to find x and y-intercepts from an equation in standard form by substituting 0 for the other variable.

$$2x - y = 6$$

To find the x-intercept: $2x - 0 = 6$
$$x = 3 \qquad \rightarrow \qquad (3,0)$$

To find the y-intercept: $2(0) - y = 6$
$$y = -6 \qquad \rightarrow \qquad (0, -6)$$

If a linear equation has no y variable, or x can be any number, then the graph is a vertical line, because it only has an x-intercept. Its slope is undefined.

In this example, the equation of the line is $x = 4$.

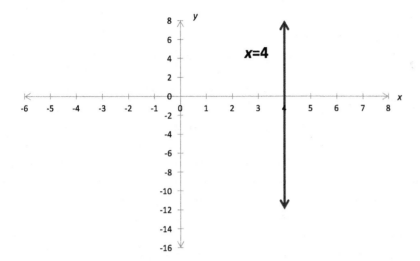

If the equation solves to **y = any number** (there is no x in the equation), then the graph is a horizontal line, because it only has a *y*-intercept. Its slope is 0 (zero). In the following example, $y = -6$.

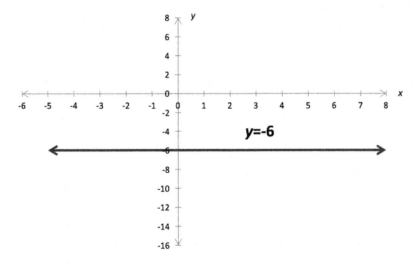

The equation of a line can be found from its graph by finding its slope and its intercept. The slope formula looks like this:

$$m = \frac{y_2 - y_1}{x_2 - x_1}$$

The equation of the line can be found using this equation:

$$Y - y_a = m(X - x_a)$$

(x_a, y_a) can be (x_1, y_1) or (x_2, y_2) If **m**, the value of the slope, is distributed through the parentheses, the equation can be rewritten into other forms of the equation of a line.

Example: Find the equation of a line through (9, –6) and (–1, 2).

To find slope:

$$m = \frac{y_2 - y_1}{x_2 - x_1}$$

$$m = \frac{-6 - 2}{9 - -1} = \frac{-8}{10} = \frac{-4}{5}$$

To find the equation of the line, substitute one of the points into the equation:

$y - y_a = m(x - x_a).$

$y - 2 = \frac{-4}{5}(x - -1)$

$y - 2 = \frac{-4}{5}x + 1(\frac{-4}{5})$

$y = \frac{-4}{5}x - \frac{4}{5} + 2$

$y = \frac{-4}{5}x + 1\frac{1}{5}$

The slope of the line is $\frac{-4}{5}$ and the *y*-intercept is $1\frac{1}{5}$,or $\frac{6}{5}$

Example: Find the slope and y-intercept of 3x + 2y = 14.

$3x + 2y = 14$

$2y = -3x + 14$

$y = \frac{-3}{2}x + 7$

The slope of the line is $\frac{-3}{2}$. The *y*-intercept of the line is 7.

The intercepts can also be found by substituting 0 in place of the other variable in the equation.

To find the *y*-intercept:

Let $x = 0$; $3(0) + 2y = 14$

$0 + 2y = 14$

$2y = 14$

$y = 7$

(0, 7) is the *y*-intercept.

To find the *x*-intercept:

Let $y = 0$; $3x + 2(0) = 14$

$3x + 0 = 14$

$3x = 14$

$x = \frac{14}{3}$

$(\frac{14}{3}, 0)$ is the *x*-intercept.

Example: Sketch the graph of the line represented by 2x + 3y = 6.

To find the *y*-intercept:

Let $x = 0$; $2(0) + 3y = 6$

$0 + 3y = 6$

$3y = 6$

$y = 2$

(0, 2) is the *y*-intercept.

To find the *x*-intercept:

Let $y = 0$; $2x + 3(0) = 6$

$2x + 0 = 6$

$2x = 6$

$x = 3$

(3, 0) is the *x*-intercept.

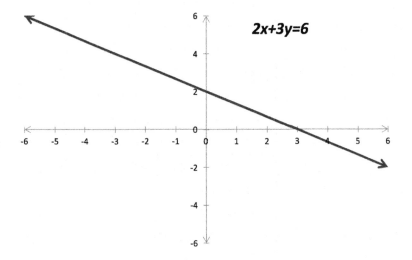

Graphing a linear inequality

A linear inequality in two variables is similar in form to a linear equation *except* that the = sign is replaced by an inequality sign of $>$, $<$, $\geq$, or $\leq$. The procedure to graph it is as follows:

1. Graph the equivalent equation with the inequality sign replaced by an equals sign. Use a solid line for this line if the inequality contains the equals sign ($\leq$ or $\geq$); use a dashed line if the inequality contains no equals sign ($<$ or $>$).

2. Pick a point on either side of the line and test whether its x- and y-values satisfy the inequality. If so, mark that region as a solution set with shading or slanted lines. If not, shade the opposite region.

Example: Identify the region that satisfies $3x + 5y < 15$.

1. We graph the equivalent equation of $3x + 5y = 15$ using a dashed line. Substituting $y = 0$ produces an x-intercept of $(5, 0)$; substituting $x = 0$ produces a y-intercept of $(0,3)$.

2. Pick a test point on either side of this line. Pick the origin for simplicity $(0, 0)$. Substitute $x = 0$ and $y = 0$ into the inequality and test:

3. $0 < 15$ is true, so accept the region containing $(0, 0)$ and shade it.

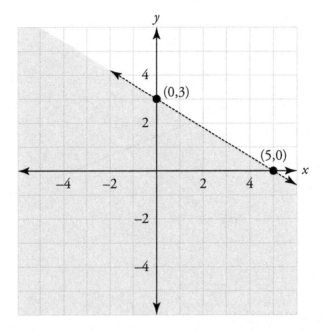

Use of "and" and "or" with inequalities

1. "And" means "intersection," the overlapping of two regions.
   It indicates the region that is common to the solutions of more than one inequality.

2. "Or" means "union," the joining of two regions. It indicates the region that is a solution of either inequality or both.

Example: Solve the inequalities 3x = 5y < 15 and y ≥ 1.

1. We found the region representing the inequality $3x + 5y < 15$ above. Shade it with horizontal lines.

2. For $y \geq 1$, graph the equivalent equation of $y = 1$. This is a horizontal line through $y = 1$. Use a solid line.

3. Use the origin $(0, 0)$ as a test point. Test the inequality with $x = 0, y = 0$: $0 \geq 1$ is false. So shade the region above the line with vertical lines.

4. The solution region is the intersection region where the two regions overlap as shown.

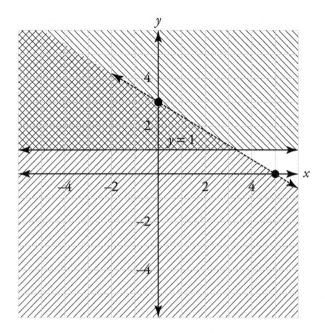

If the question had called for the solution of $3x + 5y < 15$ OR $y \geq 1$, the solution region would be as shown below.

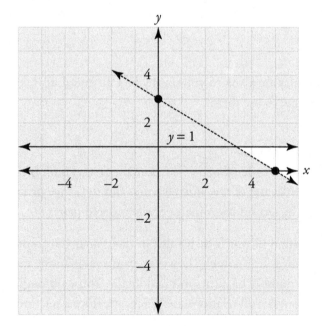

Finding Distance Between Two Points and Mid-Point

To determine the distance between two coordinate points, use the distance formula:

$$d = \sqrt{(x_2 - x_1)^2 + (y_2 - y_1)^2}$$

To determine their mid-point,

$$\left(\frac{x_1 + x_2}{2}, \frac{y_1 + y_2}{2}\right)$$

Example:

Find the distance between $(5, -2)$ and $(-3, 9)$.

$$d = \sqrt{(-3 - 5)^2 + (9 - -2)^2}$$
$$d = \sqrt{(-8)^2 + (11)^2}$$
$$d = \sqrt{64 + 121}$$
$$d = \sqrt{185}$$
$$d = 13.6$$

Example:

Find the mid-point of $(4, -6)$ and $(-10, 2)$.

$$\left(\frac{x_1 + x_2}{2}, \frac{y_1 + y_2}{2}\right)$$

$$\left(\frac{4 + -10}{2}, \frac{-6 + 2}{2}\right) \rightarrow \left(\frac{-6}{2}, \frac{-4}{2}\right) \rightarrow (-3, -2)$$

Note: These formulas are given to you on the FTCE. You don't need to memorize them, but know how to use them.

Properties of functions

A **relation** is any set of ordered pairs. The domain of a relation is the set containing all the first coordinates of the ordered pairs, and the range of a relation is the set containing all the second coordinates of the ordered pairs.

A function is a relation in which each value in the domain corresponds to only one value in the range. It is notable, however, that a value in the range may correspond to any number of values in the domain. Thus, although a function is necessarily a relation, not all relations are functions, since a relation is not bound by this rule.

On a graph, use the vertical line test to check whether a relation is a function. If any vertical line intersects the graph of a relation in more than one point, as in the graph below, then the relation is not a function.

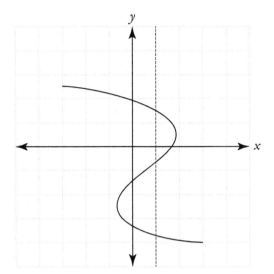

A relation is considered one-to-one if each value in the domain corresponds to only one value in the range, and each value in the range corresponds to only one value in the domain. Thus, a one-to-one relation is also a function, but it adds an additional condition.

In the same way that the graph of a relation can be examined using the vertical line test to determine whether it is a function, the horizontal line test can be used to determine if a function is a one-to-one relation. If no horizontal lines super-imposed on the plot intersect the graph of the relation in more than one place, then the relation is one-to-one (assuming it also passes the vertical line test and, therefore, is a function).

As mentioned above, a function is a relation in which each value in the domain corresponds to only one value in the range. Functions can be expressed discretely, as sets of ordered pairs, or they can be expressed more generally as formulas. For instance, the function $y = x$ is a function that represents an infinite set of ordered pairs (x, y), where each value in the domain (x) corresponds to the same value in the range (y).

Linear functions

A **linear function** can be expressed as $f(x) = mx + b$, where m and b are con-stants. It is called linear because it involves no quadratic or cubic variables, nor any square roots or cube roots of variables. No variables in a linear function have any exponent other than 1.

A linear function can be graphed as $y = mx + b$. The result is a straight line with slope m that intercepts the y-axis at $(0, b)$.

Example: $y = 2x - 1$

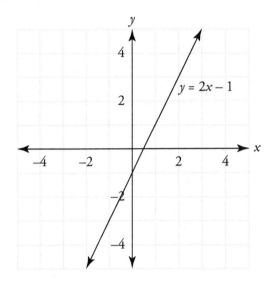

Domain and range

The **domain** of a function is the set of all possible inputs to the function. The **range** of a function is the set of all possible outputs. In some functions, both the domain and the range extend to all real numbers. Some functions have limitations on the domain, meaning that certain values are not allowed as inputs. Some functions have limitations on the range, meaning that certain values are not possible as outputs.

In the function $y = 2x + 4$, both the domain and the range extend to all real numbers. Any real number is a possible value of the input x or the output y.

In the function $y = \dfrac{1}{x - 3}$, the domain includes all real numbers except 3: x cannot equal 3, because that would cause a division by zero.

In the function $y = x^2$, the range is all positive real numbers. Since the square of a real number is always positive, the possible outputs of the function do not include any negative numbers.

Lines are linear functions, useful for modeling many real-life situations. Others situations are modeled by quadratic functions. To discuss quadratic functions, we must first review polynomial expansion and factoring.

Expanding polynomials

To multiply two binomials, use the FOIL method: First terms, Outside terms, Inside terms, Last terms.

Example: expand (3x + 1)(x − 7).

$$(3x+1)(x-7)=$$

First terms: $3x(x)+$

Outside terms: $3x(-7)+$

Inside terms: $1(x)+$

Last terms: $1(-7)$

$$= 3x^2 + (-21x) + x - 7$$
$$= 3x^2 - 20x - 7$$

Factoring polynomials

Polynomials, like integers, can be factored. The factors of a polynomial can include constants, variables, and expressions. There are various strategies for factoring a polynomial, depending on the form it's in.

Removing common factors

The first step in factoring any polynomial is to remove any common factor of all terms, using the distributive property.

Example: $8x^3 − 18x^2 − 4x = 2x(4x^2 − 9x − 2)$

Factoring the difference of two squares

If a polynomial has two terms, check if it is the difference of two squares. If it can be expressed as $a^2 − b^2$, it can be factored as $(a + b)(a − b)$.

Example: $9x^2 − 4 = (3x)^2 − (2)^2 = (3x + 2)(3x − 2)$

Factoring a trinomial in the form $x^2 + bx + c$

Look for two factors of c that add to b.

Example: *factor $x^2 + 11x + 18$*

Factors of 18: 1 and 18 (sum 19) ✗

2 and 9 (sum 11) ✓

$$x^2 + 11x + 18 = (x + 2)(x + 9)$$

Factoring a trinomial in the form $x^2 − bx + c$

Look for two factors of c that add to the absolute value of b, then make both factors negative.

Example: $x^2 - 11x + 18 = (x - 2)(x - 9)$

Factoring a trinomial in the form $x^2 + bx - c$

Look for two factors of the absolute value of c that differ by b. Make the larger factor positive and the smaller factor negative.

Example: factor $x^2 + 5x - 24$

Factors of 24: 1 and 24 (difference 23) ✗
2 and 12 (difference 10) ✗
3 and 8 (difference 5) ✓

$x^2 + 5x - 24 = (x + 8)(x - 3)$

Factoring a trinomial in the form $x^2 - bx - c$

Look for two factors of the absolute value of c that differ by the absolute value of b. Make the larger factor negative and the smaller factor positive.

Example: $x^2 - 5x - 24 = (x - 8)(x + 3)$

Quadratic equations and quadratic expressions

A **quadratic equation** is one that includes at least one squared term such as $2x^2$.

> **Definition:** The standard form of a quadratic equation is represented by $ax^2 + bx + c = 0$, where a, b, and c are real, imaginary, or complex numbers and $a \neq 0$.
>
> **Note:** Real numbers are a subset of complex numbers.

A quadratic equation, $ax^2 + bx + c = 0$, is how we "solve" a quadratic function, $y = ax^2 + bx + c$. We are typically looking for the values of x that make $y = 0$. This can be accomplished algebraically or graphically.

Examples: $3x^2 + 5x - 7 = 0$
$-3x^2 + 2x = 0$
$x^2 - 2 = 0$

A **quadratic expression** is one that includes at least one squared term; it is equivalent to the left-hand side of a quadratic equation.

Examples: $2x^2 - 2x + 9$
$4x^2 - 3x$
$-2x^2 + 6$

Quadratic equations may be solved algebraically by several methods, including taking the square root, factoring, and using the quadratic formula.

Taking the square root

If it is possible to take the square root of both sides, a quadratic equation may be solved that way.

Example: $4x^2 + 4x + 1 = 49$

$(2x + 1)^2 = 7^2$	Represent both sides as squares.
$2x + 1 = \pm 7$	Take square root of each side.
$2x + 1 = 7 \quad 2x + 1 = -7$	Find two solutions.
$2x = 6 \qquad 2x = -8$	Subtract 1 from each side.
$x = 3 \qquad x = -4$	Divide each side by 2.
$x = 3, -4$	Combine solutions.

Factoring

If the left-hand side of a quadratic equation in standard form can be factored, the equation can be solved by setting each factor to 0.

Example: solve for x: $x^2 - x - 6 = 0$

$(x + 2)(x - 3) = 0$	Equation is true if either factor equals 0.
$x + 2 = 0 \quad x - 3 = 0$	Solve by setting each factor equal to 0.
$x = -2 \qquad x = 3$	Find two solutions.
$x = -2, 3$	Combine solutions.

In general, if $x = a$ is a solution of a quadratic equation in standard form, then $x - a$ is a factor of the expression on the left-hand side of the equation, and vice versa.

Example: 3 is a solution of $x^2 + 2x - 15 = 0$,
since $3^2 + 2(3) - 15 = 9 + 6 - 15 = 0$.
Therefore, $(x - 3)$ is a factor of
$x^2 + 2x - 15: x^2 + 2x - 15 = (x - 3)(x + 5)$

Using the quadratic formula

When a quadratic equation is not factorable we use the quadratic formula, which *always yields* a solution. The solution of $ax^2 + bx + c = 0$ is given by the formula:

$$x = \frac{-b \pm \sqrt{b^2 - 4ac}}{2a}$$

This formula yields two solutions:

$$x_1 = \frac{-b + \sqrt{b^2 - 4ac}}{2a}, \quad x_2 = \frac{-b - \sqrt{b^2 - 4ac}}{2a}$$

Example: Solve for x: $3x^2 + 5x - 3 = 0$

$$a = 3; b = 5; c = -3$$

$$x = \frac{-b \pm \sqrt{b^2 - 4ac}}{2a}$$

$$= \frac{-5 \pm \sqrt{5^2 - 4(3)(-3)}}{2(3)}$$

$$= \frac{-5 \pm \sqrt{61}}{6}$$

$$x_1 = \frac{-5 + \sqrt{61}}{6}, \quad x_2 = \frac{-5 - \sqrt{61}}{6}$$

Solving Quadratics

As previously stated, "solving" a quadratic ($y = ax^2 + bx + c$) means finding the values of x that make $y = 0$. This can be difficult or time consuming, especially during a time limited test! During a multiple choice test it may be easier to try the answers and see if they work. There can be 2, 1 or 0 (no real) solutions to a quadratic.

Example:

Find the solution of $x^2 - 5x - 6 = 0$.

A. $x = 1$

B. $x = -1$

C. $x = -6, 1$

D. $x = 6, -1$

Try each choice and see if it works.

A. $(1)^2 - 5(1) - 6 = 0 \rightarrow 1 - 5 - 6 \neq 0$

B. $(-1)^2 - 5(-1) - 6 = 0 \rightarrow 1 + 5 - 6 = 0$

This works, but there may be another solution.

C. $(-6)^2 - 5(-6) - 6 = 0 \rightarrow 36 + 30 - 6 \neq 0$
   $(1)^2 - 5(1) - 6 = 0 \rightarrow 1 - 5 - 6 \neq 0$

D. $(6)^2 - 5(6) - 6 = 0 \rightarrow 36 - 30 - 6 = 0$
   $(-1)^2 - 5(-1) - 6 = 0 \rightarrow 1 + 5 - 6 = 0$

Both 6 and -1 make the equation true, so choice D is correct.

Another way to find solutions to a quadratic is to look at its graph. The graph of a quadratic is a parabola. It can open "up" or "down".

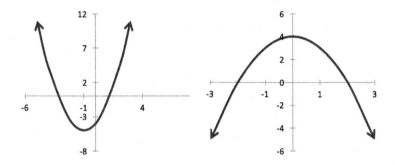

Here is an example of a quadratic with 2 solutions. The equation graphed below is $y = x^2 - 2x - 8$. Note that the parabola crosses the x-axis twice: at $x = -2$ and $x = 4$, or at the points $(-2, 0)$ and $(4, 0)$. The solutions to $x^2 - 2x - 8 = 0$ are -2 and 4.

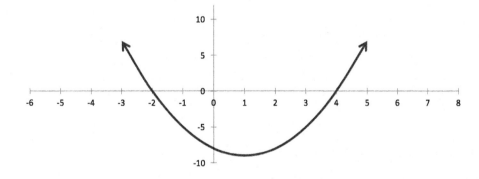

Here is an example of a quadratic with only one solution. Note that the graph touches the x-axis at only 1 point, where $x = 3$. The equation of this graph is $y = x^2 - 6x + 9$. Only a value of $x = 3$ will make $x^2 - 6x + 9 = 0$ true.

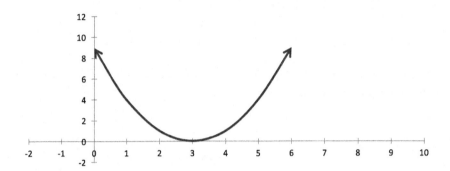

Here is an example of a quadratic with no (real) solutions. The graph does not cross the x-axis. You may recall from math class that a quadratic can have imaginary roots, but imaginary numbers are not covered here, since they are not covered on the FTCE exam. The equation of the graph below is $y = x^2 - 6x + 11$. There are no (real) solutions to $x^2 - 6x + 11 = 0$. No numbers we can put in for x will make this equation $= 0$.

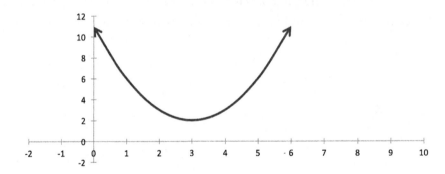

Quadratic inequalities

To solve a quadratic inequality, first gather all terms on the left side of the inequality sign, leaving zero on the right.

Example: $x^2 < 5x + 6 \rightarrow x^2 - 5x - 6 < 0$

Then replace the sign of the inequality with an equals sign and solve the resulting quadratic equation by factoring or by using the quadratic formula:

$$x^2 - 5x - 6 = 0 \rightarrow (x + 1)(x - 6) = 0 \rightarrow x = -1,6$$

The last step is to restore the inequality signs. This can be done by graphing the quadratic equation as a function. In this example, since the first term of the equation is positive, the resulting graph will be a parabola opening upward, with zeros at -1 and 6.

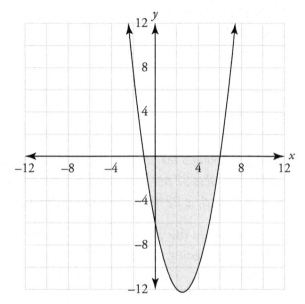

To restore the inequality signs, note that in this example, the solutions are supposed to be less than zero. Those solutions will be found in the part of the parabola that goes below the x-axis, namely the section between -1 and 6. Therefore, the solutions are $-1 < x < 6$.

SKILL 6.4 **Determine and solve equations or inequalities, graphically or algebraically, in real-world problems.**

Real-World Example Problems

Example: The YMCA wants to sell raffle tickets to raise at least $32,000. If they must pay $7,250 in expenses and prizes out of the money collected from the tickets, how many $25 tickets must they sell?

Since they want to raise *at least* $32,000, that means they would be happy to get 32,000 *or more*. This requires an inequality.

Let x = number of tickets sold.

Then $25x$ = total amount of money collected for x tickets.

The total amount of money minus expenses is greater than $32,000.

$$25x - 7,250 \geq 32,000$$

$$25x \geq 39,250$$

$$x \geq 1,570$$

If they sell 1,570 tickets or more, they will raise at least $32,000.

Example: The Simpsons went out for dinner. All four of them ordered the aardvark steak dinner. Bert paid for the four meals and included a tip of $12.00 for a total of $84.60. How much was an aardvark steak dinner?

Let x = the price of one aardvark dinner

So $4x$ = the price of four aardvark dinners

$$4x + 12 = 84.60$$
$$4x = 72.60$$
$$x = \$18.15 \text{ for each dinner}$$

Example: Lucy is thinking of taking a taxi to work. The taxi driver charges an initial fixed fee of $4 to use the taxi, plus $2 per mile. Write a linear equation that will model the cost. If her ride to work is 22 miles, how much will it cost?

The two quantities that can vary in this problem are distance travelled and total cost of the taxi ride. Begin by assigning variables. Call the total cost of the taxi ride C and the distance travelled d.

The total cost, C, is the sum of the initial cost, $4, and the miles travelled, d, multiplied by $2.

$$C = \$4 + \$2d$$

The equation is of the form $y = mx + b$. Here the slope is 2 (cost per mile), and the y-intercept is $4 (the cost when $x = 0$, or no distance is travelled).

If her ride to work is 22 miles,

$$C = \$4 + \$2(22)$$
$$C = \$4 + \$44 = \$48$$

Graph the relation. Note the value of the y-intercept. Values below $x = 0$ (0 miles travelled) have no meaning in this example.

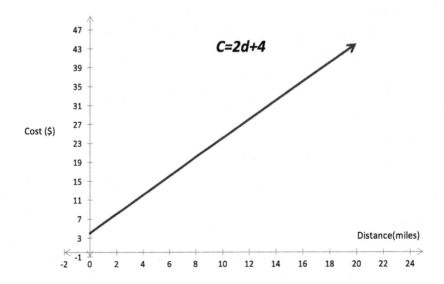

Example: Medicine doses are typically based on weight of the patient. Given the information in the table below, find a relation that relates dosage to weight.

Weight (kg)	10	20	40	60
Dosage (mg)	2	4	8	12

First identify the quantities that can change and assign variables. Weight and dosage can vary. Let us assign weight the variable W and dosage, D. Next find the relation between the variables. Examining the pattern we can write that weight divided by 5 equals dosage.

$$D = \frac{1}{5} W$$

The equation is of the form $y = mx + b$. Here the slope is $\frac{1}{5}$ (mg of medicine per kg body weight), and the y-intercept is 0 (dosage when weight = 0).

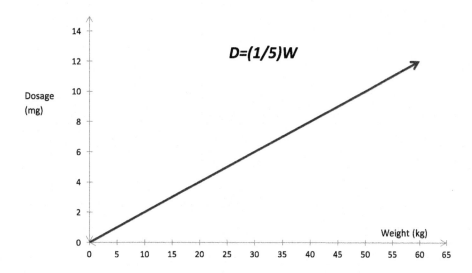

Example: Sharon's bike shop sells three speed bikes and ten speed bikes. The profit on each bike sold is $60 for a three speed bike and $75 for a ten-speed bike. They would like to make at least $300 per day. How many of each type of bike do they need to sell?

There are several combinations of three speed and ten speed bikes sold that will satisfy the $300 per day target. To show them, write an inequality and graph.

Let x = the number of three speed bikes and y = number of ten speed bikes.

(3 speed bikes sold)($60) + (10 speed bikes sold)($75) ≥ $300

$60x + 75y \geq 300$

Since this equation is greater than or equal to, the line is solid (points on the line work, or are included as solution to the problem). The shaded area above the line has other solutions, or combinations of 3-speed bikes and 10-speed bikes sold, that will work also. For example, if the shop sells 4 10-speed bikes and 7 3-speed bikes, they will make more than $300.

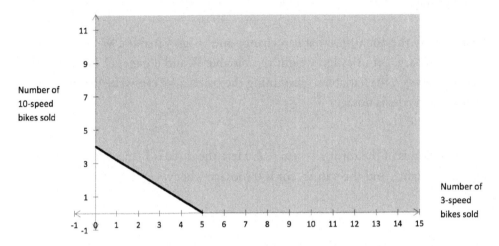

Number of 10-speed bikes sold

Number of 3-speed bikes sold

SKILL 6.5 **Graph and interpret a linear equation in real-world problems** *(e.g., use data to plot points, explain slope and y-intercept, determine additional solutions).*

Instead of writing an equation form a word problem, we may be given a graph and/or equation and be asked to interpret the information. For example, if we are given that the cost for Lucy to take a cab is (an example in the previous section):

$C = \$4 + \$2d$

We can graph the equation noting that it is of the form $y = mx + b$, with a y-intercept of 4 and a slope of 2.

These 2 pieces of information can be used to graph the equation by first putting a point at the (0,4), the y-intercept, and using the slope (rise over run) to find another point. Go up 2 and over 1 to find the point (1,6).

Alternatively, we can make a table of values and plot these, then connect the points.

d (miles)	0	2	6	10
C ($)	4	8	16	24

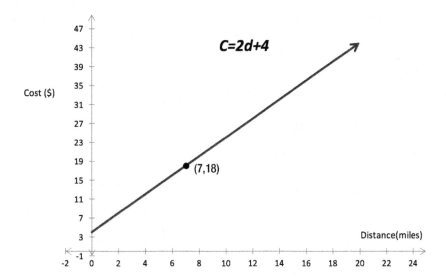

We can find cost by using the equation, or if we have a graph, read values off the graph.

Note that slope is how the quantity on vertical axis (cost) varies with a change on the horizontal axis (distance in this case) $\rightarrow \dfrac{rise}{run} \rightarrow \dfrac{y_2 - y_1}{x_2 - x_1} \rightarrow \dfrac{\text{change in cost}}{\text{change in distance}} \rightarrow$ *slope*.

Recall that the *y*-intercept is the value when $x = 0$. In this case, it is the cost (C) when 0 miles have been travelled $(d = 0)$.

SKILL 6.6 Identify relations that satisfy the definition of a function.

Recall that a function is a relation in which each value in the domain (*x* values) corresponds to only one value in the range (*y* values). Or, if we select a value for *x*, there is only one number *y* can be. Relations may be presented in a variety of forms, including tables and ordered pairs.

Examples of relations that satisfy the definition of a function:

x	−3	0	1	5
y	4	7	8	12

(0, −2), (1, 0), (2, 5), (3, 14)

x	−2	0	1	2
y	0	2	0	4

Examples of relations that do NOT satisfy the definition of a function:

(−2, 0), (0, 2), (−2, 5), (2,4)

$$
\begin{array}{ll}
x & y \\
3 \rightarrow 0 \\
3 \rightarrow 2 \\
1 \rightarrow 0 \\
2 \rightarrow 4 \\
\end{array}
$$

x	3	3	1	2
y	0	2	0	4

If given a table of values or a list of ordered pairs, look to see if any *x* value is listed more than once. If it is, and there are 2 different values for *y*, the relation is not a function.

If given a graph, the simplest way to determine if it is a function is the vertical line test. If you can draw a vertical line anywhere and cross the equation more than once, it is not a function.

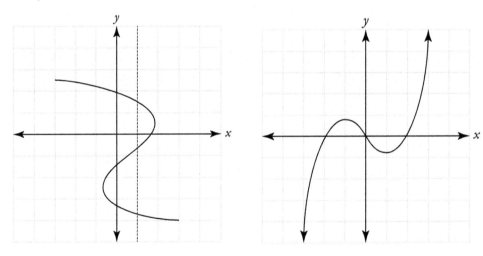

Not a Function   **Function**

When two equations or inequalities have the same (equal) slopes, they are parallel.

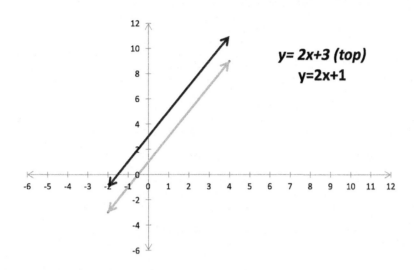

Lines that are perpendicular (intersect at a right angle) have slopes that are *negative reciprocals* of each other. For example,

$y = 3x + 2$ and $y = (\frac{-1}{3})x + 4$ are perpendicular.

Remember that when a line rises from left to right (as the lines on the graph above), the slope is *positive*. For lines with a *negative* slope, the line will fall from left to right. The slope in the graph below is $\frac{-2}{3}$. Remember that slope can be thought of as $\frac{rise}{run}$. If we start from any point on the graph, slope tells us how to get to another point. For example, if we start from the point (0, 2), we can use the slope to get to another point on the graph. Go down 2, right 3, to get to (3,0).

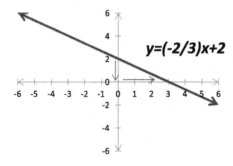

A *negative* slope tells us that as one quantity *increases*, the other *decreases*.

A *positive* slope tells us they are changing in the same way. If one is *increasing*, the other is also *increasing*. If one in *decreasing*, the other is also *decreasing*.

If given two equations and asked to compare slopes, it may be easiest to put both in slope intercept form.

Example:

Compare the slopes of the two lines:

$y = 3x + 5$

$3x - 3y = 5.$

Re-arrange the second to slope-intercept form:

$3x - 3y = 5$

$-3y = -3x + 5$

$y = x + \frac{-5}{3}$

The slope of the first line is 3. The slope of the second line is 1, so the first line has a larger slope.

If these same lines were presented on a graph, we can see that the top line, $y = 3x + 5$ has a larger slope (is steeper) than the other line.

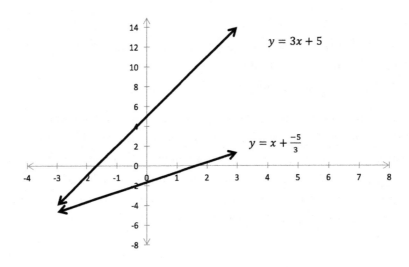

COMPETENCY 7
KNOWLEDGE OF PROBABILITY, STATISTICS, AND DATA INTERPRETATION

SKILL 7.1 **Analyze data presented in various forms** *(e.g., histograms, bar graphs, circle graphs, pictographs, line plots, tables)* **to solve problems.**

To make a **BAR GRAPH** or a **PICTOGRAPH**, determine the scale to be used for the graph. Then determine the length of each bar on the graph, or determine the number of pictures needed to represent each item of information. Be sure to include, in the legend, an explanation of the scale.

Example: A class had the following grades: 4 As, 9 Bs, 8 Cs, 1 D, and 3 Fs. Graph these on a bar graph and a pictograph.

Bar graph

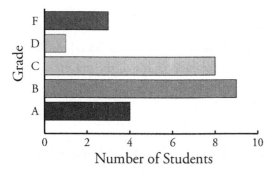

Pictograph

Grade	Number of Students
A	☺☺☺☺
B	☺☺☺☺☺☺☺☺☺
C	☺☺☺☺☺☺☺☺
D	☺
F	☺☺☺

To make a **LINE GRAPH**, determine appropriate scales for both the vertical and horizontal axes (based on the information to be graphed). Describe what each axis represents, and mark the scale at intervals on each axis. Graph the individual points of the graph, and connect the points on the graph from left to right.

> **BAR GRAPH:** a graph that compares various quantities

> **PICTOGRAPHS:** a graph that compares quantities using symbols; each symbol represents a number of items

> **LINE GRAPHS:** a graph that shows trends, often over a period of time

Example: Graph the following information using a line graph.

The number of National Merit Scholarship finalists/school year

Number of National Merit Finalists/School Year						
School	90–91	91–92	92–93	93–94	94–95	95–96
Central	3	5	1	4	6	8
Wilson	4	2	3	2	3	2

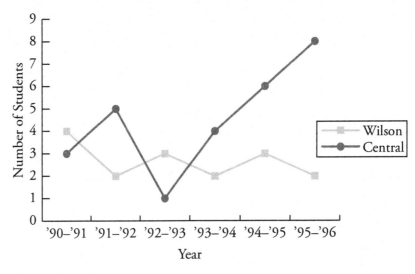

> **CIRCLE GRAPH:** also called a pie chart, this graph shows quantities in proportional sectors

To make a **CIRCLE GRAPH**, total all the information that is to be included on the graph. Determine the central angle to be used for each sector of the graph using the following formula:

$$\frac{\text{information}}{\text{total information}} \times 360° = \text{degrees in central } \sphericalangle$$

Lay out the central angles to these sizes, label each section, and include each section's percent.

Example: Graph the following information about monthly expenses on a circle graph:

MONTHLY EXPENSES					
Rent	Food	Utilities	Clothes	Church	Misc.
$400	$150	$75	$75	$100	$200

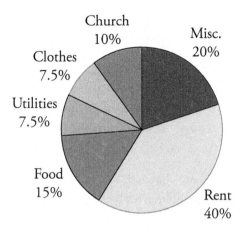

To read a bar graph or a pictograph, read the explanation of the scale that was used in the legend. Compare the length of each bar with the dimensions on the axes, and calculate the value each bar represents. On a pictograph, count the number of pictures used in the chart and calculate the value of all the pictures.

To read a circle graph, find the total of the amounts represented on the entire circle graph. To determine the actual amount that each sector of the graph represents, multiply the percent in a sector times the total amount number.

To read a chart, be sure to look at the row and column headings on the table. Use this information to evaluate the information given in the chart.

HISTOGRAMS are used to summarize information from large sets of data that can be naturally grouped into intervals. The vertical axis indicates FREQUENCY (the number of times any particular data value occurs), and the horizontal axis indicates data values or ranges of data values. The number of data values in any interval is the FREQUENCY OF THE INTERVAL.

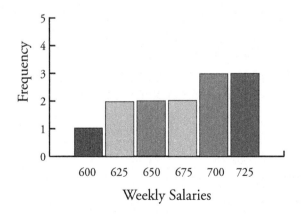

HISTOGRAMS: graphs that summarize information from large sets of data that can be naturally grouped into intervals

FREQUENCY: the number of times any particular data value occurs

FREQUENCY OF THE INTERVAL: the number of data values in any interval

Pictographs can be misleading, especially if drawn to represent 3-dimensional objects. If two or more dimensions that reflect ratio are changed, the overall visual effect can be misinterpreted.

Bar and line graphs can be misleading if the scales are changed; for example, if small-scale increments represent large numbers, the differences between sets of information will seem much less than if larger-scale increments are used.

Circle graphs, or pie charts, are excellent for comparing relative amounts. However, they cannot be used to represent absolute amounts and, if interpreted as such, they are misleading.

MEAN: the sum of a set of numbers divided by the number of items being averaged; also called the average

The arithmetic **MEAN** (or average) of a set of numbers is the sum of the numbers divided by the number of items being averaged.

Example: Find the mean of the following numbers. Round to the nearest tenth.

24.6, 57.3, 44.1, 39.8, 64.5

The sum is 230.3

The mean is $\frac{230.3}{5}$

$= 46.06$, rounded to 46.1 (nearest tenth)

MEDIAN: the middle number when a set of numbers is arranged in order

The **MEDIAN** of a set of numbers is the middle number when the numbers are arranged in order. To calculate the median, we must arrange the terms in order. If there is an even number of terms, the median is the mean of the two middle terms.

Example: Find the median.

12, 14, 27, 3, 13, 7, 17, 12, 22, 6, 16

Rearrange the terms from least to greatest.

3, 6, 7, 12, 12, 13, 14, 16, 17, 22, 27

Since there are eleven numbers, the middle would be the sixth number, or 13.

The **MODE** of a set of numbers is the number that occurs with the greatest frequency. A set can have no mode if each term appears exactly one time. Similarly, there can also be more than one mode.

Example: Find the mode.
26, 15, 37, **26**, 35, **26**, 15

   15 appears twice, but 26 appears three times. Therefore, the mode is 26.

The **RANGE** of a set of numbers is the difference between the highest and lowest data value.

Example: Given the ungrouped data below, calculate the mean and range.

15	22	28	25	34	38
18	25	30	33	19	23

Mean = 25.8333333
Range: 38 − 15 = 23

Variance and standard deviation are measures of how close to their mean a set of data are. The variance is calculated by adding up the square of each data point subtracted from the mean, then dividing by the number of data points. Standard deviation is the square root of the variance. You won't be asked to calculate variance and standard deviation on the FTCE, just to know that a bigger standard deviation means that the data are more spread out from the mean.

The lower case Greek letter sigma squared (σ^2) represents variance.

The larger the value of the variance, the larger the spread of data points from their mean.

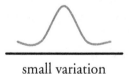

small variation   larger variation

STANDARD DEVIATION is the square root of the variance. The lower case Greek letter sigma (σ) is used to represent standard deviation.

$$\sigma = \sqrt{\sigma^2}$$

MODE: the number that occurs with the greatest frequency in a set of numbers

RANGE: the difference between the highest and lowest data value in a set of numbers

The Greek letter sigma squared (σ^2) represents variance.

STANDARD DEVIATION: the square root of the variance

A very simple example of how to calculate variance and standard deviation is shown here.

Example:

Find the variance and standard deviation of: 4, 2, 5, 3, and 1.

Mean: $\dfrac{4 + 2 + 5 + 3 + 1}{5} = 3$

Variance: $(\sigma^2) = \dfrac{(4-3)^2 + (2-3)^2 + (5-3)^2 + (3-3)^2 + (1-3)^2}{5}$

$= \dfrac{1 + 1 + 4 + 0 + 4}{5} = 2$

Standard deviation: $(\sigma) = \sqrt{2} \cong 1.4$

> Standard deviation is represented by σ.

SKILL 7.4 **Interpret the meaning of measures of central tendency** *(i.e., mean, median, mode)* **and dispersion** *(i.e., range, standard deviation)* **in the context of a real-world situation.**

Example: Is the mean, median, or mode the best measure of central tendency for the set 135, 135, 137, and 190?

The mean is 149.25, the median is 136, and the mode is 135. Thus, the median or mode is a better measure than the mean because they are both closer to the majority of the scores.

Example: The yearly salaries of the employees of Company A are $11,000, $12,000, $12,000, $15,000, $20,000, and $25,000. Which measure of central tendency would you use if you were a manager? Which would you use if you were an employee trying to get a raise?

The mean is $15,833. The median is $13,500. The mode is $12,000.

The employee would probably use the mean, since it is the largest amount. The manager would most likely use the mode, since it is the smallest.

Example:

Harry and Sandy are both students in Ms. Smith's history class. They have had 6 tests so far this semester. Given the measures of central tendency and dispersion shown in the table, which student is more likely to have had a test score of 60 for one of the tests taken this semester?

TEST SCORES IN HISTORY CLASS					
	Mean	Median	Mode	Range	σ
Harry	80.5	83	78	31	10.7
Sandy	79	78.5	77	5	1.9

It would be difficult to tell which student had a score of 60 on a test if only mean, median and mode were available. A score of 60 is quite a bit lower than the mean (average), median or mode for either student. However, Harry's scores have a range of 31 compared with Sandy's range of 5, so we would expect that Harry might have had a score of 60 on one of his tests. The standard deviation of Harry's scores is much higher than Sandy's, also indicating a much higher spread of data.

SKILL 7.5 **Analyze and evaluate how the selection of statistics** *(e.g., mean, median, mode)* **can lead to different or inappropriate interpretations in the context of a real-world situation.**

Information can be misleading if the data is not presented appropriately. If a data set contains one very high or one very low value, the mean will not be a good representative of the data set. For example, including the teacher's height in the mean height of a classroom of very young students introduces a single disproportionately high value into the data set and creates a mean that is far greater than it would be without this value.

If the data in a given set clusters around two numbers with a large gap between them, the median will not be representative of the set. For example, the median height of a family with two parents and two small children would be a misleading measure.

Modes are best used with categorical data. For example, a mode of the sale of men's shoe sizes would be helpful to a store when reordering stock of men's shoes. However, finding the mode of men's and women's shoe sizes combined would not be a good indicator of the stock that should be reordered.

Consider this set of test scores from a math class: 0, 16, 19, 65, 65, 65, 68, 69, 70, 72, 73, 73, 75, 78, 80, 85, 88, and 92. The mean of the scores is 64.06 and the median is 71. Because only three of the eighteen scores are less than the mean, the median (71) is a more descriptive measure of how the students scored on the test.

Example:

One of the statistics commonly reported by the U.S Census Bureau is median family income. For 2014, the median family income was $53,700. The mean income was $75,735. Can it be concluded that median or mean is a more accurate representation?

Median is the middle number in a group of data. So the median represents the income for which half of households had a higher income, and half of households had less income.

The mean (average) income is quite a bit higher than the median. This can be due to a variety of factors. It may be that there are either many more data points with incomes lower than the mean, fewer data points with higher incomes than the mean, or the mean may be skewed by some very high or very low numbers. There is quite a variety in population density, cost of living, average wage, etc… in the country. We cannot draw further conclusions without knowing more about the dispersion of the data. Since few people recognize the definition of "median" in median family income, it is often confused with average family income.

> ### SKILL 7.6   Solve and interpret real-world problems involving probability using counting procedures, tables, and tree diagrams.

Counting Procedures

In all the problems we have seen so far, we were given the sample space for the problem or we could easily obtain it. However, in many real-life situations, the sample space and events within it are very large and difficult to find.

There are three techniques to help find the number of elements in one event or a sample space: the counting principle, permutations, and combinations.

There are three techniques to help find the number of elements in one event or a sample space: the **counting principle**, **permutations**, and **combinations**.

The counting principle

In a sequence of two distinct events where the first one has n number of outcomes or possibilities and the second one has m number of outcomes or possibilities, the total number of possibilities of the sequence is

$n \times m$

Example: A car dealership has three Mazda models and each model comes in a choice of four colors. How many Mazda cars are available at the dealership?

Number of available Mazda cars = (3)(4) = 12

Example: If a license plate consists of three digits followed by three letters, find the possible number of licenses if:

   A. Repetition of letters and digits is not allowed.

   B. Repetition of letters and digits is allowed.

   A. Because there are twenty-six letters and ten digits and repetitions are not allowed, by using the counting principle we get:

$$\text{possible number of licenses} = (26)(25)(24)(10)(9)(8)$$
$$= 11,232,000$$

   B. If repetitions are allowed, we get:

$$\text{possible number of licenses} = (26)(26)(26)(10)(10)(10)$$
$$= 17,576,000$$

The addition principle of counting

If A and B are events, $n(A \, or \, B) = n(A) + n(B) - n(A \cap B)$

Example: In how many ways can you select a black card or a Jack from an ordinary deck of playing cards?

Let B denote the set of black cards, and let J denote the set of Jacks. Then, $n(B) = 26$, $n(J) = 4$, $n(B \cap J) = 2$, and

$$n(B \, or \, J) = n(B) + n(J) - n(B \cap A)$$
$$= 26 + 4 - 2$$
$$= 28$$

The addition principle of counting for mutually exclusive events

If A and B are mutually exclusive events, $n(A \, or \, B) = n(A) + n(B)$.

Example: A travel agency offers 40 possible trips: 14 to Asia, 16 to Europe, and 10 to South America. In how many ways can you select a trip to Asia or Europe through this agency?

Let A denote trips to Asia, and let E denote trips to Europe. Then $A \cap E = \varnothing$, and $n(A \, or \, E) = 14 + 16 = 30$.

Therefore, the number of ways you can select a trip to Asia or Europe is 30.

The multiplication principle of counting for dependent events

Let A be a set of outcomes of Stage 1 and B a set of outcomes of Stage 2.

The number of ways, $n(A \, and \, B)$ that A and B can occur in a two-stage experiment is represented by:

$$n(A \, and \, E) = n(A)n(B|A)$$

where $n(B|A)$ denotes the number of ways B can occur, given that A has already occurred.

Example: How many ways from an ordinary deck of 52 cards can 2 Jacks be drawn in succession if the first card is drawn but not replaced in the deck and then the second card is drawn?

This is a two-stage experiment where we must compute $n(A and B)$, where A is the set of outcomes for which a Jack is obtained on the first draw and B is the set of outcomes for which a Jack is obtained on the second draw.

If the first card drawn is a Jack, then there are only 3 remaining Jacks left to choose from on the second draw. Thus, drawing two cards without replacement means that the events A and B are dependent.

$$n(A and B) = n(A)n(B|A) = 4 \times 3 = 12$$

The multiplication principle of counting for independent events

Let A be a set of outcomes of Stage 1, and B a set of outcomes of Stage 2. If A and B are independent events, then the number of ways, $n(A and B)$, that A and B can occur in a two-stage experiment is represented by:

$$n(A and B) = n(A)n(B).$$

Example: How many six-letter code "words" can be formed if repetition of letters is not allowed?

With code words, a word does not have to look like a word; for example, *abcdef* could be a code word. Since we must choose a first letter and a second letter and a third letter and a fourth letter and a fifth letter and a sixth letter, this experiment has six stages.

Since repetition is not allowed there are twenty-six choices for the first letter, twenty-five for the second, twenty-four for the third, twenty-three for the fourth, twenty-two for the fifth, and twenty-one for the sixth. Therefore, we have:

n (six-letter code words without repetition of letters)

$= 26 \cdot 25 \cdot 24 \cdot 23 \cdot 22 \cdot 21$

$= 165,765,600$

Permutations

In order to understand permutations, we must first address the concept of factorials.

n factorial, written $n!$, is represented by $n! = n(n - 1)(n - 2) \ldots (2)(1)$

$5! = (5)(4)(3)(2)(1) = 120$

$3! = 3(2)(1) = 6$

By definition: $0! = 1$

$ 1! = 1$

$\frac{6!}{6!} = 1$ but $\frac{6!}{2!} \neq 3!$

$\frac{6!}{2!} = \frac{6 \cdot 5 \cdot 4 \cdot 3 \cdot 2!}{2!} = 6 \cdot 5 \cdot 4 \cdot 3 = 360$

The number of permutations represents the number of ways we can select r items from n items and arrange them in a specific order.

Write permutations as $_nP_r$ and calculate them using the following relationship:

$$_nP_r = \frac{n!}{(n - r)!}$$

Example: How many different ways can the students in a math class select a president and a vice president if seven students are available?

Because the positions of president and vice president are not equal, this question will have a number of permutations.

$$_7P_2 = \frac{7!}{(7 - 2)!} = \frac{7!}{5!} = \frac{7 \cdot 6 \cdot 5 \cdot 4 \cdot 3 \cdot 2 \cdot 1}{5 \cdot 4 \cdot 3 \cdot 2 \cdot 1} = 42$$

This problem can also be solved using the counting principle:

There are seven available students from whom to choose a president. After the math students choose a president, there are six available students from whom to choose a vice president.

Therefore, the number of ways the students can choose a president and a vice president $= 7 \cdot 6 = 42$.

> When calculating permutations, order matters. For example, 2, 3, 4 and 4, 3, 2 are counted as two different permutations. Calculating the number of permutations is not valid with experiments where replacement is allowed.

Combinations

When we are dealing with the number of COMBINATIONS, the order in which elements are selected is not important. For instance,

2, 3, 4 and 4, 2, 3 are considered one combination.

The number of combinations represents the number of ways in which r elements can be selected from n elements (in no particular order). The number of combinations is represented by $_nC_r$ and can be calculated using the following relationship.

$$_nC_r = \frac{n!}{(n - r)r!}$$

> COMBINATIONS: an unordered collection of distinct elements

Example: In how many ways can 2 students be selected from a class of 7 students to represent the class?

Since both representatives have the same position, the order is not important, and we are dealing with the number of combinations.

$$_nC_r = \frac{7!}{(7-2)!2!} = \frac{7!}{5!2!} = \frac{7 \cdot 6 \cdot 5!}{5! \cdot 2 \cdot 1} = \frac{7 \cdot 6}{2} = 21$$

Example: In a club, there are 6 women and 4 men. A committee of 2 women and 1 man is to be selected. How many different committees can be selected?

This problem has a sequence of two events. The first event involves selecting 2 women out of 6 women, and the second event involves selecting 1 man out of 4 men. We use the combination relationship to find the number of ways in events 1 and 2, and we use the counting principle to find the number of ways the sequence can happen.

Number of committees $= {}_6C_2 \cdot {}_4C_1$

$$\frac{6!}{(6-2)!2!} \cdot \frac{4!}{(4-1)!1!}$$

$$= \frac{6 \cdot 5 \cdot 4!}{4! \cdot 2 \cdot 1} \cdot \frac{4 \cdot 3!}{3! \cdot 1}$$

$$= (15) \cdot (4) = 60$$

Using Tables

Example: The results of a survey of 47 students are summarized in the table below.

	BLACK HAIR	BLONDE HAIR	RED HAIR	TOTAL
Male	10	8	6	24
Female	6	12	5	23
Total	16	20	11	47

Use the table to answer questions A through C.

A. If one student is selected at random, find the probability of selecting a male student.

$$\frac{\text{Number of male students}}{\text{Number of students}} = \frac{24}{47}$$

B. If one student is selected at random, find the probability of selecting a female with red hair.

$$\frac{\text{Number of females with red hair}}{\text{Number of students}} = \frac{5}{47}$$

C. If one student is selected at random, find the probability of selecting a student who does not have red hair.

$$\frac{\text{Number of students with red hair}}{\text{Number of students}} = \frac{11}{47}$$

$$1 - \frac{11}{47} = \frac{36}{47}$$

Remembering formulas for probability, combinations and permutations can be very confusing. A simpler way is often to construct a tree diagram.

A tree diagram is a way to show possible outcomes for an event. For example, if we flip a coin and roll a die, what is the probability of getting a head and a 4? The possible outcomes could be listed out: (H, 1), (H, 2), (H, 3), (H, 4), (H, 5), (H, 6), (T, 1), (T, 2), (T, 3), (T, 4), (T, 5), (T, 6). There are 12 possible outcomes, only one of which is a head and a 4. So the probability of getting a head and a 4 is:

$$P(H,4) = \frac{1}{12}$$

For a small set of possible outcomes, listing out the possibilities is not difficult. For a larger number of possible outcomes, a tree diagram is often a quick way to come up with these possibilities.

A tree diagram for the example above would look like this:

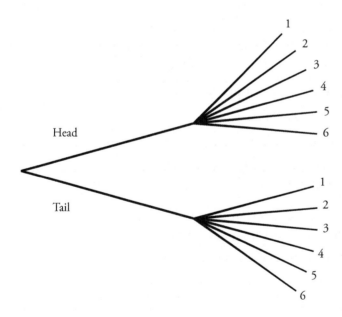

"And"

There are a few key words to look out for in probability problems. "And" generally means multiply. In the previous example, the probability of getting a head in the coin toss is $\frac{1}{2}$. The probability of getting a 4 on the die is $\frac{1}{6}$. The probability of getting a head **_and_** a 4 is the product of these two:

$$P(H \text{ and } 4) = P(H) \cdot P(4) = \frac{1}{2} \cdot \frac{1}{6} = \frac{1}{12}$$

Looking back to the tree diagram, only 1 of the 12 possibilities listed shows a head and a 4.

"Or"

The other key word to look for in probability problems is the word "or". "Or" means add. The probability of getting a 4 or a 6 is the sum of the probability of getting a 4 plus the probability of getting a 6:

$$P(4 \text{ or } 6) = P(4) + P(6) = \frac{1}{6} + \frac{1}{6} = \frac{1}{3}$$

SKILL 7.7 Infer and analyze conclusions from sample surveys, experiments, and observational studies.

When analyzing information from surveys and experiments, be mindful of how representative samples are. Be careful about inferring too much from information given.

Example:

If Betty is tasked with surveying students at her school on how to best spend a gift to the school of $500, where should she conduct her survey?

A. Ask her girls basketball team at practice (14 students)

B. Ask in her English class (24 students)

C. Ask in the cafeteria at lunch (80 people stopped to answer her questions)

D. Ask 2 random homeroom teachers from each grade to have their students fill out surveys (60 students).

A is biased because it includes only girls who play basketball.
B is better, but is likely students from only one grade.
C includes students who eat in the cafeteria only. Those that eat elsewhere may have a different choice.
D is a good random sample that includes all grades and likely a good distribution of boys and girls.

Samples can be used to extrapolate information using proportions.

Example:

A company interested in starting a bus service took a survey find out how many people in Pleasant City would use it if one were offered. In a random sample of

50 people, 12 said they would use a bus at some time during a normal day. If there are 20,000 people in the city, how many riders can the bus company expect during a normal day?

A proportion to find expected riders is:

$$\frac{12}{50} = \frac{x}{20{,}000}$$

Solving,

$$50x = 12 \cdot 20{,}000$$
$$x = 4{,}800$$

DOMAIN III
READING SKILLS

PERSONALIZED STUDY PLAN

KNOWN MATERIAL/ SKIP IT

COMPETENCY 8
KNOWLEDGE OF KEY IDEAS AND DETAILS BASED ON TEXT SELECTIONS

> **SKILL Identify textual evidence to support conclusions drawn from text.**
> **8.1**

Supporting details are specific examples, facts, ideas, illustrations, cases, and anecdotes writers use to explain, expand upon, and develop the main idea. A writer's choice of supporting materials is determined by the nature of the topic being covered and the purpose for writing the selection.

For example, an advertisement writer seeking to persuade the reader to buy a particular running shoe will emphasize only the positive characteristics of the shoe for advertisement copy. A columnist for a running magazine, on the other hand, might list the good and bad points about the same shoe in an article recommending appropriate shoes for different kinds of runners. Both major details (those that directly support the main idea) and minor details (those that provide interesting, but not always essential, information) help create a well-written and fluid passage.

In the following paragraph, the sentences in **bold** print provide a skeleton of a paragraph on the benefits of recycling. The sentences in bold are generalizations that, by themselves, do not explain the need to recycle. The sentences in *italics* add details to SHOW the general points in bold. Notice how the supporting details help you understand the necessity of recycling.

> *Both major details (those that directly support the main idea), and minor details (those that provide interesting but not always essential, information) help create a well-written and fluid passage.*

> **While one day recycling may become mandatory in all states, right now it is voluntary in many communities.** *Those of us who participate in recycling are amazed by how much material is recycled.* **For many communities, the blue-box recycling program has had an immediate effect.** *By just recycling glass, aluminum cans, and plastic bottles, we have reduced the volume of disposable trash by one-third, thus extending the useful life of local landfills by over a decade. Imagine the difference if those dramatic results were achieved nationwide.* **The number of reusable items we thoughtlessly dispose of is staggering.** *For example, Americans dispose of enough steel every day to supply Detroit car manufacturers for three months. Additionally, we dispose of enough aluminum annually to rebuild the nation's air fleet. These statistics, available from the Environmental Protection Agency (EPA), should encourage all of us to watch what we throw away.* **Clearly, recycling in our homes and in our communities directly improves the environment.**

Notice how the author's supporting examples enhance the message of the paragraph and relate to the author's thesis noted above. If you only read the boldface sentences, you have a glimpse of the topic. This paragraph of illustration, however, is developed through numerous details creating specific images: *reduced the volume of disposable trash by one-third; extended the useful life of local landfills by over a decade; enough steel every day to supply Detroit car manufacturers for three months; enough aluminum to rebuild the nation's air fleet.* If the writer had merely written a few general sentences, as those shown in bold, you would not fully understand the vast amount of trash involved in recycling or the positive results of current recycling efforts.

SKILL 8.2 **Identify explicit meaning and details within text.**

CONTEXT CLUES: help readers determine the meanings of words with which they are not familiar

CONTEXT: the sentence or sentences that surround a word

CONTEXT CLUES help readers determine the meanings of words with which they are not familiar. The **CONTEXT** of a word is the sentence or sentences that surround the word.

Read the following sentences and attempt to determine the meanings of the words in **bold** print.

> *The **luminosity** of the room was so incredible that there was no need for lights.*

If there was no need for lights, then one must assume that the word luminosity has something to do with giving off light. The definition of luminosity is "the emission of light."

> *Jamie could not understand Joe's feelings. His mood swings made understanding him somewhat of an **enigma**.*

The fact that he could not be understood made him somewhat of a puzzle. The definition of enigma is "a mystery or puzzle."

ROOTS: the basic elements of words

PREFIXES: affixes that are added to the fronts of words to form derivative words

Familiarity with **ROOTS** (the basic elements of words) and **PREFIXES** (affixes that are added to the fronts of words to form derivative words) can help you determine the meanings of unknown words.

Following are some common roots and prefixes.

COMMON ROOTS AND THEIR MEANINGS

Root	Meaning	Example
aqua	water	aqualung
astro	stars	astrology
bio	life	biology
carn	meat	carnivorous
circum	around	circumnavigate
geo	earth	geology
herb	plant	herbivorous
mal	bad	malicious
neo	new	neonatal
tele	distant	telescope

COMMON PREFIXES AND THEIR MEANINGS

Prefix	Meaning	Example
un-	not	unnamed
re-	again	reenter
il-	not	illegible
pre-	before	preset
mis-	incorrectly	misstate
in-	not	informal
anti-	against	antiwar
de-	opposite	derail
post-	after	postwar
ir-	not	irresponsible

Word Forms

Sometimes a very familiar word can appear as a different part of speech.

You may have heard that *fraud* involves a criminal misrepresentation, so when it appears as the adjective form *fraudulent* ("He was suspected of fraudulent activities"), you can make an educated guess about its meaning.

You probably know that something out of date is *obsolete*; therefore, when you read about "built-in *obsolescence*," you can detect the meaning of the unfamiliar word.

Practice Questions: Word Forms

Read the following sentences and attempt to determine the meanings of the underlined words.

1. Farmer John got a two-horse plow and went to work. Straight <u>furrows</u> stretched out behind him.

    The word <u>furrows</u> means:

    A. Long cuts made by plow

    B. Vast, open fields

    C. Rows of corn

    D. Pairs of hitched horses

2. The survivors struggled ahead, <u>shambling</u> through the terrible cold, doing their best not to fall.

    The word <u>shambling</u> means:

    A. Frozen in place

    B. Running

    C. Shivering uncontrollably

    D. Walking awkwardly

Answer Key: Word Forms

1. A

    The words "straight" and the expression "stretched out behind him" are your clues.

2. D

    The words "ahead" and "through" are your clues.

Context clues can appear within the sentence itself, within the preceding and/or following sentence(s), or in the passage as a whole.

Context clues can appear within the sentence itself, within the preceding and/or following sentence(s), or in the passage as a whole.

Sentence Clues

Often, a writer will actually define a difficult or particularly important word for you the first time it appears in a passage. Phrases like *that is*, *such as*, *which is*, or *is called* might announce the writer's intention to give just the definition you need. Occasionally, a writer will simply use a synonym (a word that means the same thing) or near-synonym joined by the word or. Look at the following examples:

> Nothing would <u>assuage</u> or lessen the child's grief.
>
> The <u>credibility</u>, that is to say the believability, of the witness was called into question by evidence of previous perjury.

Punctuation at the sentence level is often a clue to the meaning of a word. Commas, parentheses, quotation marks, and dashes tell the reader that a definition is being offered by the writer.

> A tendency toward <u>hyperbole</u>, extravagant exaggeration, is a common flaw among persuasive writers.
>
> Political <u>apathy</u>—lack of interest—can lead to the death of the state.

A writer might simply give an explanation in other words that you can understand, in the same sentence:

> The <u>xenophobic</u> townspeople were suspicious of every foreigner.

Writers also explain a word in terms of its opposite at the sentence level:

> His <u>incarceration</u> was ended, and he was elated to be out of jail.

Adjacent Sentence Clues

The context for a word goes beyond the sentence in which it appears. At times, the writer uses adjacent (adjoining) sentences to present an explanation or definition:

> The $200 for the car repair would have to come out of the <u>contingency</u> fund. Fortunately, Angela's father had taught her to keep some money set aside for just such emergencies.

The second sentence offers a clue to the definition of *contingency* as used in this sentence: "emergencies." Therefore, a fund for contingencies would be money tucked away for unforeseen and/or urgent events.

Entire Passage Clues

On occasion, you must look at an entire paragraph or passage to figure out the definition of a word or term. In the following paragraph, notice how the word *nostalgia* undergoes a form of extended definition throughout the selection rather than in just one sentence.

> The word <u>nostalgia</u> links Greek words for "away from home" and "pain." If you're feeling <u>nostalgic</u>, then, you are probably in some physical distress or discomfort, suffering from a feeling of alienation and separation from loved ones or loved places. <u>Nostalgia</u> is that awful feeling you remember you felt the first time you went away to camp or spent the weekend with a friend's family—homesickness, or some condition even more painful than that. But in common use, <u>nostalgia</u> has come to have more sentimental associations. A few years back, for example, a <u>nostalgia</u> craze had to do with the 1950s. We resurrected poodle skirts and saddle shoes, built new restaurants to look like old ones, and tried to make chicken a la king just as mother probably never made it. In TV situation comedies, we recreated a pleasant world that probably never existed and relished our <u>nostalgia</u>, longing for a homey, comfortable lost time.

SKILL 8.3 Determine inferences and conclusions based on textual evidence.

Literal Comprehension

From general to specific is a continuum. In other words, a term or phrase may be more specific than one term or more general than another one. For example, car is about the middle of the continuum; however, if I mention John Smith's car, it has become more specific. The most specific is a unique item: John Smith's 2007 Lexus, serial #000000000. Cars is a general term that can be narrowed and narrowed and narrowed to suit whatever purposes the writer has for the term. For instance, it would be possible to make a statement about all the cars in the United States, which has been narrowed somewhat from cars. It is, however, a very general term. A thesis statement is typically a generality: All the cars in the United States run on gasoline. Then specifics would be needed to prove that generalization.

In developing a line of reasoning, the choice will be either inductive, going from the specific to the general, or deductive, going from the general to the specific. Inductive reasoning might be as follows: "I tasted a green apple from my grandfather's yard when I was five years old, and it was sour. I also tasted a green apple my friend brought to school in his lunchbox when I was eight years old, and it was sour. I was in Browns' roadside market and bought some green Granny Smith apples last week, and they were sour." This is a series of specifics. From those specifics, I might draw a conclusion—a generalization—all apples are sour, and I would have reasoned inductively to arrive at that generalization.

The same simplistic argument developed deductively would begin with the generalization: all apples are sour. Then specifics would be offered to support that generalization: the sour green apple I tasted in my grandfather's orchard, the sour green apple in my friend's lunchbox, the Granny Smith apples from the market.

When reasoning is this simple and straightforward, it's easy to follow, but it's also easy to see fallacies. For example, this person hasn't tasted all the green apples in the world; and, in fact, some green apples are not sour. However, it's rarely that easy to see the generalizations and the specifics. In determining whether a point has been proven, it's necessary to do that.

Sometimes generalizations are cited on the assumption that they are commonly accepted and do not need to be supported. An example: all men die sooner or later. Examples wouldn't be needed because that is commonly accepted. Now, some people might require that "die" be defined, but even the definition of "die" is assumed in this generalization.

Some current generalizations that may assume common acceptance: Providing healthcare for all citizens is the responsibility of the government. All true patriots will support any war the government declares.

Flaws in argument, either intended or unintended, frequently have to do with generalizations and specifics. Are the specifics sufficient to prove the truth of the generality? Does a particular specific actually apply to this generalization? Many times it will depend on definitions. The question can always be asked: has the writer (or speaker) established the generalization?

Inferential Comprehension

A common fallacy in reasoning is the *post hoc ergo propter hoc* ("after this, therefore because of this") or the false-cause fallacy. These occur in cause/effect reasoning, which may either go from cause to effect or effect to cause. They happen when an inadequate cause is offered for a particular effect; when the possibility of more than one cause is ignored; and when a connection between a particular cause and a particular effect is not made.

An example of a *post hoc*: Our sales shot up thirty-five percent after we ran that television campaign; therefore the campaign caused the increase in sales. It might have been a cause, of course, but more evidence is needed to prove it.

An example of an inadequate cause for a particular effect: An Iraqi truck driver reported that Saddam Hussein had nuclear weapons; therefore, Saddam Hussein is a threat to world security. More causes are needed to prove the conclusion.

An example of ignoring the possibility of more than one possible cause: John Brown was caught out in a thunderstorm and his clothes were wet before he was rescued; therefore, he developed influenza the next day was because he got wet. Being chilled may have played a role in the illness, but Brown would have had to contract the influenza virus before he would come down with it whether or not he had gotten wet.

An example of failing to make a connection between a particular cause and an effect assigned to it. Anna fell into a putrid pond on Saturday; on Monday she came down with polio; therefore, the polio was caused by the pond. This, of course, is not acceptable unless the polio virus is found in a sample of water from the pond. A connection must be proven.

Critical Comprehension

Facts are statements that are verifiable. Opinions are statements that must be supported in order to be accepted. Facts are used to support opinions.

For example, "Jane is a bad girl" is an opinion. However, "Jane hit her sister with a baseball bat" is a *fact* upon which the opinion is based. Judgments are opinions—decisions or declarations based on observation or reasoning that express approval or disapproval. Facts report what has happened or exists and come from observation, measurement, or calculation. Facts can be tested and verified whereas opinions and judgments cannot. They can only be supported with facts.

Most statements cannot be so clearly distinguished. "I believe that Jane is a bad girl" is a fact. The speaker knows what he/she believes. However, it obviously includes a judgment that could be disputed by another person who might believe otherwise. Judgments are not usually so firm. They are, rather, plausible opinions that provoke thought or lead to factual development.

An inference is drawn from an inductive line of reasoning. The most famous one is "all men are mortal," which is drawn from the observation that everyone a person knows has died or will die and that everyone else concurs in that judgment. It is assumed to be true and for that reason can be used as proof of another conclusion: "Socrates is a man; therefore, he will die."

Sometimes the inference is assumed to be proven when it is not reliably true in all cases, such as "aging brings physical and mental infirmity." Reasoning from that *inference,* many companies will not hire anyone above a certain age. Actually, being old does not necessarily imply physical and/or mental impairment. There are many instances where elderly people have made important contributions that require exceptional ability.

An argument is a generalization that is proven or supported with facts. If the facts are not accurate, the generalization remains unproven. Using inaccurate "facts" to support an argument is called a *fallacy* in reasoning.

Some factors to consider in judging whether the facts used to support an argument are accurate are as follow:

1. Are the facts current or are they out of date? For example, if the proposition "birth defects in babies born to drug-using mothers are increasing," then the data must include the latest that is available.

2. Another important factor to consider in judging the accuracy of a fact is its source. Where was the data obtained, and is that source reliable?

3. The calculations on which the facts are based may be unreliable. It's a good idea to run one's own calculations before using a piece of derived information.

Even facts that are true and have a sharp impact on the argument may not be relevant to the case at hand.

1. Health statistics from an entire state may have no relevance, or little relevance, to a particular county or zip code. Statistics from an entire country cannot be used to prove very much about a particular state or county.

2. An analogy can be useful in making a point, but the comparison must match up in all characteristics or it will not be relevant. Analogy should be used very carefully. It is often just as likely to destroy an argument as it is to strengthen it.

The importance or significance of a fact may not be sufficient to strengthen an argument. For example, of the millions of immigrants in the U.S., using a single family to support a solution to the immigration problem will not make much difference overall even though those single-example arguments are often used to support one approach or another. They may achieve a positive reaction, but they will not prove that one solution is better than another. If enough cases were cited from a variety of geographical locations, the information might be significant.

SKILL 8.4
Discriminate among inferences, conclusions, and assumptions based on textual evidence.

See Skill 8.3

SKILL 8.5
Determine and analyze the development of central ideas or themes from one or more texts.

To discover multiple layers of meaning in a literary work, the first step is a thorough analysis, examining such things as setting, characters and characterization, plot (focusing particularly on conflicts and pattern of action), theme, tone, figures of speech, and symbolism. It's useful in looking for underlying themes to consider the author's biography, particularly with regard to setting and theme, and the date and time of the writing, paying particular attention to literary undercurrents at the time as well as political and social milieu.

Once the analysis is complete and data accumulated on the historical background, determine the overt meaning. What does the story say about the characters and their conflicts, where does the climax occur, and is there a denouement? Once the forthright, overt meaning is determined, then begin to look for undercurrents, subthemes that are related to the author's life and to what is going on in the literary, political, and social background at the time of writing.

In organization of the presentation, it's usually best to begin with an explication of the overt level of meaning and then follow up with the other messages that emerge from the text.

SKILL 8.6
Summarize one or more texts using key supporting ideas and details.

See Skills 8.5 and 8.8

SKILL 8.7 Determine how and why specific individuals, events, and ideas develop based on textual evidence.

See Skill 8.5

SKILL 8.8 Determine the cause and effect relationship(s) among individuals, events, and ideas based on textual evidence.

Cause and effect is the relationship between two things when one thing makes something else happen. Writers use this text structure to show order, inform, speculate, and change behavior. This text structure uses the process of identifying potential causes of a problem or issue in an orderly way. It is often used to teach social studies and science concepts. It is characterized by signal words such as because, so, so that, if … then, consequently, thus, since, for, for this reason, as a result of, therefore, due to, this is how, nevertheless, and accordingly.

COMPETENCY 9
KNOWLEDGE OF CRAFT AND STRUCTURE BASED ON TEXT SELECTIONS

> **SKILL 9.1** **Interpret the meaning of words and phrases as used in text** *(e.g., figurative language, connotative language, technical meanings).*

Reading literature involves a reciprocal interaction between the reader and the text.

Types of responses

Emotional

The reader can identify with the characters and situations so as to project himself into the story. The reader feels a sense of satisfaction by associating aspects of his own life with the people, places, and events in the literature. Emotional responses are observed in a reader's verbal and non-verbal reactions—laughter, comments on its effects, and retelling or dramatizing the action.

Interpretive

Interpretive responses result in inferences about character development, setting, or plot; analysis of style elements—metaphor, simile, allusion, rhythm, tone; outcomes derivable from information provided in the narrative; and assessment of the author's intent. Interpretive responses are made verbally or in writing.

Critical

Critical responses involve making value judgments about the quality of a piece of literature. Reactions to the effectiveness of the writer's style and language use are observed through discussion and written reactions.

Evaluative

Some reading response theory researchers also add a response that considers the readers considerations of such factors as how well the piece of literature represents its genre, how well it reflects the social/ ethical mores of society, and how well the author has approached the subject for freshness and slant.

COMPETENCY 10

KNOWLEDGE OF THE INTEGRATION OF INFORMATION AND IDEAS BASED ON TEXT SELECTIONS

SKILL Evaluate and relate content presented in diverse formats.
10.1

Visual representations of information that simply store descriptive information in a form available for general use are called repository **tables**. They usually contain primary data, which summarizes raw data. They are not intended to analyze the data, so analysis is left to the reader or user of the table. A good example of a repository table would be a report of birth statistics by the federal Health and Human Services Department. An analytical table is constructed from some sort of analysis of primary or secondary data, possibly from a repository table or from the raw data itself. An example of an analytical table would be one that compares birth statistics in 1980 to birth statistics in 2005 for the country as a whole. It might also break down the data and present comparisons by state.

Graphs also present data in visual form. Whereas tables are useful for showing large numbers of specific, related facts or statistics in a brief space, trends, movements, distributions and cycles are more readily apparent in a graph. However, although graphs can present statistics in a more interesting and comprehensible form than tables, they are less accurate. For this reason, the two will often be shown together.

While the most obvious use for **maps** is to locate places geographically, maps also can show specific geographic features such as roads, mountains, rivers, and so on. They can also show information according to geographic distribution, such as population, housing, manufacturing centers, and so on.

A wide range of **illustrations** may be used to illuminate the text in a document. They may also be a part of a graphic layout designed to make the page more attractive.

Some possibilities for the analysis of data, whether presented in tables, charts, graphs, maps, or other illustrations, are as follows:

- **Qualitative descriptions**—Drawing conclusions about the quality of a particular treatment or course of action as revealed by the illustration.

- **Quantitative descriptions**—How much do the results of one particular treatment or course of action differ from another one, and is that variation significant?

- **Classification**—Is worthwhile information derived from breaking down the information into classifications?

- **Estimations**—Is it possible to estimate future performance on the basis of the information in the illustration?

- **Comparisons**—Is it useful to make comparisons based on the data?

- **Relationships**—Are relationships between components revealed by scrutinizing the data?

- **Cause-and-effect relationships**—Does the data suggest that there were cause-and-effect relationships that were not previously apparent?

- **Mapping and modeling**—If the data were mapped and a model drawn up, would the point of the document be demonstrated or refuted?

Questions to ask regarding an illustration include the following: Why is it in this document? What was the writer's purpose in putting it in the document, and why at this particular place? Does it make a point clearer? What implications are inherent in a table that shows birth statistics in all states or even in some selected states? What does that have to do with the point and purpose of this piece of writing? Is there adequate preparation in the text for the inclusion of the illustration? Does the illustration underscore or clarify any of the points made in the text? Is there a clear connection between the illustration and the subject matter of the text?

> **SKILL 10.2** **Evaluate specific claims in text based on relevancy, sufficiency, and validity or reasoning.**

INDUCTIVE THINKING: the process of finding a pattern from a group of examples

INDUCTIVE THINKING is the process of finding a pattern from a group of examples. That pattern is the conclusion that this set of examples seems to indicate. It may be a correct conclusion, or it may be an incorrect conclusion because other examples may not follow the predicted pattern.

DEDUCTIVE THINKING: the process of arriving at a conclusion based on other statements that are all known to be true

DEDUCTIVE REASONING is the process of arriving at a conclusion based on other statements that are all known to be true.

A symbolic argument consists of a set of premises and a conclusion in the format of if [premise 1 and premise 2] then [conclusion].

An argument is **valid** when the conclusion follows necessarily from the premises. An argument is **invalid** or a fallacy when the conclusion does not follow from the premises.

There are four standard forms of valid arguments that you must remember.

1. Law of Detachment   If p, then q (premise 1)
        p,   (premise 2)
        Therefore, q

2. Law of Contraposition   If p, then q
        not q,
        Therefore not p

3. Law of Syllogism   If p, then q
        If q, then r
        Therefore if p, then r

4. Disjunctive Syllogism p or q
        not p
        Therefore, q

Example: Can a conclusion be reached from these two statements?

     A. All swimmers are athletes.
         All athletes are scholars.

In "if-then" form, these would be:

If you are a swimmer, then you are an athlete.
If you are an athlete, then you are a scholar.

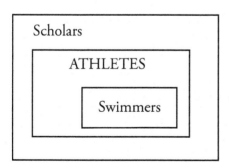

Clearly, if you are a swimmer, then you are also an athlete. This includes you in the group of scholars.

     B. All swimmers are athletes.
         All wrestlers are athletes.

In "if-then" form, these would be:

If you are a swimmer, then you are an athlete.
If you are a wrestler, then you are an athlete.

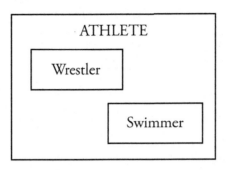

Clearly, if you are a swimmer or a wrestler, then you are also an athlete. This swimmer does NOT allow you to come to any other conclusions. A swimmer may or may NOT also be a wrestler. Therefore, NO CONCLUSION IS POSSIBLE.

Example: Determine whether statement A, B, C, or D can be deduced from the following:

    i. If John drives the big truck, then the shipment will be delivered.
    ii. The shipment will not be delivered.

    A. John does not drive the big truck.

    B. John drives the big truck.

    C. The shipment will not be delivered.

    D. None of the above conclusion is true.

Let p: John drives the big truck.
    q: The shipment is delivered.

Statement (i) gives $p \rightarrow q$, statement (ii) gives $\sim q$. This is the Law of Contraposition.

Therefore, the logical conclusion is $\sim p$ or "John does not drive the big truck." So the answer is response A.

Example: Given that:

    i. Peter is a Jet Pilot or Peter is a Navigator.
    ii. Peter is not a Jet Pilot.

Determine which conclusion can be logically deduced.

    A. Peter is not a Navigator.

B. Peter is a Navigator.

C. Peter is neither a Jet Pilot nor a Navigator.

D. None of the above is true.

Let p: Peter is a Jet Pilot

q: Peter is a Navigator.

So we have p ? q from statement (i)

$\sim p$ from statement (ii)

So choose response B.

SKILL 10.3 Synthesize information from a range of texts to develop a coherent explanation of a process, phenomenon, concept, or theme.

Content areas such as science, mathematics, history, and social studies rely on textbooks and other materials that use primarily expository text to introduce, explain, and illustrate new subject matter. From a reading perspective, students face several challenges when approaching these texts, such as deciphering unfamiliar vocabulary and adapting to new structures of content organization, which directly impact their ability to understand, synthesize, and apply the information contained therein.

Students lacking a solid foundation of reading strategies will likely experience difficulties in developing the competencies needed to master a subject area's academic requirements. At the secondary level, reading and understanding is only the beginning. Students are expected to absorb, evaluate, and form opinions and theories about topics within the subject matter, and then discuss, write about, and apply what they've learned on high level.

Metacognitive reading development strategies can help students engage effectively with their reading materials across the curriculum. The sample strategies below can be employed through structured activities that occur before reading, during reading, and after reading.

Before Reading

- **Incorporate prior knowledge:** Draw a connection between students' previous experiences—both personal and educational—and the topic at hand. A student who has helped out in the family garden, for example, will have a visual and basic vocabulary starting point for the study of plant physiology.

- **Make predictions about what will be learned:** Encourage students to identify what they think they will learn from the text, based on clues in the material (e.g., book titles, chapter headings, pictures, etc.)

- **Prepare questions:** Write specific questions to be answered during reading.

During Reading

- **Use context cues:** Utilize other words and concepts in the same sentence or paragraph to determine the meaning of an unfamiliar word.

- **Reread challenging text:** Practice rereading a selection of text to check for understanding.

- **Use visualizing techniques:** Mental pictures formed during the reading of text can aid in comprehension and retention of information. Read alouds, followed by a discussion of how these mental pictures factually reflect the text, provide opportunity for practicing and reinforcing this technique at all grade levels.

- **Make inferences:** Much of human communication relies on our ability to "read between the lines" of explicit statements and make logical guesses that fill in the blanks of information not provided. Similarly, for textbooks, making inferences means making connections to information extending beyond the text and subject matter at hand. For example, a geography book making the simple declaration that Brazil has a tropical climate can allow the student to deduce a wealth of information not stated in the text (e.g., tropical climates have warm year-round temperatures and high precipitation levels; therefore, certain crops will grow successfully and can positively impact the local economy).

- **Check the predictions made before reading:** Use the text to confirm earlier predictions about content and answer the questions posed prior to reading.

After Reading

- **Summarize information:** Students who understand the information they have read should be able to restate what they have learned in an organized manner. This activity can be practiced in both written and oral forms.

- **Make critical evaluations:** Encourage students to respond to the text with the ideas and opinions they've formed during reading. Facilitate discussions by devising questions that lead students to make qualitative and evaluative judgments about the content they've read.

> **SKILL 10.4** **Analyze multiple texts to differentiate approaches authors take to develop similar themes** (e.g., mode, author's craft, genre, point of view).

To discover multiple layers of meaning of literary works, the first step is a thorough analysis, examining such things as setting, characters and characterization, plot (focusing particularly on conflicts and pattern of action), theme, tone, figures of speech, and symbolism. It's useful in looking for underlying themes to consider the author's biography, particularly with regard to setting and theme, and the date and time of the writing, paying particular attention to literary undercurrents at the time as well as political and social milieu.

Once the analysis is complete and data accumulated on the historical background, determine the overt meaning. What does the story say about the characters and their conflicts, where does the climax occur, and is there a denouement? Once the overt meaning is determined, begin to look for undercurrents, subthemes that are related to the author's life and to what is going on in the literary, political, and social background at the time of writing.

In organization of the presentation, it's usually best to begin with an explication of the overt level of meaning and then follow up with the other messages that emerge from the text.

Paying attention to the genre of the written work is important as well. The **GENRE** is categorized by the style, form, and content of a story. Some examples are: Historical Fiction, Science Fiction, Fantasy, Biography, and Mystery.

> **GENRE** is categorized by the style, form, and content of a story

The point of view is also a critical part of the analysis. The point of view is the angle at which things are being considered in the written piece. It can be categorized in one of the following basic ways:

1. **First person**—uses the pronoun 'I' or 'we'

2. **Second person**—utilizes the pronoun 'you'

3. **Third person**—employs the use of the pronouns 'he,' 'she,' 'it,' 'they,' or a name

Writers use a point of view to effectively convey their ideas to the reader.

DOMAIN IV
ESSAY

PERSONALIZED STUDY PLAN

		KNOWN MATERIAL/ SKIP IT

PAGE	COMPETENCY AND SKILL	
164	**11: Essay**	☐
	11.1: Determine the purpose of writing to task and audience	☐
	11.2: Provide a section that effectively introduces the topic	☐
	11.3: Formulate a relevant thesis or claim	☐
	11.4: Organize ideas and details effectively	☐
	11.5: Provide adequate, relevant support by citing ample textual evidence; response may also include anecdotal experiences for added support	☐
	11.6: Use of a variety of transitional devices effectively throughout and within a written text	☐
	11.7: Demonstrate a proficient use of college-level, standard written English (e.g., varied word choice, syntax, language conventions, semantics)	☐
	11.8: Provide a concluding statement or section that follows from, or supports, the argument or information presented	☐
	11.9: Use a variety of sentence patterns effectively	☐
	11.10: Maintain consistent point of view	☐
	11.11: Apply the conventions of standard English (e.g., avoid inappropriate use of slang, jargon, clichés)	☐

The General Knowledge Essay subtest requires that the examinee select from two topics and organize and compose an original essay about one of them in 50 minutes.

The intent of the essay test component is to show that you can, in the time allotted, compose and write an original essay that addresses the topic in an effective, well-organized manner with good grammar and spelling.

An examinee is absolutely not permitted to memorize an essay from another source and present it as an original essay. Doing so is considered cheating, and if the essay is identified as being preprepared, all tests taken that day will be invalidated and no scores will be received. In addition, the incident will be reported to the Department's Bureau of Professional Practices Services.

GENERAL STRATEGIES FOR WRITING THE ESSAY	
Watch the time	Use all the time wisely. You should neither run out of time before you are done, nor write an incomplete essay because you did not use all the time allowed.
Read the instructions carefully and select one of the topics	Determine what the topic is asking. Think of how the topic relates to what you know, what you have learned, and what experiences you have had so that you can provide concrete details rather than vague generalities.
Take a few minutes to prewrite	Jot down your first ideas. Sketch a quick outline or group your ideas together with arrows or numbers.
Write a thesis statement that provides a clear focus for your essay	In your thesis, state a point of view that guides the purpose and scope of your essay. Consider the larger point you're trying to convey to the reader and what you want the reader to understand about the topic. Avoid a thesis statement framed as a fact statement, a question, or an announcement.
Develop the essay while considering your purpose	Develop paragraphs fully and give examples and reasons that support your thesis. Indent each new paragraph. Note that a good essay may be longer or shorter than the basic five-paragraph format of some short essays. The key is to *develop* a topic by using concrete, informative details.
Tie your main ideas together with a brief conclusion	Provide a concluding paragraph that ties together the essay's points and offers insights about the topic. Avoid a conclusion that merely restates the thesis and repeats the supporting details.
Revise/proofread the essay so that it conforms to standard English	Look for particular errors you tend to make. Mark errors, then correct them. You will never be penalized for clearly crossing out errors. Look for words, sentences, or even paragraphs that need changing. Write legibly so that the reader knows what you have written.

Determine the purpose of writing to task and audience.

Topic Analysis

Even before you select a topic, determine what each prompt is asking you to discuss. This first decision is crucial. If you pick a topic that you do not understand well or about which you have little to say, you will have difficulty developing your essay. Take a few moments to analyze each topic carefully before you chose a topic and begin to write.

Topic A: A modern invention that can be considered a wonder of the world

In general, the topic prompts have two parts:

1. The SUBJECT of the topic

2. An ASSERTION about the subject

The subject is a modern invention. In this prompt, the word modern indicates you should discuss something invented recently, at least in this century. The word invention indicates you should write about something created by humans (not natural phenomena such as mountains or volcanoes). You may discuss an invention that has potential for harm, such as chemical weapons or the atomic bomb, or you may discuss an invention that has the potential for good, such as the computer, DNA testing, television, or antibiotics.

> **ASSERTION:** a statement of point of view

The **ASSERTION** is that the invention has such powerful or amazing qualities that it should be considered a wonder of the world. The assertion states your point of view about the subject and it limits the range of possible discussion. In this essay, you should discuss particular qualities or uses of the invention you choose, not just how it was invented or whether it should have been invented at all.

> Some topic prompts lend themselves to essays with an argumentative edge, one in which you take a stand on a particular issue and persuasively prove your point.

Note also that this particular topic encourages you to use examples to show the reader that a particular invention is a modern wonder. Some topic prompts lend themselves to essays with an argumentative edge, one in which you take a stand on a particular issue and persuasively prove your point. In this case, you undoubtedly could offer examples or illustrations of the many "wonders" and uses of the particular invention you chose.

Be aware that misreading or misinterpreting the topic prompt can lead to serious problems. If you misread or misinterpret words, or read the topic too quickly, you may write an essay that does not address the topic. Misreading can also lead to an essay that addresses only part of the topic prompt rather than the entire topic.

See also Skill 2.3

SKILL 11.2 **Provide a section that effectively introduces the topic.**

See Skill 11.4

SKILL 11.3 **Formulate a thesis or statement of main idea.**

To develop a complete essay, spend a few minutes planning. Jot down your ideas and quickly sketch an outline. Although you may feel under pressure to begin writing, you will write more effectively if you plan your major points.

Prewriting

Before actually writing, you will need to generate content and develop a writing plan. Three prewriting techniques can be helpful.

Brainstorming

When brainstorming, quickly create a list of words and ideas that are connected to the topic. Let your mind roam free to generate as many relevant ideas as possible in a few minutes. For example, on the topic of computers you may write:

> *computer—modern invention*
>
> *types—personal computers, microchips in smartphones and watches*
>
> *wonder—acts like an electronic brain*
>
> *uses—science, medicine, offices, homes, schools*
>
> *problems—too much reliance; the machines are not perfect*

This list could help you focus on the topic, and it states the points you could develop in the body paragraphs. The brainstorming list keeps you on track and is well worth the few minutes it takes to jot down the ideas. While you have not yet ordered the ideas, seeing them on paper is an important step.

Questioning

Questioning helps you focus as you mentally ask a series of exploratory questions about the topic. You may use the most basic questions: who, what, where, when, why, and how.

> **"What** is my subject?"
> [computers]
>
> **"What** types of computers are there?"
> [personal computers, microchip computers]
>
> **"Why** have computers been a positive invention?"
> [act as an electronic brain in machinery and equipment; help solve complex scientific problems]
>
> **"How** have computers been a positive invention?"
> [used to make improvements in:
> • Science (space exploration, moon landings)
> • Medicine (MRIs, CT scans, surgical tools, research models)
> • Business (PCs, FAX, telephone equipment)
> • Education (computer programs for math, languages, science, social studies)
> • Personal tasks (family budgets, tax programs, healthy diet plans)]

> **"How** can I show that computers are good?"
> [cite numerous examples]
>
> **"What** problems do I see with computers?"
> [too much reliance; not yet perfect]
>
> **"What** personal experiences would help me develop examples to respond to this topic?
> [my own experiences using computers]

Of course, you may not have time to write out the questions completely. You might just write the words *who, what, where, when, why,* and *how* and the major points next to each. An abbreviated list might look like this:

> **What:** computers/modern wonder/making life better
>
> **How:** through technological improvements: lasers, calculators, smartphones, MRIs
>
> **Where:** in science and space exploration, medicine, schools, offices, homes

In a few moments, your questions should help you focus on the topic and generate interesting ideas and points to make in the essay. Later in the writing process, you can look back at the list to be sure you have made your key points.

Clustering

Some visual thinkers find clustering an effective prewriting method. When clustering, you draw a box in the center of your paper and write your topic within that box. Then, you draw lines from the center box connecting it to small satellite boxes that contain related ideas. Note the cluster below on computers:

Sample Cluster

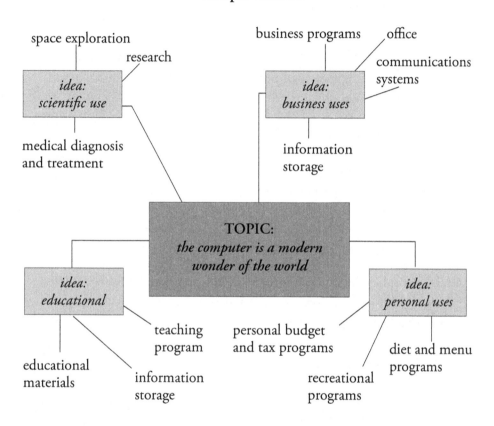

Writing the Thesis

After focusing on the topic and generating your ideas, you will form your **THESIS**, the controlling idea of your essay. The thesis is your general statement to the reader that expresses your point of view and guides your essay's purpose and scope. A strong thesis will enable you either to explain your subject or to take an arguable position about it. A good thesis statement is neither too narrow nor too broad.

THESIS: the controlling idea of an essay

Subject and Assertion of the Thesis

From the statement of the general topic, you analyzed the topic in terms of its two parts: subject and assertion. On the teacher certification exam, your thesis or viewpoint on a particular topic is stated in two important points:

1. The *subject* of the paper.

2. The *assertion* about the subject

The **SUBJECT OF THE THESIS** relates directly to the topic prompt but expresses the specific area you have chosen to discuss. (Remember, the exam topic will be general and will allow you to choose a particular subject related to the topic.) For example, the computer is one of many modern inventions you might choose to write about.

The **ASSERTION OF THE THESIS** is your viewpoint, or opinion, about the subject. The assertion provides the motive or purpose for your essay, and it may be an arguable point or one that explains or illustrates a point of view.

For example, you may present an argument for or against a particular issue. You may contrast two people, objects, or methods to show that one is better than the other. You may analyze a situation in all aspects and make recommendations for improvement. You may assert that a law or policy should be adopted, changed, or abandoned. You may also explain to your reader, as in the computer example, that a situation or condition exists; rather than argue a viewpoint, you would use examples to illustrate your assertion about the essay's subject.

Specifically, the subject of Topic A is *the computer*. The assertion is that *it is a modern wonder that has improved our lives*, and *we rely on it*. Now you quickly have created a workable thesis in a few moments:

> The computer is a modern wonder of the world that has improved our lives and that we have come to rely on.

Guidelines for Writing Thesis Statements

The following guidelines are not a formula for writing thesis statements, but rather are general strategies for making your thesis statement clear and effective.

1. State a particular point of view about the topic with both a subject and an assertion. The thesis should give the essay purpose and scope and thus provide the reader a guide. If the thesis is vague, your essay may be undeveloped because you do not have an idea to assert or a point to explain. Weak thesis statements are often framed as facts, questions, or announcements:

A. Avoid a fact statement as a thesis. While a fact statement may provide a subject, it generally does not include a point of view about the subject that provides the basis for an extended discussion. Example: *Recycling saved our community over $10,000 last year.* This fact statement provides a detail, not a point of view. Such a detail might be found within an essay, but it does not state a point of view.

B. Avoid framing the thesis as a vague question. In many cases, rhetorical questions do not provide a clear point of view for an extended essay. Example: *How do people recycle?* This question neither asserts a point of view nor helpfully guides the reader to understand the essay's purpose and scope.

C. Avoid the "announcer" topic sentence that merely states the topic you will discuss. Example: *I will discuss ways to recycle.* This sentence states the subject, but the scope of the essay is only suggested. Again, this statement does not assert a viewpoint that guides the essay's purpose. It merely "announces" that the writer will write about the topic.

2. Start with a workable thesis. You might revise your thesis as you begin writing and discover your own point of view.

3. If feasible and appropriate, perhaps state the thesis in multipoint form, expressing the scope of the essay. By stating the points in parallel form, you clearly lay out the essay's plan for the reader. Example: *To improve the environment, we can recycle our trash, elect politicians who see the environment as a priority, and support lobbying groups that work for environmental protection.*

4. Because of the exam time limit, place your thesis in the first paragraph to key the reader to the essay's main idea.

SKILL 11.4 Organize ideas and details effectively.

Creating a Working Outline

A good thesis gives structure to your essay and helps focus your thoughts. When forming your thesis, look at your prewriting strategy—clustering, questioning, or brainstorming. Then, decide quickly which two or three major areas you will discuss. Remember, you must limit the scope of the paper because of the time factor.

The OUTLINE lists the main points as topics for each paragraph. Looking at the prewriting cluster on computers, you might choose several areas in which computers help us; for example, in science and medicine, business, and education. You might also consider people's reliance on this "wonder" and include at least one paragraph about this reliance. A formal outline for this essay might look like the one below:

> **OUTLINE:** a list of the main points of a thesis that will be used as topics for each paragraph

I. Introduction and thesis

II. Computers used in science and medicine

III. Computers used in business

IV. Computers used in education

V. People's reliance on computers

VI. Conclusion

Under time pressure, however, you may use a shorter organizational plan, such as abbreviated key words in a list. For example:

1. intro: wonders of the computer -OR-	a. intro: wonders of computers—science
2. science	b. in the space industry
3. med	c. in medical technology
4. schools	d. conclusion
5. business	
6. conclusion	

Developing the Essay

With a working thesis and an outline, you can begin writing the essay. The essay should be divided into three main sections:

1. The introduction sets up the essay and leads to the thesis statement.

2. The body paragraphs are developed with concrete information leading from the topic sentences.

3. The conclusion ties the essay together.

Introduction

Put your thesis statement into a clear, coherent opening paragraph. One effective device is to use a funnel approach, in which you begin with a brief description of the broader issue and then move to a clearly focused, specific thesis statement.

Consider the following possible introductions to the essay on computers. The length of each is obviously different. Read each, and consider the other differences.

Does each introduce the subject generally?

Does each lead to a stated thesis?

Does each relate to the topic prompt?

Introduction 1: *Computers are used every day. They have many uses. Some people who use them are workers, teachers, and doctors.*

Analysis: This introduction does give the general topic—computers are used every day—but it does not explain what those uses are. This introduction does not offer a point of view in a clearly stated thesis, nor does it convey the idea that computers are a modern wonder.

Introduction 2: *Computers are used just about everywhere these days. I don't think there's an office around that doesn't use computers, and we use them a lot in all kinds of jobs. Computers are great for making life easier and work better. I don't think we'd get along without the computer.*

Analysis: This introduction gives the general topic as computers and mentions one area that uses computers. The thesis states that people could not get along without computers, but it does not state the specific areas the essay will discuss. Note, too, that the meaning is not helped by vague diction, such as *a lot* and *great*.

Introduction 3: *Each day, we either use computers or see them being used around us. We wake to the sound of a digital alarm operated by a microchip. Our cars run by computerized machinery. We use computers to help us learn. We receive phone calls and letters transferred from computers across continents. Our astronauts walked on the moon and returned safely, all because of computer technology. The computer is a wonderful electronic brain that we have come to rely on, and it has changed our world through advances in science, business, and education.*

Analysis: This introduction is the most thorough and fluent because it provides interest in the general topic and offers specific information about computers as a modern wonder. It also leads to a thesis that directs the reader to the scope of the discussion—advances in science, business, and education.

Topic Sentences

Just as the essay must have an overall focus reflected in the thesis statement, each paragraph must have a central idea reflected in the topic sentence. A good topic sentence provides transition from the previous paragraph and relates to the essay's thesis. Good topic sentences, therefore, provide unity throughout the essay.

Consider the following potential topic sentences. Determine whether each provides transition and clearly states the subject of the paragraph.

> *Just as the essay must have an overall focus that is reflected in the thesis statement, each paragraph must have a central idea reflected in the topic sentence.*

Topic Sentence 1: *Computers are used in science.*

Analysis: This sentence simply states the topic: Computers are used in science. It does not relate to the thesis nor provide transition from the introduction. The reader still does not know how computers are used in science.

Topic Sentence 2: *Now I will talk about computers used in science.*

Analysis: Like the faulty "announcer" thesis statement, this "announcer" topic sentence is vague and merely names the topic.

Topic Sentence 3: *First, computers used in science have improved our lives.*

Analysis: The transition word *First* helps link the introduction and this paragraph. It adds unity to the essay. It does not, however, give specifics about the improvements computers have made in our lives.

Topic Sentence 4: *First used in scientific research and spaceflights, computers are now used extensively in the diagnosis and treatment of disease.*

Analysis: This sentence is the most thorough and fluent. It provides specific areas that will be discussed in the paragraph and it offers more than an announcement of the topic. The writer gives concrete information about the content of the paragraph that will follow.

SUMMARY GUIDELINES FOR WRITING TOPIC SENTENCES
Specifically relate the topic to the thesis statement
State clearly and concretely the subject of the paragraph
Provide some transition from the previous paragraph
Avoid topic sentences that are facts, questions, or announcements

SKILL 11.5 Provide adequate, relevant support by citing ample textual evidence; response may also include anecdotal experiences for added support.

Citing textual evidence supports the analysis of a piece of writing through what the text explicitly says, as well as what might be inferred from it. Locating direct support from the text ensures that an answer is correct and supported thoroughly.

In order to do this, a writer must first state his or her clear idea. The next step is locating the information from the text that led to the idea. Locating specific examples, and using quotations to share them exactly as they were found in the information, is an important step. This validates that the idea that has been shared is being specifically supported. The writer then follows up with an explanation as to how the quoted text shows or summarizes the given idea. Sentence starters might include: *This highlights, This reveals, This illustrates, This is because,* or *This means.*

Often, we must use our background knowledge and information we believe to be true as we write. Using **inferences** requires the writer to "read between the lines" and discern what the author has shared in his or her work. An author does not always reveal everything to his or her reader.

Showing evidence is still possible with the same model. The write shares an idea, cites the idea from the given text, and then explains the idea further. The explanation will most likely include background knowledge, anecdotal evidence, and details from the story that validate the writer's thoughts and ideas.

SKILL 11.6 **Use of a variety of transitional devices effectively throughout and within a written text.**

TRANSITIONS are words and phrases that connect sentences, phrases, and ideas. This allows for text to be smooth and flow well, without being choppy and difficult to follow. Transitions logically connect one part to the next, and they work best when connecting the end of one paragraph to an upcoming paragraph. They may show contrast between ideas, show a similarity or comparison, add to another point in the essay, denote time, or sum up points, or illustrate details.

> **TRANSITIONS:** words and phrases that connect sentences, phrases, and ideas

Some common phrases utilized for effective transitions are:

- for example
- for instance
- with the result that
- therefore
- consequently
- especially
- in particular
- indeed
- although
- at any rate
- at least

Transitions play an important role in allowing the reader to understand the logical sequence of ideas.

> **SKILL 11.7** **Demonstrate proficient use of college-level, standard written English** *(e.g., varied word choice, syntax, language conventions, semantics).*

See Skills 1.2, 1.3, 1.4, 2.1, and 2.3

> **SKILL 11.8** **Provide a concluding statement or section that follows from, or supports, the argument or information presented.**

The conclusion serves as the opportunity to have a final say on the issues that have been written in the piece of work. It enables the writer to summarize his or her thoughts, and may propel the reader to have a new view on the subject.

Effective conclusions synthesize what has been written, may include thought-provoking insight, a solution to an issue, further questions to think about, or might parallel insights from the paper's introduction.

A conclusion is essentially the writer's last chance to comment on the subject, making a lasting final impression.

> **SKILL 11.9** **Use a variety of sentence patterns effectively.**

See Skills 1.2 and 1.3

> **SKILL 11.10** **Maintain consistent point of view.**

Point of view defines the focus a writer assumes in relation to a given topic. It is extremely important to maintain a consistent point of view in order to create coherent paragraphs. Point of view is related to matters of person, tense, tone, and number.

- **Person:** A shift in the form that indicates whether a person is speaking (first), is being spoken to (second), or is being spoken about (third) can disrupt the continuity of a passage. In your essay, it is recommended that you write in the third person because it is often considered to be the most formal of the modes of person. If you do decide to use the more informal first or second person (I, you, we) in your essay, be careful not to shift between first, second, and third person from sentence to sentence or paragraph to paragraph.

- **Tense:** Verbs tenses indicate the time of an action or state of being: the past, present, or future. It is important, usually, to stick to a selected tense, though this may not always be the case. For instance, in an essay about the history of environmental protection, it might be necessary to include a paragraph about past environmental catastrophes or a paragraph about the future benefits or consequences of protecting the Earth.

- **Tone:** The tone of an essay varies greatly with the purpose, subject, and audience. It is best to assume a formal tone for this essay.

- **Number:** Words change when their meanings are singular or plural. Make sure that you do not shift number needlessly; if a meaning is singular in one sentence, do not make it plural in a subsequent sentence.

SKILL 11.11 **Apply the conventions of standard English** (e.g., avoid inappropriate use of slang, jargon, clichés).

SLANG is defined as very informal usage of vocabulary and idiom that is characteristically more metaphorical, playful, elliptical, vivid, and ephemeral than ordinary language. The phrase *to hit the road*, meaning "to leave," is a good example of slang. Slang is fine in conversation between friends, but it is extremely inappropriate in formal writing.

Slang is often specific to a social group or geographic region. Because it is so colloquial, slang can be easily misunderstood. Moreover, using slang can affect how seriously readers regard your writing. The only time that slang may be appropriate in formal writing is when it is being used in a quote or dialogue.

JARGON is defined as the language, especially the vocabulary, peculiar to a particular trade, profession, or group, for instance, *medical jargon*. Because jargon pertains to the vocabulary used by a limited or specialized group of people, using jargon can hinder clear and effective communication to a general reading public.

Jargon, like slang, has its own time and place. If you are writing for a specialized audience, specialized language will communicate meaning effectively and show the audience that you are familiar with the terms associated with that specialized

SLANG: informal usage of vocabulary and idiom that is characteristically more metaphorical, playful, elliptical, vivid, and ephemeral than ordinary language

The phrase to hit the road, *meaning "to leave," is a good example of slang.*

JARGON: language, especially the vocabulary, peculiar to a particular trade, profession, or group

field. If, however, you are writing for a more general audience, jargon will be unintelligible gibberish and, perhaps, even offensive. If readers feel that an author is being pretentious or boastful, they may find the jargon distasteful.

A **CLICHÉ** is defined as a trite, stereotyped expression that has lost originality, ingenuity, and impact by long overuse. The sayings *older but wiser* and *strong as an ox* are examples of clichés. The use of clichés weakens writing due to lack of creativity, thoughtfulness, and personal perspective. Clichés are boring and sometimes even offensive, and they are best avoided when one is writing an original piece. Rather than using tired expressions to convey an idea, rethink the idea that is being conveyed and reword it with correct vocabulary and specific details.

See also Domain 1, Competency 3

> **CLICHÉ:** a trite, stereotyped expression

> *The sayings* **older but wiser** *and* **strong as an ox** *are examples of clichés.*

SAMPLE TEST

SAMPLE TEST

English Test

DIRECTIONS: Choose the underlined word or phrase that is unnecessary within the context of the passage.

(Easy) (Skill 1.3)

1. The <u>expanding</u> number of television channels has <u>prompted</u> cable operators to raise their prices, <u>even</u> <u>though</u> many consumers do not want to pay a higher <u>increased</u> amount for their service.

   A. expanding

   B. prompted

   C. even though

   D. increased

(Average) (Skill 1.3)

2. <u>Considered by many to be</u> one of the worst <u>terrorist</u> incidents <u>on American soil</u> was the bombing of the Oklahoma City Federal Building, which will be remembered <u>for years to come</u>.

   A. Considered by many to be

   B. terrorist

   C. on American soil

   D. for years to come

(Average) (Skill 1.3)

3. The <u>flu</u> epidemic struck <u>most of</u> the <u>respected</u> faculty and students of The Woolbright School, forcing the Boynton Beach School Superintendent to close it down <u>for two weeks</u>.

   A. flu

   B. most of

   C. respected

   D. for two weeks

DIRECTIONS: Choose the word or phrase that is the best option for completing the sentence.

(Average) (Skill 2.1)

4. Many of the clubs in Boca Raton are noted for their _____ elegance.

   A. vulgar

   B. tasteful

   C. ordinary

(Average) (Skill 2.1)

5. When a student is expelled from school, the parents are usually _____ in advance.

   A. rewarded

   B. congratulated

   C. notified

(Average) (Skill 2.1)

6. Before appearing in court, the witness was _____ the papers requiring her to show up.

   A. condemned

   B. served

   C. criticized

(Average) (Skill 2.1)

7. Because George's _____ bothering him, he apologized for crashing his father's car.

   A. feelings were

   B. conscience was

   C. guiltiness was

(Rigorous) (Skill 2.1)

8. The charity art auction _____ every year at Mizner Park includes a wide selection of artists showcasing their work.

   A. attended

   B. presented

   C. displayed

DIRECTIONS: For the underlined sentence(s), choose the option that expresses the meaning with the most fluency and the clearest logic within the context. If the underlined sentence should not be changed, choose Option A, which shows no change.

(Average) (Skill 2.3)

9. John wanted to join his friends on the mountain-climbing trip. <u>Seeing that the weather had become dark and stormy, John knew he would stay safe indoors.</u>

   A. Seeing that the weather had become dark and stormy, John knew he would stay safe indoors.

   B. The weather had become dark and stormy, and John knew he would stay indoors, and he would be safe.

   C. Because the weather had become dark and stormy, John knew he would stay indoors, where he would be safe.

   D. Because the weather had become dark, as well as stormy, John knew he would stay safe indoors.

(Average) (Skill 2.3)

10. A few hours later, the storm subsided, so John left the cabin to join his friends. <u>Even though he was tired from the four-mile hike the day before; he climbed the mountain in a few hours.</u>

    A. Even though he was tired from the four-mile hike the day before, he climbed the mountain in a few hours.

    B. He was tired from the four-mile hike the day before; he climbed the mountain in a few hours.

    C. He climbed the mountain in a few hours, John was tired from the four-mile hike the day before.

    D. Seeing as he was tired from the day before, when he went on a four-mile hike, John climbed the mountain in a few hours.

(Rigorous) (Skill 2.3)

11. Selecting members of a president's cabinet can often be an aggravating process. **Either there are too many or too few qualified candidates for a certain position, and then they have to be confirmed by the Senate, where there is the possibility of rejection.**

    A. Either there are too many or too few qualified candidates for a certain position, and then they have to be confirmed by the Senate, where there is the possibility of rejection.

    B. Qualified candidates for certain positions face the possibility of rejection, when they have to be confirmed by the Senate.

    C. The Senate has to confirm qualified candidates, who face the possibility of rejection.

    D. Because the Senate has to confirm qualified candidates; they face the possibility of rejection.

(Rigorous) (Skill 2.3)

12. Treating patients for drug and/or alcohol abuse is sometimes a difficult process. **Even though there are a number of different methods for helping the patient overcome a dependency, there is no way of knowing which is best in the long run.**

    A. Even though there are a number of different methods for helping the patient overcome a dependency, there is no way of knowing which is best in the long run.

    B. Even though different methods can help a patient overcome a dependency, there is no way to know which is best in the long run.

    C. Even though there is no way to know which way is best in the long run, patients can overcome their dependencies when they are helped.

    D. There is no way to know which method will help the patient overcome a dependency in the long run, even though there are many different ones.

(Rigorous) (Skill 2.3)

13. Many factors account for the decline in quality of public education. **Overcrowding, budget cutbacks, and societal deterioration which have greatly affected student learning.**

    A. Overcrowding, budget cutbacks, and societal deterioration which have greatly affected student learning.

    B. Student learning has been greatly affected by overcrowding, budget cutbacks, and societal deterioration.

    C. Due to overcrowding, budget cutbacks, and societal deterioration, student learning has been greatly affected.

    D. Overcrowding, budget cutbacks, and societal deterioration have affected students learning greatly.

(Easy) (Skill 2.3)

14. Choose the sentence that logically and correctly expresses the comparison.

    A. The Empire State Building in New York is taller than buildings in the city.

    B. The Empire State Building in New York is taller than any other building in the city.

    C. The Empire State Building in New York is tallest than other buildings in the city.

DIRECTIONS: The passage below contains many errors. Read the passage. Then answer each test item by choosing the option that corrects an error in the underlined portion(s). No more than one underlined error will appear in each item. If no error exists, choose "No change is necessary."

Climbing to the top of Mount Everest is an adventure. One which everyone—whether physically fit or not—seems eager to try. The trail stretches for miles, the cold temperatures are usually frigid and brutal.

Climbers must endure severel barriers on the way, including other hikers, steep jagged rocks, and lots of snow. Plus, climbers often find the most grueling part of the trip is their climb back down, just when they are feeling greatly exhausted. Climbers who take precautions are likely to find the ascent less arduous than the unprepared. donning heavy flannel shirts, gloves, and hats, climbers prevented hypothermia, as well as simple frostbite. A pair of rugged boots is also one of the necesities. If climbers are to avoid becoming dehydrated, there is beverages available for them to transport as well.

Once climbers are completely ready to begin their lengthy journey, they can comfortable enjoy the wonderful scenery. Wide rock formations dazzle the observers eyes with shades of gray and white, while the peak forms a triangle that seems to touch the sky. Each of the climbers are reminded of the splendor and magnifisence of God's great Earth.

(Rigorous) (Skill 2.3)

15. Climbing to the top of Mount Everest is an <u>adventure. One</u> which <u>everyone—whether</u> physically fit or not—<u>seems</u> eager to try.

   A. adventure, one

   B. everyone, whether

   C. seem

   D. No change is necessary

(Rigorous) (Skills 3.1 and 3.3)

16. The <u>trail</u> stretches for <u>miles</u>, the cold temperatures are <u>usually</u> frigid and brutal.

   A. trails

   B. miles;

   C. usual

   D. No change is necessary

(Average) (Skills 3.1 and 3.3)

17. By donning heavy flannel shirts, boots, and <u>hats, climbers</u> <u>prevented</u> <u>hypothermia,</u> as well as simple frostbite.

   A. hats climbers

   B. can prevent

   C. hypothermia;

   D. No change is necessary

(Average) (Skill 3.5)

18. Plus, climbers often find the most grueling part of the trip is <u>their</u> climb back <u>down, just</u> when they <u>are</u> feeling greatly exhausted.

   A. his

   B. down; just

   C. were

   D. No change is necessary

(Easy) (Skills 3.1 and 3.3)

19. If climbers are to avoid <u>becoming</u> dehydrated, there <u>is</u> beverages available for <u>them</u> to transport as well.

    A. becomming

    B. are

    C. him

    D. No change is necessary

(Rigorous) (Skills 3.1 and 3.3)

20. Each of the climbers <u>are</u> reminded of the splendor and <u>magnificence</u> of <u>God's</u> great Earth.

    A. is

    B. magnifisence

    C. Gods

    D. No change is necessary

(Average) (Skill 3.6)

21. Once climbers are completely prepared for <u>their</u> lengthy <u>journey</u>, <u>they</u> can <u>comfortable</u> enjoy the wonderful scenery.

    A. they're

    B. journey; they

    C. comfortably

    D. No change is necessary

(Average) (Skill 3.7)

22. <u>Climbers who</u> take precautions are likely to find the ascent <u>less difficult</u> <u>than</u> the unprepared.

    A. Climbers, who

    B. least difficult

    C. then

    D. No change is necessary

(Rigorous) (Skill 2.2)

23. Climbers must endure <u>severel</u> barriers <u>on the way, including</u> other <u>hikers</u>, steep jagged rocks, and lots of snow.

    A. several

    B. on the way: including

    C. hikers'

    D. No change is necessary

(Rigorous) (Skill 2.2)

24. A pair of rugged boots <u>is</u> <u>also one</u> of the <u>necesities</u>.

    A. are

    B. also, one

    C. necessities

    D. No change is necessary

(Rigorous) (Skill 2.2)

25. Wide rock formations dazzle the <u>observers eyes</u> with shades of gray and <u>white, while</u> the peak <u>forms</u> a triangle that seems to touch the sky.

    A. observers' eyes

    B. white; while

    C. formed

    D. No change is necessary

DIRECTIONS: The passage below contains several errors. Read the passage. Then answer each test item by choosing the option that corrects an error in the underlined portion(s). No more than one underlined error will appear in each item. If no error exists, choose "No change is necessary."

Every job places different kinds of demands on their employees. For example, whereas such jobs as accounting and bookkeeping require mathematical ability; graphic design requires creative/artistic ability.

Doing good at one job does not usually guarantee success at another. However, one of the elements crucial to all jobs are especially notable: the chance to accomplish a goal.

The accomplishment of the employees vary according to the job. In many jobs the employees become accustom to the accomplishment provided by the work they do every day.

In medicine, for example, all doctors test them selves by treating badly injured or critically ill people. In the operating room, a team of Surgeons, is responsible for operating on many of these patients. In addition to the feeling of accomplishment that the workers achieve, some jobs also give a sense of identity to the employees'. Profesions like law, education, and sales offer huge financial or emotional rewards. Politicians are public servants: who work for the federal and state governments. President obama is basically employed by the American people to make laws and run the country.

Finally; the contributions that employees make to their companies and to the world cannot be taken for granted. Through their work, employees are performing a service for their employers and are contributing something to the world.

(Rigorous) (Skill 2.2)

26. The <u>accomplishment</u> of the <u>employees</u> <u>vary</u> according to the job.

   A. accomplishment,

   B. employee's

   C. varies

   D. No change is necessary

(Average) (Skill 2.2)

27. In many jobs the employees <u>become accustom</u> to the accomplishment <u>provided</u> by the work they do every day.

   A. became

   B. accustomed

   C. provides

   D. No change is necessary

(Rigorous) (Skill 2.2)

28. <u>However,</u> one of the elements crucial to all jobs <u>are</u> especially <u>notable:</u> the accomplishment of a goal.

   A. However

   B. is

   C. notable;

   D. No change is necessary

(Average) (Skill 2.2)

29. In medicine, for example, all doctors <u>test them self</u> by treating badly injured and critically ill people.

   A. tests

   B. themselves

   C. critical

   D. No change is necessary

(Rigorous) (Skill 3.1)

30. Every job <u>places</u> different kinds of demands on <u>their</u> <u>employees</u>.

    A. place

    B. its

    C. employes

    D. No change is necessary

(Rigorous) (Skill 2.1)

31. Doing <u>good</u> at one job does not <u>usually</u> guarantee <u>success</u> at another.

    A. well

    B. usualy

    C. succeeding

    D. No change is necessary

(Average) (Skill 3.1)

32. <u>Profesions</u> like law, <u>education,</u> and sales <u>offer</u> huge financial or emotional rewards.

    A. Professions

    B. education;

    C. offered

    D. No change is necessary

(Easy) (Skill 3.1)

33. Politicians <u>are</u> public <u>servants: who</u> <u>work</u> for the federal and state governments.

    A. were

    B. servants who

    C. worked

    D. No change is necessary

(Average) (Skill 3.11)

34. <u>For example,</u> <u>whereas</u> such jobs as accounting and bookkeeping require mathematical <u>ability;</u> graphic design requires creative/artistic ability.

    A. For example

    B. whereas,

    C. ability,

    D. No change is necessary

(Easy) (Skills 3.10 and 3.11)

35. In addition to the feeling of accomplishment that the workers <u>achieve,</u> some jobs also <u>give</u> a sense of self-identity to the <u>employees'</u>.

    A. acheive

    B. gave

    C. employees

    D. No change is necessary

(Average) (Skill 3.11)

36. <u>Finally;</u> the contributions that employees make to <u>their</u> companies and to the world cannot be <u>taken</u> for granted.

    A. Finally,

    B. thier

    C. took

    D. No change is necessary

(Easy) (Skill 3.12)

37. In the <u>operating room,</u> a team of <u>Surgeons, is</u> responsible for operating on many of <u>these</u> patients.

    A. operating room:

    B. surgeons is

    C. those

    D. No change is necessary

(Easy) (Skill 3.12)

38. President <u>obama</u> is basically employed <u>by</u> the American people to <u>make</u> laws and run the country.

   A. Obama

   B. to

   C. made

   D. No change is necessary

DIRECTIONS: The passage below contains several errors. Read the passage. Then answer each test item by choosing the option that corrects an error in the underlined portion(s). No more than one underlined error will appear in each item. If no error exists, choose "No change is necessary."

The discovery of a body at Paris Point marina in Boca Raton shocked the residents of Palmetto Pines, a luxury condominium complex located next door to the marina.

The victim is a thirty-five-year-old woman who had been apparently bludgeoned to death and dumped in the ocean late last night. Many neighbors reported terrible screams, gunshots: as well as the sound of a car backfiring loudly to Boca Raton Police shortly after midnight. The woman had been spotted in the lobby of Palmetto Pines around ten thirty, along with an older man, estimated to be in his fifties, and a younger man, in his late twenties.

"Apparently, the victim had been driven to the complex by the older man, and was seen arguing with him when the younger man intervened," said Sheriff Fred Adams, "all three of them left the building together and walked to the marina, where gunshots rang out an hour later." Deputies found five bullets

on the sidewalk and some blood, along with a steel pipe that is assumed to be the murder weapon. Two men were seen fleeing the scene in a red Mercedes short after, rushing toward the Interstate.

The Palm Beach County Coroner, Melvin Watts, said he concluded the victim's skull had been crushed by a blunt tool, which resulted in a brain hemorrhage. As of now, there is no clear motive for the murder.

(Easy) (Skill 3.8)

39. Two men <u>were</u> seen fleeing the scene in a red Mercedes <u>short</u> after, <u>rushing</u> toward the Interstate.

   A. are

   B. shortly

   C. rushed

   D. No change is necessary

(Easy) (Skills 3.2, 3.10, and 3.11)

40. As of <u>now,</u> <u>there</u> <u>is</u> no clear motive for the murder.

   A. now;

   B. their

   C. was

   D. No change is necessary

Answer Key: English Test

1. D	11. C	21. C	31. A
2. A	12. B	22. D	32. A
3. C	13. B	23. A	33. B
4. B	14. B	24. C	34. C
5. C	15. A	25. A	35. C
6. B	16. B	26. C	36. A
7. B	17. B	27. B	37. B
8. B	18. D	28. B	38. A
9. D	19. B	29. B	39. B
10. A	20. A	30. B	40. D

Rigor Table: English Test

RIGOR TABLE	
Rigor level	Questions
Easy 20%	1, 14, 19, 33, 35, 37, 38, 39, 40
Average 42%	2, 3, 4, 5, 6, 7, 9, 10, 17, 18, 21, 22, 27, 29, 32, 34, 36
Rigorous 38%	8, 11, 12, 13, 15, 16, 20, 23, 24, 25, 26, 28, 30, 31

English Test with Rationales

DIRECTIONS: Choose the underlined word or phrase that is unnecessary within the context of the passage.

(Easy) (Skill 1.3)

1. The <u>expanding</u> number of television channels has <u>prompted</u> cable operators to raise their prices, <u>even though</u> many consumers do not want to pay a higher <u>increased</u> amount for their service.

    A. expanding

    B. prompted

    C. even though

    D. increased

    Answer: D. increased

    The word "increased" is redundant when used after the word "higher" and should be removed. All the other words are necessary within the context of the sentence.

(Average) (Skill 1.3)

2. <u>Considered by many to be</u> one of the worst <u>terrorist</u> incidents <u>on American soil</u> was the bombing of the Oklahoma City Federal Building, which will be remembered <u>for years to come</u>.

    A. Considered by many to be

    B. terrorist

    C. on American soil

    D. for years to come

Answer: A. Considered by many to be

Considered by many to be is a wordy phrase and unnecessary in the context of the sentence. All other words are necessary within the context of the sentence.

(Average) (Skill 1.3)

3. The <u>flu</u> epidemic struck <u>most of</u> the <u>respected</u> faculty and students of The Woolbright School, forcing the Boynton Beach School Superintendent to close it down <u>for two weeks</u>.

    A. flu

    B. most of

    C. respected

    D. for two weeks

    Answer: C. respected

    The fact that the faculty might have been *respected* is not necessary to in the purpose of the sentence. The other words and phrases are all necessary to complete the meaning of the sentence.

DIRECTIONS: Choose the word or phrase that is the best option for completing the sentence.

(Average) (Skill 2.1)

4. Many of the clubs in Boca Raton are noted for their _____ elegance.

    A. vulgar

    B. tasteful

    C. ordinary

    Answer: B. tasteful

"Tasteful" means beautiful or charming, which would correspond to an elegant club. The words "vulgar" and "ordinary" have negative connotations.

(Average) (Skill 2.1)

5. When a student is expelled from school, the parents are usually _____ in advance.

    A. rewarded

    B. congratulated

    C. notified

    Answer: C. notified

    "Notified" means informed or told, which fits into the logic of the sentence. The words "rewarded" and "congratulated" are positive actions, which don't make sense in the context of an expulsion.

(Average) (Skill 2.1)

6. Before appearing in court, the witness was _____ the papers requiring her to show up.

    A. condemned

    B. served

    C. criticized

    Answer: B. served

    "Served" means given, which makes sense in the context of the sentence. "Condemned" and "criticized" do not make sense within the context of the sentence.

(Average) (Skill 2.1)

7. Because George's _____ bothering him, he apologized for crashing his father's car.

    A. feelings were

    B. conscience was

    C. guiltiness was

    Answer: B. conscience was

    Option B shows the correct word choice because a *conscience* would motivate someone to confess. Option A is incorrect because *feelings* is not as accurate as conscience. Option C is incorrect because *guiltiness* is less descriptive of George's motive for confession than conscience.

(Rigorous) (Skill 2.1)

8. The charity art auction _____ every year at Mizner Park includes a wide selection of artists showcasing their work.

    A. attended

    B. presented

    C. displayed

    Answer: B. presented

    The word "presented" makes more sense in the context of the sentence than "attended" or "displayed."

DIRECTIONS: For the underlined sentence(s), choose the option that expresses the meaning with the most fluency and the clearest logic within the context. If the underlined sentence should not be changed, choose Option A, which shows no change.

(Average) (Skill 2.3)

9. John wanted to join his friends on the mountain-climbing trip. <u>Seeing that the weather had become dark and stormy, John knew he would stay safe indoors.</u>

    A. Seeing that the weather had become dark and stormy, John knew he would stay safe indoors.

    B. The weather had become dark and stormy, and John knew he would stay indoors, and he would be safe.

    C. Because the weather had become dark and stormy, John knew he would stay indoors, where he would be safe.

    D. Because the weather had become dark, as well as stormy, John knew he would stay safe indoors.

    Answer: D. Because the weather had become dark, as well as stormy, John knew he would stay safe indoors.

    This sentence best subordinates the idea of dark and stormy weather to John's knowledge. Option A is incorrect because *Seeing that* is an awkward construction. Option B does not subordinate any idea to any other. Option C is incorrect because the idea that John would be safe shouldn't be subordinate to staying indoors.

(Average) (Skill 2.3)

10. A few hours later, the storm subsided, so John left the cabin to join his friends. <u>Even though he was tired from the four-mile hike the day before; he climbed the mountain in a few hours.</u>

    A. Even though he was tired from the four-mile hike the day before, he climbed the mountain in a few hours.

    B. He was tired from the four-mile hike the day before; he climbed the mountain in a few hours.

    C. He climbed the mountain in a few hours, John was tired from the four-mile hike the day before.

    D. Seeing as he was tired from the day before, when he went on a four-mile hike, John climbed the mountain in a few hours.

    Answer: A. Even though he was tired from the four-mile hike the day before, he climbed the mountain in a few hours.

    The idea that John was tired from the four-mile hike the day before is subordinate to the idea of John climbing the mountain. Options B and C do not subordinate the idea of John being tired from the four-mile hike to John climbing the mountain. In Option D, the modifying phrase *Seeing as ... before* makes no logical sense in the context of the sentence.

(Rigorous) (Skill 2.3)

11. Selecting members of a president's cabinet can often be an aggravating process. **Either there are too many or too few qualified candidates for a certain position, and then they have to be confirmed by the Senate, where there is the possibility of rejection.**

    A. Either there are too many or too few qualified candidates for a certain position, and then they have to be confirmed by the Senate, where there is the possibility of rejection.

    B. Qualified candidates for certain positions face the possibility of rejection, when they have to be confirmed by the Senate.

    C. The Senate has to confirm qualified candidates, who face the possibility of rejection.

    D. Because the Senate has to confirm qualified candidates; they face the possibility of rejection.

    Answer: C. The Senate has to confirm qualified candidates, who face the possibility of rejection.

    Option C is the most straightforward and concise sentence. Option A is too unwieldy with the wordy *Either … or* phrase at the beginning. Option B doesn't make it clear that candidates face rejection by the Senate. Option D illogically implies that candidates face rejection because they have to be confirmed by the Senate.

(Rigorous) (Skill 2.3)

12. Treating patients for drug and/or alcohol abuse is sometimes a difficult process. **Even though there are a number of different methods for helping the patient overcome a dependency, there is no way of knowing which is best in the long run.**

    A. Even though there are a number of different methods for helping the patient overcome a dependency, there is no way of knowing which is best in the long run.

    B. Even though different methods can help a patient overcome a dependency, there is no way to know which is best in the long run.

    C. Even though there is no way to know which way is best in the long run, patients can overcome their dependencies when they are helped.

    D. There is no way to know which method will help the patient overcome a dependency in the long run, even though there are many different ones.

    Answer: B. Even though different methods can help a patient overcome a dependency, there is no way to know which is best in the long run.

    Option B is concise and logical. Option A tends to ramble with the use of "there are" and the verbs "helping" and "knowing." Option C is awkwardly worded and repetitive in the first part of the sentence, and vague in the second part because it never indicates how the patients can be helped. Option D contains the unnecessary phrase *even though there are many different ones.*

(Rigorous) (Skill 2.3)

13. Many factors account for the decline in quality of public education. <u>Overcrowding, budget cutbacks, and societal deterioration which have greatly affected student learning.</u>

   A. Overcrowding, budget cutbacks, and societal deterioration which have greatly affected student learning.

   B. Student learning has been greatly affected by overcrowding, budget cutbacks, and societal deterioration.

   C. Due to overcrowding, budget cutbacks, and societal deterioration, student learning has been greatly affected.

   D. Overcrowding, budget cutbacks, and societal deterioration have affected students learning greatly.

   Answer: B. Student learning has been greatly affected by overcrowding, budget cutbacks, and societal deterioration.

   Option B is concise and best explains the causes of the decline in student learning. The unnecessary use of "which" in Option A makes the sentence feel incomplete. Option C makes a weak connection between the reasons for the decline in public education and the fact that student learning has been affected. Option D incorrectly places the adverb "greatly" after the noun "learning," instead of before "affected."

(Easy) (Skill 2.3)

14. Choose the sentence that logically and correctly expresses the comparison.

   A. The Empire State Building in New York is taller than buildings in the city.

   B. The Empire State Building in New York is taller than any other building in the city.

   C. The Empire State Building in New York is tallest than other buildings in the city.

   Answer: B. The Empire State Building in New York is taller than any other building in the city.

   Because the Empire State Building is a building in New York City, the phrase "any other" must be included. Option A is incorrect because the Empire State Building is implicitly compared to itself since it is one of the buildings. Option C is incorrect because "tallest" is the incorrect form of the adjective.

DIRECTIONS: The passage below contains many errors. Read the passage. Then answer each test item by choosing the option that corrects an error in the underlined portion(s). No more than one underlined error will appear in each item. If no error exists, choose "No change is necessary."

Climbing to the top of Mount Everest is an adventure. One which everyone—whether physically fit or not—seems eager to try. The trail stretches for miles, the cold temperatures are usually frigid and brutal.

Climbers must endure severel barriers on the way, including other hikers, steep jagged rocks, and lots of snow. Plus, climbers often find the most grueling part of the trip is their climb back down, just when they are feeling greatly exhausted. Climbers who take precautions are likely to find the ascent less arduous than the unprepared. donning heavy flannel shirts, gloves, and hats, climbers prevented hypothermia, as well as simple frostbite. A pair of rugged boots is also one of the necesities. If climbers are to avoid becoming dehydrated, there is beverages available for them to transport as well.

Once climbers are completely ready to begin their lengthy journey, they can comfortable enjoy the wonderful scenery. Wide rock formations dazzle the observers eyes with shades of gray and white, while the peak forms a triangle that seems to touch the sky. Each of the climbers are reminded of the splendor and magnifisence of God's great Earth.

(Rigorous) (Skill 2.3)

15. **Climbing to the top of Mount Everest is an <u>adventure. One</u> which <u>everyone—whether</u> physically fit or not—<u>seems</u> eager to try.**

    A. adventure, one

    B. everyone, whether

    C. seem

    D. No change is necessary

    Answer: A. adventure, one

    A comma is needed between "adventure" and "one" to avoid making the second part of the sentence a fragment. In Option B a comma after "everyone" would not be appropriate when a dash is used on the other side of "not." In Option C the singular verb "seems" is needed to agree with the singular subject "everyone."

(Rigorous) (Skills 3.1 and 3.3)

16. **The <u>trail</u> stretches for <u>miles,</u> the cold temperatures are <u>usually</u> frigid and brutal.**

    A. trails

    B. miles;

    C. usual

    D. No change is necessary

    Answer: B. miles;

    A semicolon, not a comma, is needed to separate the first independent clause from the second independent clause. Option A is incorrect because the plural subject "trails" needs the singular verb "stretch." Option C is incorrect because the adverb form "usually," not the adjective "usual," is needed to modify the adjective "frigid."

(Average) (Skills 3.1 and 3.3)

17. **By donning heavy flannel shirts, boots, and <u>hats, climbers</u> <u>prevented</u> <u>hypothermia</u>, as well as simple frostbite.**

    A. hats climbers

    B. can prevent

    C. hypothermia;

    D. No change is necessary

    Answer: B. can prevent

    The verb "prevented" is in the past tense and must be changed to the present "can prevent" to be consistent. Option A is incorrect because a comma is needed after a long introductory phrase. Option C is incorrect because the semicolon creates a fragment of the phrase *as well as simple frostbite.*

(Average) (Skill 3.5)

18. Plus, climbers often find the most grueling part of the trip is <u>their</u> climb back <u>down, just</u> when they <u>are</u> feeling greatly exhausted.

   A. his

   B. down; just

   C. were

   D. No change is necessary

Answer: D. No change is necessary

The present tense must be used consistently throughout, therefore Option C is incorrect. Option A is incorrect because the singular pronoun "his" does not agree with the plural antecedent "climbers." Option B is incorrect because a comma, not a semicolon, is needed to separate the dependent clause from the main clause.

(Easy) (Skills 3.1 and 3.3)

19. If climbers are to avoid <u>becoming</u> dehydrated, there <u>is</u> beverages available for <u>them</u> to transport as well.

   A. becomming

   B. are

   C. him

   D. No change is necessary

Answer: B. are

The plural verb "are" must be used with the plural subject "beverages." Option A is incorrect because becoming is spelled with only one *m*. Option C is incorrect because the plural pronoun "them" is needed to agree with the plural referent "climbers."

(Rigorous) (Skills 3.1 and 3.3)

20. Each of the climbers <u>are</u> reminded of the splendor and <u>magnificence</u> of <u>God's</u> great Earth.

   A. is

   B. magnifisence

   C. Gods

   D. No change is necessary

Answer: A. is

The singular verb "is" agrees with the singular subject "each." Option B is incorrect because "magnificence" is misspelled. Option C is incorrect because an apostrophe is needed to show possession.

(Average) (Skill 3.6)

21. Once climbers are completely prepared for <u>their</u> lengthy <u>journey,</u> <u>they</u> can <u>comfortable</u> enjoy the wonderful scenery.

   A. they're

   B. journey; they

   C. comfortably

   D. No change is necessary

Answer: C. comfortably

The adverb form "comfortably," not the adjective "comfortable," is needed to modify the verb phrase can enjoy. Option A is incorrect because the possessive plural pronoun is spelled "their." Option B is incorrect because a semicolon would make the first half of the item seem like an independent clause when the subordinating conjunction "once" makes that clause dependent.

(Average) (Skill 3.7)

22. <u>Climbers who</u> take precautions are likely to find the ascent <u>less difficult</u> <u>than</u> the unprepared.

    A. Climbers, who

    B. least difficult

    C. then

    D. No change is necessary

    Answer: D. No change is necessary

    No change is needed. Option A is incorrect because a comma would make the phrase *who take precautions* seem less restrictive or less essential to the sentence. Option B is incorrect because *less* is appropriate when two items—the prepared and the unprepared—are compared. Option C is incorrect because the comparative adverb "than," not "then," is needed.

(Rigorous) (Skill 2.2)

23. Climbers must endure <u>severel</u> barriers <u>on the way, including</u> other <u>hikers</u>, steep jagged rocks, and lots of snow.

    A. several

    B. on the way: including

    C. hikers'

    D. No change is necessary

    Answer: A. several

    The word several is misspelled in the text. Option B is incorrect because a comma, not a colon, is needed to set off the modifying phrase. Option C is incorrect because no apostrophe is needed after "hikers" since it is not a possessive form.

(Rigorous) (Skill 2.2)

24. A pair of rugged boots <u>is</u> <u>also one</u> of the <u>necesities</u>.

    A. are

    B. also, one

    C. necessities

    D. No change is necessary

    Answer: C. necessities

    The word "necessities" is misspelled in the text. Option A is incorrect because the singular verb "is" must agree with the singular noun "pair" (a collective singular). Option B is incorrect because if "also" is set off with commas (which is a potential correction), it must be set off on both sides.

(Rigorous) (Skill 2.2)

25. Wide rock formations dazzle the <u>observers eyes</u> with shades of gray and <u>white, while</u> the peak <u>forms</u> a triangle that seems to touch the sky.

    A. observers' eyes

    B. white; while

    C. formed

    D. No change is necessary

    Answer: A. observers' eyes

    An apostrophe is needed to show the plural possessive form "observers' eyes." Option B is incorrect because the semicolon would make the second half of the item seem like an independent clause when the subordinating conjunction "while" makes that clause dependent. Option C is incorrect because "formed" is in the wrong tense.

DIRECTIONS: The passage below contains several errors. Read the passage. Then answer each test item by choosing the option that corrects an error in the underlined portion(s). No more than one underlined error will appear in each item. If no error exists, choose "No change is necessary."

Every job places different kinds of demands on their employees. For example, whereas such jobs as accounting and bookkeeping require mathematical ability; graphic design requires creative/artistic ability.

Doing good at one job does not usually guarantee success at another. However, one of the elements crucial to all jobs are especially notable: the chance to accomplish a goal.

The accomplishment of the employees vary according to the job. In many jobs the employees become accustom to the accomplishment provided by the work they do every day.

In medicine, for example, all doctors test them selves by treating badly injured or critically ill people. In the operating room, a team of Surgeons, is responsible for operating on many of these patients. In addition to the feeling of accomplishment that the workers achieve, some jobs also give a sense of identity to the employees'. Profesions like law, education, and sales offer huge financial or emotional rewards. Politicians are public servants: who work for the federal and state governments. President obama is basically employed by the American people to make laws and run the country.

Finally; the contributions that employees make to their companies and to the world cannot be taken for granted. Through their work, employees are performing a service for their employers and are contributing something to the world.

(Rigorous) (Skill 2.2)

26. The <u>accomplishment</u> of the <u>employees</u> <u>vary</u> according to the job.

   A. accomplishment,

   B. employee's

   C. varies

   D. No change is necessary

Answer: C. varies

The singular verb "varies" is needed to agree with the singular subject "accomplishment." Option A is incorrect because a comma after "accomplishment" would suggest that the modifying phrase "of the employees" is not essential to the sentence. Option B is incorrect because "employees" is not possessive.

(Average) (Skill 2.2)

27. **In many jobs the employees <u>become accustom</u> to the accomplishment <u>provided</u> by the work they do every day.**

   A. became

   B. accustomed

   C. provides

   D. No change is necessary

Answer: B. accustomed

The past participle "accustomed" is needed with the verb "become." Option A is incorrect because the verb tense does not need to change to the past "became." Option C is incorrect because "provides" is the wrong tense.

(Rigorous) (Skill 2.2)

28. <u>However,</u> one of the elements crucial to all jobs <u>are</u> especially <u>notable</u>: the accomplishment of a goal.

    A. However

    B. is

    C. notable;

    D. No change is necessary

    Answer: B. is

    The singular verb "is" agrees with the singular subject "one." Option A is incorrect because a comma is needed to set off the transitional word "however." Option C is incorrect because a colon, not a semicolon, is needed to set off an item.

(Average) (Skill 2.2)

29. In medicine, for example, all doctors <u>test them self</u> by treating badly injured and critically ill people.

    A. tests

    B. themselves

    C. critical

    D. No change is necessary

    Answer: B. themselves

    The reflexive pronoun "themselves" is needed (them self is nonstandard and never correct). Option A is incorrect because the plural verb "test" is needed to agree with the plural subject "doctors." Option C is incorrect because the adverb "critically" is needed to modify the adjective "ill."

(Rigorous) (Skill 3.1)

30. Every job <u>places</u> different kinds of demands on <u>their</u> <u>employees</u>.

    A. place

    B. its

    C. employes

    D. No change is necessary

    Answer: B. its

    The singular possessive pronoun "its" must agree with its antecedent "job," which is singular also. Option A is incorrect because "place" is a plural form and the subject, "job," is singular. Option C is incorrect because the correct spelling of "employees" is given in the sentence.

(Rigorous) (Skill 2.1)

31. Doing <u>good</u> at one job does not <u>usually</u> guarantee <u>success</u> at another.

    A. well

    B. usualy

    C. succeeding

    D. No change is necessary

    Answer: A. well

    The adverb "well" modifies the verb "doing." Option B is incorrect because "usually" is spelled correctly in the sentence. Option C is incorrect because "succeeding" is in the wrong tense.

(Average) (Skill 3.1)

32. <u>Profesions</u> like law, <u>education,</u> and sales <u>offer</u> huge financial or emotional rewards.

    A. Professions

    B. education;

    C. offered

    D. No change is necessary

    Answer: A. Professions

    Option A is correct because "professions" is misspelled in the sentence. Option B is incorrect because a comma, not a semicolon, is needed after "education." In Option C "offered" is in the wrong tense.

(Easy) (Skill 3.1)

33. <u>Politicians</u> <u>are</u> public <u>servants: who</u> <u>work</u> for the federal and state governments.

    A. were

    B. servants who

    C. worked

    D. No change is necessary

    Answer: B. servants who

    A colon is not needed to set off the introduction of the sentence. In Option A, "were" is the incorrect tense of the verb. In Option C "worked" is in the wrong tense of the verb.

(Average) (Skill 3.11)

34. <u>For example</u>, <u>whereas</u> such jobs as accounting and bookkeeping require mathematical <u>ability;</u> graphic design requires creative/artistic ability.

    A. For example

    B. whereas,

    C. ability,

    D. No change is necessary

    Answer: C. ability,

    An introductory dependent clause is set off with a comma, not a semicolon. Option A is incorrect because the transitional phrase *for example* should be set off with a comma. Option B is incorrect because the adverb "whereas" functions like "while" and does not need a comma after it.

(Easy) (Skills 3.10 and 3.11)

35. In addition to the feeling of accomplishment that the workers <u>achieve</u>, some jobs also <u>give</u> a sense of self-identity to the <u>employees'</u>.

    A. acheive

    B. gave

    C. employees

    D. No change is necessary

    Answer: C. employees

    Option C is correct because "employees" is not possessive. Option A is incorrect because "achieve" is spelled correctly in the sentence. Option B is incorrect because "gave" is the wrong tense.

(Average) (Skill 3.11)

36. <u>Finally;</u> the contributions that employees make to <u>their</u> companies and to the world cannot be <u>taken</u> for granted.

A. Finally,

B. thier

C. took

D. No change is necessary

Answer: A. Finally,

"Finally" is a transitional word that should be separated by a comma from the rest of the sentence. Option B is incorrect because "their" is misspelled. Option C is incorrect because "took" is the wrong form of the verb.

(Easy) (Skill 3.12)

37. In the <u>operating room,</u> a team of <u>Surgeons, is</u> responsible for operating on many of <u>these</u> patients.

A. operating room:

B. surgeons is

C. those

D. No change is necessary

Answer: B. surgeons is

Surgeons is not a proper name so it does not need to be capitalized. Also, a comma is not needed to break up a *team of surgeons* from the rest of the sentence. Option A is incorrect because a comma, not a colon, is needed to set off an item. Option C is incorrect because "those" is an incorrect pronoun.

(Easy) (Skill 3.12)

38. President <u>obama</u> is basically employed <u>by</u> the American people to <u>make</u> laws and run the country.

A. Obama

B. to

C. made

D. No change is necessary

Answer: A. Obama

Obama is a proper name and should be capitalized. Option B, "to," does not fit with the verb employed. Option C uses the wrong form of the verb.

DIRECTIONS: The passage below contains several errors. Read the passage. Then answer each test item by choosing the option that corrects an error in the underlined portion(s). No more than one underlined error will appear in each item. If no error exists, choose "No change is necessary."

The discovery of a body at Paris Point marina in Boca Raton shocked the residents of Palmetto Pines, a luxury condominium complex located next door to the marina.

The victim is a thirty-five-year-old woman who had been apparently bludgeoned to death and dumped in the ocean late last night. Many neighbors reported terrible screams, gunshots: as well as the sound of a car backfiring loudly to Boca Raton Police shortly after midnight. The woman had been spotted in the lobby of Palmetto Pines around ten thirty, along with an older man, estimated to be in his fifties, and a younger man, in his late twenties.

"Apparently, the victim had been driven to the complex by the older man, and was seen arguing with him when the younger man intervened," said Sheriff Fred Adams, "all three of them left the building together and walked to the marina, where gunshots rang out an hour later." Deputies found five bullets on the sidewalk and some blood, along with a steel pipe that is assumed to be the murder weapon. Two men were seen fleeing the scene in a red Mercedes short after, rushing toward the Interstate.

The Palm Beach County Coroner, Melvin Watts, said he concluded the victim's skull had been crushed by a blunt tool, which resulted in a brain hemorrhage. As of now, there is no clear motive for the murder.

(Easy) (Skill 3.8)

39. Two men <u>were</u> seen fleeing the scene in a red Mercedes <u>short</u> after, <u>rushing</u> toward the Interstate.

    A. are

    B. shortly

    C. rushed

    D. No change is necessary

Answer: B. shortly

The adverb "shortly" is needed to modify the adverb "after," not the adjective "short." Option A incorrectly uses the present tense "are" instead of the past tense were. Option C, "rushed," is the wrong form of the verb.

(Easy) (Skills 3.2, 3.10, and 3.11)

40. As of <u>now, there is</u> no clear motive for the murder.

    A. now;

    B. their

    C. was

    D. No change is necessary

Answer: D. No change is necessary

Option A is incorrect because a comma, not a semicolon, is needed to separate the independent clause from the dependent clause. Option B creates a misspelling. Option C uses the incorrect tense, "was," which doesn't fit with the present tense phrase "as of now."

Mathematics Test

(Skill 4.3)

1. Insert mathematical symbols to make the given calculation correct.

    $3 + 5 \cdot 4 - 1 = 18$

    A. Place parentheses around $5 \cdot 4$

    B. Place parentheses around $3 + 5$

    C. Place parentheses around $4 - 1$

    D. No symbols are needed. The calculation is already correct.

(Skill 4.2)

2. The admission price to tour the Haunted House has been changed from \$25 to \$30. What is the percent of change in the admission price?

    A. 5%

    B. 16.7%

    C. 20%

    D. 25%

(Skill 4.1)

3. $(-2.1 \times 10^4)(4.2 \times 10^{-5}) =$

    A. 8.82

    B. -8.82

    C. -0.882

    D. 0.882

(Skill 4.1)

4. Solve $|2x - 5| + 2 = 45$

    A. -19

    B. 19

    C. 24

    D. Both A and C

(Skill 4.1)

5. Choose the set in which the members are **not** equivalent.

    A. $\frac{1}{2}$, 0.5, 50%

    B. $\frac{10}{5,}$ 2.0, 200%

    C. $\frac{3}{8}$, 0.385, 38.5%

    D. $\frac{7}{10}$, 0.7, 70%

(Skill 4.1)

6. Put the following in order from smallest to largest:

    $3^2, -\pi, 2^3, 4\frac{2}{3}, -5, -8.1, \sqrt{6}$

    A. $-5, -8.1, \sqrt{6}, -\pi, 4\frac{2}{3}, 3^2, 2^3$

    B. $-5, -8.1, -\pi, \sqrt{6}, 4\frac{2}{3}, 2^3, 3^2$

    C. $-8.1, -5, -\pi, \sqrt{6}, 4\frac{2}{3}, 2^3, 3^2$

    D. $3^2, -\pi, 2^3, 4\frac{2}{3}, -5, -8.1, \sqrt{6}$

(Skill 4.2)

7. Simplify: $2\frac{2}{5} \div \frac{2}{3}$

    A. $2\frac{2}{5}$

    B. $1\frac{3}{5}$

    C. $2\frac{3}{5}$

    D. $3\frac{3}{5}$

(Skill 5.3)

8. The figure below shows a running track in the shape of a rectangle with semi-circles at each end.

    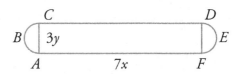

    Calculate the distance around the track.

(Skill 5.2)

9. On a map, 10 miles corresponds to $\frac{3}{4}$ inch. If two cities are 3 inches apart on this map, what is the actual distance in miles between them?

   A. 12.25

   B. 22.5

   C. 30

   D. 40

(Skill 5.2)

10. The owner of a rectangular piece of land 40 yards in length and 30 yards in width wants to divide it into two parts. She plans to join two opposite corners with a fence as shown in the diagram below. The cost of the fence will be approximately $25 per linear foot. What is the estimated total cost for the fence?

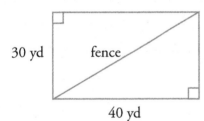

30 yd   fence   40 yd

(Skill 5.4)

11. The price of gas is $3.27 per gallon. Your tank holds 15 gallons of fuel. You are using two tanks of gas a week. Approximately how much will you save each week if the price of gas goes down to $2.30 per gallon?

   A. $26.00

   B. $29.00

   C. $15.00

   D. $17.00

(Skill 5.2)

12. At the lake, the ratio is 16 ducks to 9 geese. Suppose there are 192 ducks. How many geese are there?

   A. 21

   B. 108

   C. 7

   D. 1,728

(Skill 5.1)

13. Which of the following is true about a parallelogram?

   A. The opposite sides are congruent.

   B. The diagonals are congruent.

   C. All four angles are congruent.

   D. The sum of the interior angles is 180°.

(Skill 5.1)

14. Find the surface area of a box 3 feet wide, 5 feet tall, and 4 feet deep.

   A. 47 sq. ft.

   B. 60 sq. ft.

   C. 94 sq. ft

   D. 188 sq. ft.

(Skill 5.1)

15. If a cylinder has a radius of 5 and a height of 10, find the volume.

   A. 50π

   B. 100π

   C. 250π

   D. 500π

(Skill 5.4)

16. Anna can run 5 miles per hour. How many feet per minute does she run?

    A. $0.06 \frac{feet}{minute}$

    B. $17.6 \frac{feet}{minute}$

    C. $63,360 \frac{feet}{minute}$

    D. $440 \frac{feet}{minute}$

(Skill 5.3)

17. What unit of measurement could be used to describe the spread of a forest fire in a unit time?

    A. 10 square yards per second

    B. 10 yards per minute

    C. 10 feet per hour

    D. 10 cubic feet per hour

(Skill 6.2)

18. If n represents a number, which one of the following is the correct interpretation for the expression $8 - 2n$?

    A. Six times a number

    B. Twice a number subtracted from eight

    C. Twice eight minus a number

    D. Eight subtracted from twice a number

(Skill 6.6)

19. Which of the following sets of ordered pairs does not represent a function?

    A. $\{(1,-1), (2,-2), (3,-3)\}$

    B. $\{(3,1), (4,1), (5,1)\}$

    C. $\{(1,3), (1,4), (1,5)\}$

    D. All of the above do represent functions.

(Skill 6.3)

20. Which equation matches the data in the table?

x	3	4	5	6
y	7	8	9	10

    A. $y = 2x - 1$

    B. $y = 2x + 1$

    C. $y = -x + 10$

    D. $y = x + 4$

(Skill 6.4)

21. The fees charged by a parking garage are as follows:

Hours	1	2	3	4	5
Fee	$12	$19	$26	$33	$40

    How would you summarize the fees charged?

    A. $12 an hour

    B. $5 plus $7 per hour

    C. $15 an hour with a $3 discount

    D. $4 plus $8 per hour

(Skill 6.1)

22. Solve for x: $7 - 5x = 7x - 11 - 3x$

    A. -2

    B. 2

    C. 0

    D. $-1\frac{1}{2}$

(Skill 6.3)

23. Solve for y: $4x - 3y = 9$

    A. $y = 4x - 9$

    B. $y = 4x + 3$

    C. $y = 3 - \dfrac{4}{3}x$

    D. $y = \dfrac{4}{3}x - 3$

(Skill 6.3)

24. What is the equation of the graph shown below?

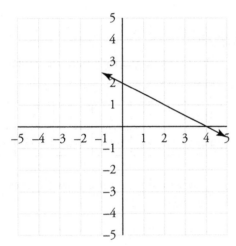

    A. $x + 2y = 4$

    B. $x - 2y = 4$

    C. $2x + y = 4$

    D. $x + 2y = -4$

(Skill 6.1)

25. Choose the expression that is **not** equivalent to $5x + 3y + 15z$:

    A. $5(x + 3z) + 3y$

    B. $3(x + y + 5z)$

    C. $3y + 5(x + 3z)$

    D. $5x + 3(y + 5z)$

(Skill 6.2)

26. Which choice below represents the phrase "3 less than 5 times a number?"

    A. $3 - 5n$

    B. $5n - 3$

    C. $3 < 5n$

    D. $5(n - 3)$

(Skill 6.1)

27. Which choice below could correctly appear during the solving of the given equation?

    $15 + 3x = -8x$

    A. $15 = -5x$

    B. $18 = -8x$

    C. $15 = 11x$

    D. $15 + 11x = 0$

(Skill 6.3)

28. Find the zeros of the function $f(x) = x^2 - 12x - 13$.

    A. -1

    B. 0

    C. 13

    D. Both A and C

(Skill 6.3)

29. Which number line shows the solution to $7x - 5 \geq 9x - 17$?

(Skill 6.7)

30. Which of the following equations has the same slope as $6x + 3y = 9$?

    A. $y = -2x+8$

    B. $y = 2x+8$

    C. $y = 6x+8$

    D. $y = -6x+8$

(Skill 7.1)

31. Which statement is true about George's budget?

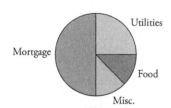

    A. George spends the greatest portion of his income on food

    B. George spends twice as much on utilities as he does on his mortgage

    C. George spends twice as much on utilities as he does on food

    D. George spends the same amount on food and utilities as he does on mortgage

(Skill 7.4)

32. Mary did comparison shopping on her favorite brand of coffee. Over half of the stores priced the coffee at $1.70. Most of the remaining stores priced the coffee at $1.80, except for a few who charged $1.90. Which of the following statements about the distribution of prices is true?

    A. The mean and the mode are the same

    B. The mean is greater than the mode

    C. The mean is less than the mode

    D. The mean is less than the median

(Skill 7.4)

33. Corporate salaries are listed for several employees. Which is the best measure of central tendency?

    $24,000, $24,000, $26,000, $28,000, $30,000, $120,000

    A. Mean

    B. Median

    C. Mode

    D. There is no best measure

(Skill 7.6)

34. The table below shows the distribution of majors for a group of college students.

MAJOR	PROPORTION OF STUDENTS
Mathematics	0.32
Photography	0.26
Journalism	0.19
Engineering	0.21
Criminal Law	0.02

If we know that a student, chosen at random, is not majoring in mathematics or engineering, what is the probability that the student is majoring in journalism?

A. 0.19

B. 0.36

C. 0.40

D. 0.81

(Skill 7.6)

35. A drawer contains 5 black socks, 3 blue socks, and 2 red socks. Without looking at the socks you draw, what is the probability that you will draw two black socks in two draws?

A. $\frac{2}{9}$

B. $\frac{1}{4}$

C. $\frac{17}{18}$

D. $\frac{1}{18}$

(Skill 7.6)

36. How many unique sandwiches can be made considering choices of white or wheat bread, meat choices of turkey, ham or roast beef, and an option of butter, mayonnaise, mustard, or no condiment?

A. 234

B. 64

C. 24

D. 9

(Skill 7.4)

37. The ages of the participants in a hula-hoop contest are as follows: 10, 18, 22, 17, 77, 19, 13, 20, 10, 15. Which measure would most accurately represent the data as a whole?

A. range

B. mode

C. mean

D. median

(Skill 7.2)

38. Hiroshi surveys his classmates to find what percent of them come to school on the bus, by car, by subway, by bicycle, or on foot. What is the best way to display his results?

A. A line graph

B. A box plot

C. A scatterplot

D. A circle graph

(Skill 7.1)

39. The following chart shows the yearly average number of international tourists visiting Palm Beach for 1990–1994. How many more international tourists visited Palm Beach in 1994 than in 1991?

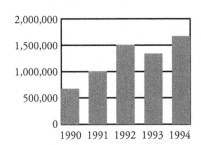

A. 100,000

B. 600,000

C. 1,600,000

D. 8,000,000

(Skill 7.3)

40. Which of the following statements is false about the data: 2, 4, 6, 8, 10?

A. The mean is 6

B. The median is 6

C. There is no mode

D. The range is 10

(Skill 7.3)

41. A student has taken three tests in his algebra class for which the mean score is 88. He will take one more test and his final grade will be the mean of all four tests. He wants to achieve a final grade of 90. Which one of the following is the correct procedure to determine the score he needs on the fourth test?

A. He needs a score of 92 since $\frac{(88 + 92)}{2} = 90$

B. He needs a score of 89.5 since $\frac{(88 + 90 + 90 + 90)}{4} = 89.5$

C. He needs a score of 96 since $\frac{(88 + 88 + 88 + 96)}{4} = 90$

D. He cannot achieve a final grade of 90 since each of his scores on the first three tests is less than 90

(Skill 7.6)

42. What is the probability of flipping 3 coins and getting 2 tails and 1 head?

A. $\frac{3}{8}$

B. $\frac{1}{8}$

C. $\frac{1}{3}$

D. $\frac{1}{2}$

(Skill 7.5)

43. In many states, you can get a driver's license when you turn 16. Which of the age statistic choices below would best represent when a person gets a license?

A. mean

B. median

C. mode

D. variance

(Skill 7.6)

44. In a card game, you get another turn if the card you draw is red or if it is a jack, queen, king, or ace. You are the first to draw from a full deck of 52 cards. What is the chance you will get another turn?

   A. $\frac{2}{13}$

   B. $\frac{4}{13}$

   C. $\frac{1}{2}$

   D. $\frac{17}{26}$

(Skill 7.7)

45. Jesse is trying to find out how many boys attend his school. To get an estimate, he counts the girls and boys in 3 of his classes and finds there are 58 boys and 62 girls. If his school has a total of 560 students, how many boys attend his school?

   A. 271

   B. 289

   C. 325

   D. 347

Answer Key: Mathematics Test

1. C	11. B	21. B	31. C	41. C
2. C	12. B	22. B	32. B	42. A
3. C	13. A	23. D	33. B	43. C
4. D	14. C	24. A	34. C	44. D
5. C	15. C	25. B	35. A	45. A
6. C	16. D	26. B	36. C	
7. D	17. A	27. D	37. D	
8. D	18. B	28. D	38. D	
9. D	19. C	29. B	39. B	
10. D	20. D	30. A	40. D	

Mathematics Test with Rationales

1. Insert mathematical symbols to make the given calculation correct.

    $3 + 5 \cdot 4 - 1 = 18$

    A. Place parentheses around $5 \cdot 4$

    B. Place parentheses around $3 + 5$

    C. Place parentheses around $4 - 1$

    D. No symbols are needed. The calculation is already correct.

    Answer: C.

    Without inserting any symbols, the problem's answer is 22 as multiplication must be completed before the addition and subtraction. Choice C turns the calculation into
    $3 + 5 \cdot (4 - 1)$
    $3 + 5 \cdot 3$
    $3 + 15$
    18

(Skill 4.2)

2. The admission price to tour the Haunted House has been changed from $25 to $30. What is the percent of change in the admission price?

    A. 5%

    B. 16.7%

    C. 20%

    D. 25%

    Answer: C.

    First use subtraction to find the change in dollars: $30 - 25 = 5$. Then compare the change to the original to find the percent:
    $\frac{5}{25} = 0.2 = 20\%$

(Skill 4.1)

3. $(-2.1 \times 10^4)(4.2 \times 10^{-5}) =$

    A. 8.82

    B. -8.82

    C. -0.882

    D. 0.882

    Answer: C.

    First, multiply -2.1 by 4.2 to get -8.82. Then, multiply 10^4 by 10^{-5} to get 10^{-1}.
    $-8.82 \times 10^{-1} = -0.882$.

(Skill 4.1)

4. Solve $|2x - 5| + 2 = 45$

    A. -19

    B. 19

    C. 24

    D. Both A and C

    Answer: D.

    First isolate the absolute value expression, then set up two equations to solve.

    $$|2x - 5| = 43$$
    $$2x - 5 = -43 \text{ or } 2x - 5 = 43$$
    $$2x = -38 \text{ or } 2x = 48$$
    $$x = -19 \text{ or } x = 24$$

(Skill 4.1)

5. Choose the set in which the members are not equivalent.

    A. $\frac{1}{2}$, 0.5, 50%

    B. $\frac{10}{5}$, 2.0, 200%

    C. $\frac{3}{8}$, 0.385, 38.5%

    D. $\frac{7}{10}$, 0.7, 70%

Answer: C.

$\frac{3}{8}$ is equivalent to .375 and 37.5%.

(Skill 4.1)

6. **Put the following in order from smallest to largest:**

$3^2, -\pi, 2^3, 4\frac{2}{3}, -5, -8.1, \sqrt{6}$

A. $-5, -8.1, \sqrt{6}, -\pi, 4\frac{2}{3}, 3^2, 2^3$

B. $-5, -8.1, -\pi, \sqrt{6}, 4\frac{2}{3}, 2^3, 3^2$

C. $-8.1, -5, -\pi, \sqrt{6}, 4\frac{2}{3}, 2^3, 3^2$

D. $3^2, -\pi, 2^3, 4\frac{2}{3}, -5, -8.1, \sqrt{6}$

Answer: C.

First put the numbers in decimal form so they may be easily compared,

$3^2 = 9, -\pi \approx -3.14, 2^3 = 8,$
$4\frac{2}{3} = 4.67, \sqrt{6} \approx 2.45$

$9, -3.14, 8, 4.67, -5, -8.1, 2.45$

Then arrange in order beginning with the largest negative number:

$-8.1, -5, -3.14, 2.45, 4.67, 8, 9 \rightarrow$

$-8.1, -5, -\pi, \sqrt{6}, 4\frac{2}{3}, 2^3, 3^2$

(Skill 4.2)

7. **Simplify:** $2\frac{2}{5} \div \frac{2}{3}$

A. $2\frac{2}{5}$

B. $1\frac{3}{5}$

C. $2\frac{3}{5}$

D. $3\frac{3}{5}$

Answer: D.

First convert to improper fractions,

$\frac{12}{5} \div \frac{2}{3}$

Change to a multiplication problem by using the reciprocal of the fraction after the division sign, cancel common factors, multiply numerators together and denominators together. Simplify.

$\frac{12}{5} \cdot \frac{3}{2} = \frac{6}{5} \cdot \frac{3}{1} = \frac{18}{5} = 3\frac{3}{5}$

(Skill 5.3)

8. **The figure below shows a running track in the shape of a rectangle with semicircles at each end.**

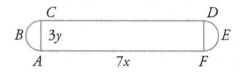

Calculate the distance around the track.

A. $6\pi y + 14x$

B. $3\pi y + 7x$

C. $6\pi y + 7x$

D. $3\pi y + 14x$

Answer: D.

The two semicircles of the track create one circle with a diameter $3y$. The circumference of a circle is $C = \pi d$ so $C = 3\pi y$. The length of both sides of the track is $7x$ each side, so the total circumference around the track is $3\pi y + 7x + 7x = 3\pi y + 14x$

(Skill 5.2)

9. **On a map, 10 miles corresponds to $\frac{3}{4}$ inch. If two cities are 3 inches apart on this map, what is the actual distance in miles between them?**

   A. 12.25

   B. 22.5

   C. 30

   D. 40

Answer: D.

Let x represent the distance in miles between the two cities. Then $\frac{\frac{3}{4}}{3} = \frac{10}{x}$. Cross-multiply to get $\frac{3}{4}x = (10)(3) = 30$. Then $x = \frac{30}{\frac{3}{4}} = 40$.

(Skill 5.2)

10. **The owner of a rectangular piece of land 40 yards in length and 30 yards in width wants to divide it into two parts. She plans to join two opposite corners with a fence as shown in the diagram below. The cost of the fence will be approximately $25 per linear foot. What is the estimated total cost for the fence?**

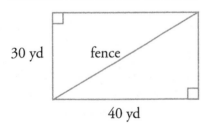

   A. $1,250

   B. $62,500

   C. $5,250

   D. $3,750

Answer: D.

Find the length of the diagonal by using the Pythagorean theorem. Let x be the length of the diagonal.

$30^2 + 40^2 = x^2 \rightarrow 900 + 1600 = x^2$

$2500 = x^2 \rightarrow \sqrt{2500} = \sqrt{x^2}$

$x = 50$ yards

Convert to feet.
$\frac{50 \text{ yards}}{x \text{ feet}} = \frac{1 \text{ yard}}{3 \text{ feet}} \rightarrow 150$ feet

The fence costs $25 per linear foot, so the cost is (150 ft)($25) = $3,750.

(Skill 5.4)

11. **The price of gas is $3.27 per gallon. Your tank holds 15 gallons of fuel. You are using two tanks of gas a week. Approximately how much will you save each week if the price of gas goes down to $2.30 per gallon?**

   A. $26.00

   B. $29.00

   C. $15.00

   D. $17.00

Answer: B.

15 gallons × 2 tanks = 30 gallons a week
= 30 gallons × $3.27 = $98.10
30 gallons × $2.30 = $69.00
$98.10 − $69.00 = $29.10 is approximately $29.00.

(Skill 5.2)

12. At the lake, the ratio is 16 ducks to 9 geese. Suppose there are 192 ducks. How many geese are there?

    A. 21

    B. 108

    C. 7

    D. 1,728

Answer: B.

Set up the proportion: $\frac{16}{9} = \frac{192}{g}$.
Solve for g.
$16g = (192)(9)$
$16g = 1728$
$g = 108$

(Skill 5.1)

13. Which of the following is true about a parallelogram?

    A. The opposite sides are congruent.

    B. The diagonals are congruent.

    C. All four angles are congruent.

    D. The sum of the interior angles is 180°.

Answer: A.

Choices B and C are true for rectangles. Choice D is true for triangles.

(Skill 5.1)

14. Find the surface area of a box 3 feet wide, 5 feet tall, and 4 feet deep.

    A. 47 sq. ft.

    B. 60 sq. ft.

    C. 94 sq. ft

    D. 188 sq. ft.

Answer: C.

The top and bottom faces measure 3 ft. by 4 ft., so the surface area of the top and bottom together is 2(12) = 24. The front and back measure 3 ft. by 5 ft., so the surface area of those two faces is 2(15) = 30. The left and right sides by 4 ft. by 5 ft., so the surface area of those two faces is 2(20) = 40. The total surface area is therefore 24 + 30 + 40 = 94 square feet.

(Skill 5.1)

15. If a cylinder has a radius of 5 and a height of 10, find the volume.

    A. 50π

    B. 100π

    C. 250π

    D. 500π

Answer: C.

Applying the formula for the volume of a cylinder, $V = \pi r^2 h$, gives $\pi \cdot 5^2 \cdot 10 = 250\pi$

(Skill 5.4)

16. Anna can run 5 miles per hour. How many feet per minute does she run?

    A. $0.06 \frac{feet}{minute}$

    B. $17.6 \frac{feet}{minute}$

    C. $63,360 \frac{feet}{minute}$

    D. $440 \frac{feet}{minute}$

Answer: D.

$$\frac{5 \ miles}{1 \ hour} \cdot \frac{1 \ hour}{60 \ minutes} \cdot \frac{5280 \ feet}{1 \ mile}$$

$$= 440 \ \frac{feet}{minute}$$

(Skill 5.3)

17. **What unit of measurement could be used to describe the spread of a forest fire in a unit time?**

    A. 10 square yards per second

    B. 10 yards per minute

    C. 10 feet per hour

    D. 10 cubic feet per hour

Answer: A.

The only appropriate answer is one that describes an *area* of forest consumed per unit time. Only answer A is a unit of area measurement.

(Skill 6.2)

18. **If *n* represents a number, which one of the following is the correct interpretation for the expression 8 − 2*n*?**

    A. Six times a number

    B. Twice a number subtracted from eight

    C. Twice eight minus a number

    D. Eight subtracted from twice a number

Answer: B.

The expression 2*n* means twice a number. Since 8 precedes 2*n* in the given expression, this means that 2*n* is being subtracted from 8.

(Skill 6.6)

19. **Which of the following sets of ordered pairs does not represent a function?**

    A. $\{(1,-1), (2,-2), (3,-3)\}$

    B. $\{(3,1), (4,1), (5,1)\}$

    C. $\{(1,3), (1,4), (1,5)\}$

    D. All of the above do represent functions.

Answer: C.

A function cannot have more than one output value (*y*) for the same input (*x*).

(Skill 6.3)

20. **Which equation matches the data in the table?**

x	3	4	5	6
y	7	8	9	10

    A. $y = 2x - 1$

    B. $y = 2x + 1$

    C. $y = -x + 10$

    D. $y = x + 4$

Answer: D.

Each *y* value is 4 greater than its *x* value, which is the relationship demonstrated by choice D.

(Skill 6.4)

21. The fees charged by a parking garage are as follows:

Hours	1	2	3	4	5
Fee	$12	$19	$26	$33	$40

How would you summarize the fees charged?

A. $12 an hour

B. $5 plus $7 per hour

C. $15 an hour with a $3 discount

D. $4 plus $8 per hour

Answer: B.

Choice B satisfies each entry in the table. For instance, at 4 hours the calculation is $5 + 7(4) = 33$.

(Skill 6.1)

22. **Solve for x: $7 - 5x = 7x - 11 - 3x$**

A. -2

B. 2

C. 0

D. $-1\frac{1}{2}$

Answer: B.

First add $5x$ to both sides to get all the x terms on one side.

Then $7 = 7x - 11 - 3x + 5x$. Combine all the x terms: $7 = 9x - 11$. Add 11 to both sides to get $18 = 9x$. Dividing both sides by 9, $x = 2$.

(Skill 6.3)

23. **Solve for y: $4x - 3y = 9$**

A. $y = 4x - 9$

B. $y = 4x + 3$

C. $y = 3 - \dfrac{4}{3}x$

D. $y = \dfrac{4}{3}x - 3$

Answer: D.

Original equation: $4x - 3y = 9$, subtract $4x$ from both sides

$-3y = -4x + 9$, divide each term by -3

$y = \dfrac{4}{3}x - 3$

(Skill 6.3)

24. **What is the equation of the graph shown below?**

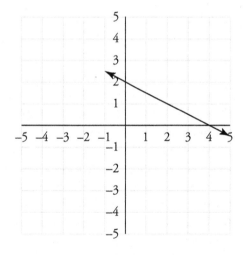

A. $x + 2y = 4$

B. $x - 2y = 4$

C. $2x + y = 4$

D. $x + 2y = -4$

Answer: A.

When $y = 0$, solving for x yields 4, giving the point $(4, 0)$. When $x = 0$, solving for y yields 2, giving the point $(0, 2)$. These are the intercepts of the given graph.

(Skill 6.1)

25. **Choose the expression that is not equivalent to $5x + 3y + 15z$:**

    A. $5(x + 3z) + 3y$

    B. $3(x + y + 5z)$

    C. $3y + 5(x + 3z)$

    D. $5x + 3(y + 5z)$

    Answer: B.

    $5x + 3y + 15z = (5x + 15z) + 3y = 5(x + 3z) + 3y$ A is equivalent

    $= 5x + (3y + 15z) = 5x + 3(y + 5z)$ D is equivalent

    $= 3y + (5x + 15z) = 3y + 5(x + 3z)$ C is equivalent

    We can solve all of these using the associative property and then factoring. However, in B $3(x + y + 5z)$ by distributive property $= 3x + 3y + 15z$, which does not equal $5x + 3y + 15z$.

(Skill 6.2)

26. **Which choice below represents the phrase "3 less than 5 times a number?"**

    A. $3 - 5n$

    B. $5n - 3$

    C. $3 < 5n$

    D. $5(n - 3)$

Answer: B.

Choice B expresses the operations in the correct order. Choice C expresses 3 *is* less than 5 times a number.

(Skill 6.1)

27. **Which choice below could correctly appear during the solving of the given equation?**

    $15 + 3x = -8x$

    A. $15 = -5x$

    B. $18 = -8x$

    C. $15 = 11x$

    D. $15 + 11x = 0$

Answer: D.

Choice D arises when $8x$ is added to both sides of the equation.

(Skill 6.3)

28. **Find the zeros of the function $f(x) = x^2 - 12x - 13$.**

    A. -1

    B. 0

    C. 13

    D. Both A and C

Answer: D.

Set $f(x)$ equal to 0 and solve by factoring:

$$x^2 - 12x - 13 = 0$$
$$(x - 13)(x + 1) = 0$$
$$x = 13, -1$$

(Skill 6.3)

29. **Which number line shows the solution to $7x - 5 \geq 9x - 17$?**

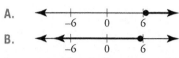

A.

B.

C.

D.

Answer: B.

First gather all the *x*-terms on one side of the inequality and the numbers on the other.

$$7x - 5 \geq 9x - 17$$

$$-2x \geq -12$$

Dividing both sides of an inequality by a negative number reverses the inequality sign. So division by -2 on both sides results in x ≤ 6, which is graphed in choice B.

(Skill 6.7)

30. **Which of the following equations has the same slope as $6x + 3y = 9$?**

A. $y = -2x+8$

B. $y = 2x+8$

C. $y = 6x+8$

D. $y = -6x+8$

Answer: A.

Put $6x + 3y = 9$ into slope-intercept form, $y = mx + b$.

$y = -2x + 3$

m, slope, is -2, so the equation with an *x* coefficient of -2 has the same slope.

(Skill 7.1)

31. **Which statement is true about George's budget?**

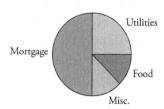

A. George spends the greatest portion of his income on food

B. George spends twice as much on utilities as he does on his mortgage

C. George spends twice as much on utilities as he does on food

D. George spends the same amount on food and utilities as he does on mortgage

Answer: C.

The wedge representing utilities is twice as large as the wedge representing food.

(Skill 7.4)

32. **Mary did comparison shopping on her favorite brand of coffee. Over half of the stores priced the coffee at $1.70. Most of the remaining stores priced the coffee at $1.80, except for a few who charged $1.90. Which of the following statements about the distribution of prices is true?**

A. The mean and the mode are the same

B. The mean is greater than the mode

C. The mean is less than the mode

D. The mean is less than the median

Answer: B.

Over half the stores priced the coffee at $1.70, so this is the mode. The mean is slightly over $1.70 because other stores priced the coffee at over $1.70.

(Skill 7.4)

33. Corporate salaries are listed for several employees. Which is the best measure of central tendency?

$24,000, $24,000, $26,000, $28,000, $30,000, $120,000

A. Mean

B. Median

C. Mode

D. There is no best measure

Answer: B.

The median provides the best measure of central tendency in this case because the mode is the lowest number and the mean is disproportionately skewed by the outlier $120,000.

(Skill 7.6)

34. The table below shows the distribution of majors for a group of college students.

MAJOR	PROPORTION OF STUDENTS
Mathematics	0.32
Photography	0.26
Journalism	0.19
Engineering	0.21
Criminal Law	0.02

If we know that a student, chosen at random, is not majoring in mathematics or engineering, what is the probability that the student is majoring in journalism?

A. 0.19

B. 0.36

C. 0.40

D. 0.81

Answer: C.

The proportion of students majoring in math or engineering is $0.32 + 0.21 = 0.53$. This means that the proportion of students not majoring in math or engineering is $1.00 - 0.53 = 0.47$. The proportion of students majoring in journalism out of those not majoring in math or engineering is $\frac{0.19}{0.47} = 0.404$.

(Skill 7.6)

35. A drawer contains 5 black socks, 3 blue socks, and 2 red socks. Without looking at the socks you draw, what is the probability that you will draw two black socks in two draws?

A. $\frac{2}{9}$

B. $\frac{1}{4}$

C. $\frac{17}{18}$

D. $\frac{1}{18}$

Answer: A.

In this example of conditional probability, the probability of drawing a black sock on the first draw is $\frac{5}{10}$. The problem implies that there is no replacement, so the probability of drawing a black sock on the second draw is $\frac{4}{9}$. Multiply the two probabilities and reduce to lowest terms.

(Skill 7.6)

36. How many unique sandwiches can be made considering choices of white or wheat bread, meat choices of turkey, ham or roast beef, and an option of butter, mayonnaise, mustard, or no condiment?

A. 234

B. 64

C. 24

D. 9

Answer: C.

Model the Fundamental Counting Principle with 3 events: 2 bread choices, 3 meat choices, and 4 possibilities for condiments. $2 \cdot 3 \cdot 4 = 24$

(Skill 7.4)

37. The ages of the participants in a hula-hoop contest are as follows: 10, 18, 22, 17, 77, 19, 13, 20, 10, 15. Which measure would most accurately represent the data as a whole?

A. range

B. mode

C. mean

D. median

Answer: D.

The data set contains an outlier. The range including the outlier would represent too wide a variation of the data, most of which falls within a narrow range. The mode would be a value smaller than all the other data items. The mean would be too large, skewed by the presence of the outlier. Only the median would have a value representative of the data as a whole.

(Skill 7.2)

38. Hiroshi surveys his classmates to find what percent of them come to school on the bus, by car, by subway, by bicycle, or on foot. What is the best way to display his results?

A. A line graph

B. A box plot

C. A scatterplot

D. A circle graph

Answer: D.

A circle graph, or pie chart, typically represents percent values.

(Skill 7.1)

39. The following chart shows the yearly average number of international tourists visiting Palm Beach for 1990–1994. How many more international tourists visited Palm Beach in 1994 than in 1991?

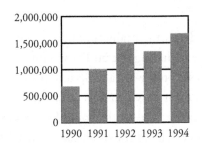

A. 100,000

B. 600,000

C. 1,600,000

D. 8,000,000

Answer: B.

The number of tourists in 1991 was 1,000,000 and the number in 1994 was 1,600,000. Subtract to get a difference of 600,000.

(Skill 7.3)

40. Which of the following statements is false about the data: 2, 4, 6, 8, 10?

A. The mean is 6

B. The median is 6

C. There is no mode

D. The range is 10

Answer: D.

In this case that median is 6, which is also the mean:

$$\frac{2+4+6+8+10}{5} = \frac{30}{5}$$

Since none of the data values appear more than once, there is no mode. However, the range is $10 - 2 = 8$, not 10, so choice D is false.

(Skill 7.3)

41. A student has taken three tests in his algebra class for which the mean score is 88. He will take one more test and his final grade will be the mean of all four tests. He wants to achieve a final grade of 90. Which one of the following is the correct procedure to determine the score he needs on the fourth test?

A. He needs a score of 92 since $\frac{(88 + 92)}{2}$ = 90

B. He needs a score of 89.5 since $\frac{(88 + 90 + 90 + 90)}{4}$ = 89.5

C. He needs a score of 96 since $\frac{(88 + 88 + 88 + 96)}{4}$ = 90

D. He cannot achieve a final grade of 90 since each of his scores on the first three tests is less than 90

Answer: C.

The sum of all four tests must be $(90)(4)$ = 360 in order to achieve a mean score of 90. Since he has averaged 88 on his first three tests, the sum of his scores thus far is $(88)(3)$ = 264. Therefore he needs a score of $360 - 264$ = 96 on his fourth test.

(Skill 7.6)

42. What is the probability of flipping 3 coins and getting 2 tails and 1 head?

    A. $\frac{3}{8}$

    B. $\frac{1}{8}$

    C. $\frac{1}{3}$

    D. $\frac{1}{2}$

    Answer: A.

    The simplest way to find the answer can be found by listing out all the possible combinations or making a tree diagram. There are 8 total combinations. Three result in 2 tails and 1 head.

(Skill 7.5)

43. In many states, you can get a driver's license when you turn 16. Which of the age statistic choices below would best represent when a person gets a license?

    A. mean

    B. median

    C. mode

    D. variance

    Answer: C.

    People younger than 16 can't get a license, so the mean will be skewed by people older than 16 getting a license for the first time. The median will also be skewed in this same manner.

(Skill 7.6)

44. In a card game, you get another turn if the card you draw is red or if it is a jack, queen, king, or ace. You are the first to draw from a full deck of 52 cards. What is the chance you will get another turn?

    A. $\frac{2}{13}$

    B. $\frac{4}{13}$

    C. $\frac{1}{2}$

    D. $\frac{17}{26}$

    Answer: D.

    The cards that would give you another turn include all 26 red cards, plus the two black jacks, queens, kings, and aces, making a total of 34 out of 52 or $\frac{17}{26}$.

(Skill 7.7)

45. Jesse is trying to find out how many boys attend his school. To get an estimate, he counts the girls and boys in 3 of his classes and finds there are 58 boys and 62 girls. If his school has a total of 560 students, how many boys attend his school?

    A. 271

    B. 289

    C. 325

    D. 347

    Answer: A.

    Find the proportion of boys in the classes he counted. Use this to find the number in the entire school by setting up a proportion.

    $$\frac{58 \text{ boys}}{58 + 62 \text{ total students}} = \frac{x \text{ boys}}{560}$$

    $\rightarrow 270.7 \rightarrow 271$ boys

Reading Test

DIRECTIONS: Read the following passage and answer the questions that follow.

This writer has often been asked to tutor hospitalized children with cystic fibrosis. While undergoing all the precautionary measures to see these children (for example, scrubbing thoroughly and donning a face mask and sterile gown), she has wondered why parents subject these children to the pressures of schooling and trying to catch up on what they have missed because of hospitalization, which is a normal part of cystic fibrosis patients' lives. These children undergo so many tortuous treatments a day that it seems cruel to expect them to learn as normal children do, especially when their life expectancies are so short.

(Average) (Skill 8.1)

1. **What is the main idea of this passage?**

   A. There is a lot of preparation involved in visiting a patient with cystic fibrosis

   B. Children with cystic fibrosis are incapable of living normal lives

   C. Certain concessions should be made for children with cystic fibrosis

   D. Children with cystic fibrosis die young

(Easy) (Skill 8.2)

2. **How is the author so familiar with the procedures used when visiting a child with cystic fibrosis?**

   A. She has read about it

   B. She works in a hospital

   C. She is the parent of one

   D. She often tutors them

(Average) (Skill 8.3)

3. **What is meant by the word "precautionary" in the second sentence?**

   A. Careful

   B. Protective

   C. Medical

   D. Sterilizing

(Average) (Skill 9.5)

4. **What is the author's purpose?**

   A. To inform

   B. To entertain

   C. To describe

   D. To narrate

(Rigorous) (Skill 9.5)

5. **What type of organizational pattern does the author use?**

   A. Classification

   B. Example, clarification, and definition

   C. Comparison and contrast

   D. Cause and effect

(Rigorous) (Skill 8.4)

6. The author states that it is "cruel" to expect children with cystic fibrosis to learn as "normal" children do. Is this a fact or an opinion?

    A. Fact

    B. Opinion

(Rigorous) (Skill 8.3)

7. Is there evidence of bias in this paragraph?

    A. Yes

    B. No

(Rigorous) (Skill 9.2)

8. What is the author's tone?

    A. Sympathetic

    B. Cruel

    C. Disbelieving

    D. Cheerful

(Rigorous) (Skill 9.3)

9. What organizational structure is used in the last sentence of this passage?

    A. Addition

    B. Summary

    C. Example

    D. Comparison and contrast

(Rigorous) (Skill 9.5)

10. Is the author's argument about schooling children with cystic fibrosis valid or invalid?

    A. Valid

    B. Invalid

DIRECTIONS: Read the following passage and answer the questions that follow.

Disciplinary practices have been found to affect diverse areas of child development such as moral values, obedience to authority, and performance at school. Even though the dictionary has a specific definition for the word "discipline," the concept is still open to interpretation by people of different cultures.

There are four types of disciplinary styles: assertion of power, withdrawal of love, reasoning, and permissiveness. Assertion of power involves the use of force to discourage unwanted behavior. Withdrawal of love involves making the love of a parent or authority figure a condition of a child's good behavior. Reasoning involves persuading a child to behave one way rather than another. Permissiveness involves allowing children to do as they please and face the consequences of their actions.

(Average) (Skill 8.2)

11. What is the main idea of this passage?

    A. Different people have different ideas of what discipline is

    B. Permissiveness is the most widely used disciplinary style

    C. Most people agree on their definition of discipline

    D. There are four disciplinary styles

(Easy) (Skill 10.4)

12. **Name the four types of disciplinary styles.**

   A. Reasoning, power assertion, morality, and permissiveness

   B. Morality, reasoning, permissiveness, and withdrawal of love

   C. Withdrawal of love, permissiveness, assertion of power, and reasoning

   D. Permissiveness, morality, reasoning, and power assertion

(Easy) (Skill 10.2)

13. **What does the technique of reasoning involve?**

   A. Persuading children to behave in a certain way

   B. Allowing children to do as they please

   C. Using force to discourage unwanted behavior

   D. Making love a condition of good behavior

(Easy) (Skill 10.1)

14. **What is the meaning of the word "diverse" in the first sentence?**

   A. Many

   B. Related to children

   C. Disciplinary

   D. Moral

(Easy) (Skill 9.5)

15. **What is the author's purpose in writing this passage?**

   A. To describe

   B. To narrate

   C. To entertain

   D. To inform

(Rigorous) (Skill 9.3)

16. **What is the overall organizational pattern of this passage?**

   A. Statement support

   B. Cause and effect

   C. Classification

   D. Summary

(Rigorous) (Skill 9.3)

17. **What organizational structure is used in the first sentence of the second paragraph?**

   A. Addition

   B. Location/spatial order

   C. Clarification

   D. Example

(Average) (Skill 8.4)

18. **The author states that "assertion of power involves the use of force to discourage unwanted behavior." Is this a fact or an opinion?**

   A. Fact

   B. Opinion

(Average) (Skill 8.3)

19. **Is this passage biased?**

   A. Yes

   B. No

(Average) (Skill 9.2)

20. **What is the author's tone?**

   A. Disbelieving

   B. Angry

   C. Informative

   D. Optimistic

(Rigorous) (Skill 8.1)

21. **From reading this passage we can conclude that:**

    A. The author is a teacher

    B. The author has many children

    C. The author has written a book about discipline

    D. The author has done research on discipline

DIRECTIONS: Read the following passage and answer the questions that follow.

One of the most difficult problems plaguing American education is the assessment of teachers. No one denies that teachers should be answerable for what they do, but what exactly does that mean? The *Oxford American Dictionary* defines accountability as the obligation to give a reckoning or explanation for one's actions.

Do students have to learn for teaching to have taken place? Historically, teaching has not been defined in this restrictive manner; teachers were thought to be responsible for the quantity and quality of material covered and for the way in which it was presented. However, some definitions of teaching now imply that students must learn in order for teaching to have taken place.

As a teacher who tries my best to keep current on all the latest teaching strategies, I believe that those teachers who do not bother even to pick up an educational journal every once in a while should be kept under close watch. There are many teachers out there who have been teaching for decades and refuse to change their ways even if research has proven that their methods are outdated and ineffective. There is no place in the profession of teaching for these types of individuals. It is time that the American educational system clean house, for the sake of our children.

(Average) (Skill 8.2)

22. **What is the main idea of the passage?**

    A. Teachers should not be answerable for what they do

    B. Teachers who do not do their job should be fired

    C. The author is a good teacher

    D. Assessment of teachers is a serious problem in society today

(Easy) (Skill 8.1)

23. **The author states that teacher assessment is a problem for:**

    A. Elementary schools

    B. Secondary schools

    C. American education

    D. Families

(Easy) (Skill 8.1)

24. **Where does the author get her definition of "accountability?"**

    A. *Webster's Dictionary*

    B. *Encyclopedia Britannica*

    C. *The Oxford American Dictionary*

    D. *World Book Encyclopedia*

(Easy) (Skill 8.2)

25. **What is meant by the word "plaguing" in the first sentence?**

    A. Causing problems

    B. Causing illness

    C. Causing anger

    D. Causing failure

(Average) (Skill 8.2)

26. What is the meaning of the word "reckoning" in the third sentence?

    A. Thought

    B. Answer

    C. Obligation

    D. Explanation

(Average) (Skill 9.5)

27. What is the author's purpose in writing this?

    A. To entertain

    B. To narrate

    C. To describe

    D. To persuade

(Average) (Skill 9.3)

28. What is the author's overall organizational pattern?

    A. Classification

    B. Cause and effect

    C. Definition

    D. Comparison and contrast

(Rigorous) (Skill 9.3)

29. What is the organizational pattern of the second paragraph?

    A. Cause and effect

    B. Classification

    C. Addition

    D. Example, clarification, and definition

(Average) (Skill 8.4)

30. "Teachers who do not keep current on educational trends should be fired." Is this a fact or an opinion?

    A. Fact

    B. Opinion

(Rigorous) (Skill 8.3)

31. Is there evidence of bias in this passage?

    A. Yes

    B. No

(Average) (Skill 9.2)

32. The author's tone is one of:

    A. Disbelief

    B. Excitement

    C. Support

    D. Concern

(Rigorous) (Skill 9.4)

33. Is the author's argument valid?

    A. Yes

    B. No

(Rigorous) (Skill 8.1)

34. From the passage, one can infer that:

    A. The author considers herself a good teacher

    B. Poor teachers will be fired

    C. Students have to learn for teaching to take place

    D. The author will be fired

DIRECTIONS: Read the following paragraph and answer the questions that follow.

Mr. Smith gave instructions for the painting to be hung on the wall. And then it leaped forth before his eyes: the little cottages on the river, the white clouds floating over the valley, and the green of the towering mountain ranges that were seen in the distance. The painting was so vivid that it seemed almost real. Mr. Smith was now absolutely certain that the painting had been worth the money.

(Average) (Skill 8.1)

35. **What is the main idea of this passage?**

    A. The painting that Mr. Smith purchased was expensive

    B. Mr. Smith purchased a painting

    C. Mr. Smith was pleased with the quality of the painting he had purchased

    D. The painting depicted cottages and valleys

(Average) (Skill 8.2)

36. **What does the author mean by the expression "it leaped forth before his eyes"?**

    A. The painting fell off the wall

    B. The painting appeared so real it was almost three-dimensional

    C. The painting struck Mr. Smith in the face

    D. Mr. Smith was hallucinating

(Average) (Skill 9.2)

37. **What is the meaning of the word "vivid" in the third sentence?**

    A. Lifelike

    B. Dark

    C. Expensive

    D. Big

(Rigorous) (Skill 9.5)

38. **The author's purpose is to:**

    A. Inform

    B. Entertain

    C. Persuade

    D. Narrate

(Rigorous) (Skill 8.3)

39. **Is this passage biased?**

    A. Yes

    B. No

(Rigorous) (Skill 8.1)

40. **From the last sentence, one can infer that:**

    A. The painting was expensive

    B. The painting was cheap

    C. Mr. Smith was considering purchasing the painting

    D. Mr. Smith thought the painting was too expensive and decided not to purchase it

Answer Key: Reading Test

1. C	11. A	21. D	31. A
2. D	12. C	22. D	32. D
3. B	13. A	23. C	33. B
4. C	14. A	24. C	34. A
5. B	15. D	25. A	35. C
6. B	16. C	26. D	36. B
7. A	17. D	27. D	37. A
8. A	18. A	28. C	38. D
9. B	19. B	29. D	39. B
10. B	20. C	30. B	40. A

Rigor Table: Reading Test

RIGOR TABLE	
Rigor level	Questions
Easy 20%	2, 12, 13, 14, 15, 23, 24, 25
Average 40%	1, 3, 4, 11, 18, 19, 20, 22, 26, 27, 28, 30, 32, 35, 36, 37
Rigorous 40%	5, 6, 7, 8, 9, 10, 16, 17, 21, 29, 31, 33, 34, 38, 39, 40

Reading Test with Rationales

DIRECTIONS: Read the following passage and answer the questions that follow.

This writer has often been asked to tutor hospitalized children with cystic fibrosis. While undergoing all the precautionary measures to see these children (for example, scrubbing thoroughly and donning a face mask and sterile gown), she has wondered why parents subject these children to the pressures of schooling and trying to catch up on what they have missed because of hospitalization, which is a normal part of cystic fibrosis patients' lives. These children undergo so many tortuous treatments a day that it seems cruel to expect them to learn as normal children do, especially when their life expectancies are so short.

(Average) (Skill 8.1)
1. **What is the main idea of this passage?**

    A. There is a lot of preparation involved in visiting a patient with cystic fibrosis

    B. Children with cystic fibrosis are incapable of living normal lives

    C. Certain concessions should be made for children with cystic fibrosis

    D. Children with cystic fibrosis die young

    Answer: C. Certain concessions should be made for children with cystic fibrosis

    The author states that she wonders "why parents subject these children to the pressures of schooling," and that "it seems cruel to expect them to learn as normal children do." In making these statements, she seems to express the belief that these children should not have to do everything that "normal" children do.

They have enough to deal with—their illness itself.

(Easy) (Skill 8.2)
2. **How is the author so familiar with the procedures used when visiting a child with cystic fibrosis?**

    A. She has read about it

    B. She works in a hospital

    C. She is the parent of one

    D. She often tutors them

    Answer: D. She often tutors them

    The writer states this fact in the opening sentence as a supporting detail.

(Average) (Skill 8.3)
3. **What is meant by the word "precautionary" in the second sentence?**

    A. Careful

    B. Protective

    C. Medical

    D. Sterilizing

    Answer: B. Protective

    Details such as "sterilized gown" and "scrubbing thoroughly" help readers understand the meaning of the word "precautionary" in this context.

(Average) (Skill 9.5)

4. **What is the author's purpose?**

   A. To inform

   B. To entertain

   C. To describe

   D. To narrate

   Answer: C. To describe

   This author is simply describing her experience in working with children with cystic fibrosis.

(Rigorous) (Skill 9.5)

5. **What type of organizational pattern does the author use?**

   A. Classification

   B. Example, clarification, and definition

   C. Comparison and contrast

   D. Cause and effect

   Answer: B. Example, clarification, and definition

   The author mentions tutoring children with cystic fibrosis in her opening sentence and goes on to explain and elaborate on her main idea. She focuses extensively on how little time the children have due to hospitalization and a shortened life span.

(Rigorous) (Skill 8.4)

6. **The author states that it is "cruel" to expect children with cystic fibrosis to learn as "normal" children do. Is this a fact or an opinion?**

   A. Fact

   B. Opinion

   Answer: B. Opinion

   The fact that she states that it "seems" cruel indicates that there is no evidence to support this belief.

(Rigorous) (Skill 8.3)

7. **Is there evidence of bias in this paragraph?**

   A. Yes

   B. No

   Answer: A. Yes

   The writer clearly feels sorry for these children, and her writing reflects these personal feelings.

(Rigorous) (Skill 9.2)

8. **What is the author's tone?**

   A. Sympathetic

   B. Cruel

   C. Disbelieving

   D. Cheerful

   Answer: A. Sympathetic

   The author states that "it seems cruel to expect them to learn as normal children do," thereby indicating that she feels sorry for them.

(Rigorous) (Skill 9.3)

9. **What organizational structure is used in the last sentence of this passage?**

    A. Addition

    B. Summary

    C. Example

    D. Comparison and contrast

Answer: B. Summary

In mentioning that their life expectancies are short, she is reiterating her point that it is cruel to expect them to learn as other children do.

(Rigorous) (Skill 9.5)

10. **Is the author's argument about schooling children with cystic fibrosis valid or invalid?**

    A. Valid

    B. Invalid

Answer: B. Invalid

Even though the writer's argument may make good sense to many readers, it is biased and is not supported by any concrete facts or evidence.

DIRECTIONS: Read the following passage and answer the questions that follow.

Disciplinary practices have been found to affect diverse areas of child development such as moral values, obedience to authority, and performance at school. Even though the dictionary has a specific definition for the word "discipline," the concept is still open to interpretation by people of different cultures.

There are four types of disciplinary styles: assertion of power, withdrawal of love, reasoning, and permissiveness. Assertion of power involves the use of force to discourage unwanted behavior. Withdrawal of love involves making the love of a parent or authority figure a condition of a child's good behavior. Reasoning involves persuading a child to behave one way rather than another. Permissiveness involves allowing children to do as they please and face the consequences of their actions.

(Average) (Skill 8.2)

11. **What is the main idea of this passage?**

    A. Different people have different ideas of what discipline is

    B. Permissiveness is the most widely used disciplinary style

    C. Most people agree on their definition of discipline

    D. There are four disciplinary styles

Answer: A. Different people have different ideas of what discipline is

Choice C is not true; in fact, the passage states the opposite. Choice B could be true, but the passages does not give any evidence to support this. Choice D is one of the many facts listed in the passage, not the main idea.

(Easy) (Skill 10.4)

12. **Name the four types of disciplinary styles.**

    A. Reasoning, power assertion, morality, and permissiveness

    B. Morality, reasoning, permissiveness, and withdrawal of love

    C. Withdrawal of love, permissiveness, assertion of power, and reasoning

    D. Permissiveness, morality, reasoning, and power assertion

    Answer: C. Withdrawal of love, permissiveness, assertion of power, and reasoning

    This supporting detail is directly stated in the second paragraph.

(Easy) (Skill 10.2)

13. **What does the technique of reasoning involve?**

    A. Persuading children to behave in a certain way

    B. Allowing children to do as they please

    C. Using force to discourage unwanted behavior

    D. Making love a condition of good behavior

    Answer: A. Persuading children to behave in a certain way

    This supporting fact is directly stated in the second paragraph.

(Easy) (Skill 10.1)

14. **What is the meaning of the word "diverse" in the first sentence?**

    A. Many

    B. Related to children

    C. Disciplinary

    D. Moral

    Answer: A. Many

    Any of the other choices would be redundant in this sentence, and none are correct definitions of the word "diverse."

(Easy) (Skill 9.5)

15. **What is the author's purpose in writing this passage?**

    A. To describe

    B. To narrate

    C. To entertain

    D. To inform

    Answer: D. To inform

    The author is providing the reader with information about disciplinary practices.

(Rigorous) (Skill 9.3)

16. **What is the overall organizational pattern of this passage?**

    A. Statement support

    B. Cause and effect

    C. Classification

    D. Summary

Answer: C. Classification

The author has taken a subject, in this case the subject of discipline, and developed it point by point by stating the general category and then explaining its related styles.

(Rigorous) (Skill 9.3)

17. **What organizational structure is used in the first sentence of the second paragraph?**

    A. Addition

    B. Location/spatial order

    C. Clarification

    D. Example

    Answer: D. Example

    The author states the types of disciplinary styles and then gives an example of each.

(Average) (Skill 8.4)

18. **The author states that "assertion of power involves the use of force to discourage unwanted behavior." Is this a fact or an opinion?**

    A. Fact

    B. Opinion

    Answer: A. Fact

    The author is stating an established definition of assertion of power.

(Average) (Skill 8.3)

19. **Is this passage biased?**

    A. Yes

    B. No

    Answer: B. No

    A reader could research discipline and find this information.

(Average) (Skill 9.2)

20. **What is the author's tone?**

    A. Disbelieving

    B. Angry

    C. Informative

    D. Optimistic

    Answer: C. Informative

    The author appears to simply be stating facts.

(Rigorous) (Skill 8.1)

21. **From reading this passage we can conclude that:**

    A. The author is a teacher

    B. The author has many children

    C. The author has written a book about discipline

    D. The author has done research on discipline

    Answer: D. The author has done research on discipline

    Given all the facts mentioned in the passage, this is the only inference one can make. The other answers, while possibly true statements about the author, are not supported by any evidence in the content or style of the passage.

DIRECTIONS: Read the following passage and answer the questions that follow.

One of the most difficult problems plaguing American education is the assessment of teachers. No one denies that teachers should be answerable for what they do, but what exactly does that mean? The *Oxford American Dictionary* defines accountability as the obligation to give a reckoning or explanation for one's actions.

Do students have to learn for teaching to have taken place? Historically, teaching has not been defined in this restrictive manner; teachers were thought to be responsible for the quantity and quality of material covered and for the way in which it was presented. However, some definitions of teaching now imply that students must learn in order for teaching to have taken place.

As a teacher who tries my best to keep current on all the latest teaching strategies, I believe that those teachers who do not bother even to pick up an educational journal every once in a while should be kept under close watch. There are many teachers out there who have been teaching for decades and refuse to change their ways even if research has proven that their methods are outdated and ineffective. There is no place in the profession of teaching for these types of individuals. It is time that the American educational system clean house, for the sake of our children.

(Average) (Skill 8.2)

22. **What is the main idea of the passage?**

    A. Teachers should not be answerable for what they do

    B. Teachers who do not do their job should be fired

    C. The author is a good teacher

    D. Assessment of teachers is a serious problem in society today

    Answer: D. Assessment of teachers is a serious problem in society today

    Most of the passage is dedicated to elaborating on why teacher assessment is such a problem.

(Easy) (Skill 8.1)

23. **The author states that teacher assessment is a problem for:**

    A. Elementary schools

    B. Secondary schools

    C. American education

    D. Families

    Answer: C. American education

    This fact is directly stated in the first paragraph.

(Easy) (Skill 8.1)

24. **Where does the author get her definition of "accountability?"**

    A. *Webster's Dictionary*

    B. *Encyclopedia Britannica*

    C. *The Oxford American Dictionary*

    D. *World Book Encyclopedia*

Answer: C. *The Oxford American Dictionary*

The supporting details in the first paragraph make this definition clear.

(Easy) (Skill 8.2)

25. **What is meant by the word "plaguing" in the first sentence?**

    A. Causing problems

    B. Causing illness

    C. Causing anger

    D. Causing failure

    Answer: A. Causing problems

    Other words in the first sentence, such as "difficult" and "problems," help define "plaguing" in this context.

(Average) (Skill 8.2)

26. **What is the meaning of the word "reckoning" in the third sentence?**

    A. Thought

    B. Answer

    C. Obligation

    D. Explanation

    Answer: D. Explanation

    The meaning of this word is directly stated in the same sentence.

(Average) (Skill 9.5)

27. **What is the author's purpose in writing this?**

    A. To entertain

    B. To narrate

    C. To describe

    D. To persuade

    Answer: D. To persuade

    The majority of the statements in this passage are opinions seemingly intended to convince the reader that teachers who are lazy or who do not keep current should be fired.

(Average) (Skill 9.3)

28. **What is the author's overall organizational pattern?**

    A. Classification

    B. Cause and effect

    C. Definition

    D. Comparison and contrast

    Answer: C. Definition

    The author identifies teacher assessment as a problem and spends the rest of the passage defining why it is considered a problem.

(Rigorous) (Skill 9.3)

29. **What is the organizational pattern of the second paragraph?**

A. Cause and effect

B. Classification

C. Addition

D. Example, clarification, and definition

Answer: D. Example, clarification, and definition

The author states a question in the first paragraph. The second paragraph explains and expands upon this question.

(Average) (Skill 8.4)

30. **"Teachers who do not keep current on educational trends should be fired." Is this a fact or an opinion?**

A. Fact

B. Opinion

Answer: B. Opinion

There may be those who can be good teachers by using old methods.

(Rigorous) (Skill 8.3)

31. **Is there evidence of bias in this passage?**

A. Yes

B. No

Answer: A. Yes

The entire third paragraph is the author's opinion on the matter, with no supporting facts or examples.

(Average) (Skill 9.2)

32. **The author's tone is one of:**

A. Disbelief

B. Excitement

C. Support

D. Concern

Answer: D. Concern

The author appears concerned with the future of education.

(Rigorous) (Skill 9.4)

33. **Is the author's argument valid?**

A. Yes

B. No

Answer: B. No

In the third paragraph, the author appears to be resentful of lazy teachers.

(Rigorous) (Skill 8.1)

34. **From the passage, one can infer that:**

A. The author considers herself a good teacher

B. Poor teachers will be fired

C. Students have to learn for teaching to take place

D. The author will be fired

Answer: A. The author considers herself a good teacher

The first sentence of the third paragraph alludes to this.

DIRECTIONS: Read the following paragraph and answer the questions that follow.

Mr. Smith gave instructions for the painting to be hung on the wall. And then it leaped forth before his eyes: the little cottages on the river, the white clouds floating over the valley, and the green of the towering mountain ranges that were seen in the distance. The painting was so vivid that it seemed almost real. Mr. Smith was now absolutely certain that the painting had been worth the money.

(Average) (Skill 8.1)

35. **What is the main idea of this passage?**

    A. The painting that Mr. Smith purchased was expensive

    B. Mr. Smith purchased a painting

    C. Mr. Smith was pleased with the quality of the painting he had purchased

    D. The painting depicted cottages and valleys

    Answer: C. Mr. Smith was pleased with the quality of the painting he had purchased

    Every sentence in the paragraph alludes to this fact.

(Average) (Skill 8.2)

36. **What does the author mean by the expression "it leaped forth before his eyes"?**

    A. The painting fell off the wall

    B. The painting appeared so real it was almost three-dimensional

    C. The painting struck Mr. Smith in the face

    D. Mr. Smith was hallucinating

Answer: B. The painting appeared so real it was almost three-dimensional

This is almost directly stated in the third sentence.

(Average) (Skill 9.2)

37. **What is the meaning of the word "vivid" in the third sentence?**

    A. Lifelike

    B. Dark

    C. Expensive

    D. Big

Answer: A. Lifelike

This idea is reinforced by the second half of the same sentence.

(Rigorous) (Skill 9.5)

38. **The author's purpose is to:**

    A. Inform

    B. Entertain

    C. Persuade

    D. Narrate

Answer: D. Narrate

The author is simply narrating or telling the story of Mr. Smith and his painting.

(Rigorous) (Skill 8.3)

39. **Is this passage biased?**

   A. Yes

   B. No

   Answer: B. No

   The author appears to be simply relating what happened when Mr. Smith had his new painting hung on the wall.

(Rigorous) (Skill 8.1)

40. **From the last sentence, one can infer that:**

   A. The painting was expensive

   B. The painting was cheap

   C. Mr. Smith was considering purchasing the painting

   D. Mr. Smith thought the painting was too expensive and decided not to purchase it

   Answer: A. The painting was expensive

   The correct answer is A. Choice B is incorrect because, had the painting been cheap, chances are that Mr. Smith would not have considered his purchase. Choices C and D are ruled out by the fact that the painting had already been purchased, as is clear in the phrase "…the painting had been worth the money."

CONSTRUCTED RESPONSE WRITING PREVIEW

After the sample test questions conclude, you will be asked to write an essay of your own. The testing people will present you with what is known as a test-prompt, question, situation, or passage, upon which you will be asked to write an opinion.

Assert yourself in a thesis statement. Take a stance in which you believe; do not worry if you are right or wrong. This test does not evaluate you or judge you on your opinion. It judges you on how well and confidently you can express your opinion. So you need to believe in yourself, and express yourself with conviction.

Second, you need to convey *why* you feel the way you do. A really good essay goes beyond merely asserting a belief: it offers a variety of reasons in support of this belief.

These reasons flow as naturally from the pen as if you were explaining to a friend why, for instance, you had decided to become a teacher in the first place—or any key decision in your life that matters. Why did you choose teaching? Why the certain specialty within teaching that you are now seeking? What are your greatest hopes from the career in that specialty (the subject and age group)? You can see that the reasons lead to more specific levels of inquiry.

In keeping with the above, include concrete details that readers can visualize to help support your reasons; these are known as examples.

Again, to liken essay writing to conversation, you ought to be a friendly neighbor. Try to find some good in the viewpoint opposing yours; it may come naturally to the person sitting across from you. You ought to include the merits of the opposite viewpoint in the body of your essay.

Overall, however, you will want to conclude by restating your personal conviction, giving it a new and resounding emphasis.

Sample Question Prompt

Topic: Classroom safety

In the past few years, we have seen a rise in the sudden eruption of violence in secondary schools, leading to permanent trauma and loss of life. Given the copycat nature of this situation, should students in public secondary schools be submitted to random searches?

While an imperfect instrument, search would benefit the students, the schools, and the community. Searches can benefit the school's students as a whole. They can contribute to the safety of the student group in the most literal sense of this word. Students should not feel they are entering a high-risk situation when they attend school, but rather feel free to immerse themselves in learning without fear or nervousness. In order for this to happen, the students must feel that someone has instituted safeguards for them. If the whole student body is routinely, or randomly, searched as they enter the building through a backpack or belongings search, real and felt security will come into play. It will then affect both the real safely level of the student community, and their comfort level—and level of trust.

Others to benefit from these searches are the teachers and administrators themselves. It is preposterous to think of these nurturing adults as in the front line of fire. Nor should the leaders of the school in any way be "set against" the students in this battle to establish a safe environment: for the truth is that the safety is something all crave, and it is therefore imperative that such searches as are beneficial be carried out by security people—such as police officers—from outside the school, rather than by the administration or the teachers themselves, whose bond with students is implicitly one of mutual trust. All students must be deemed alike in school policy eyes, for the true community to function.

This last point highlights a possible drawback of searches. If student searches go too far, they break down the sense of community by creating divisiveness; then their very mission of community healing has failed. If they are too vigorously pursued in a sort of witch-hunt style, causing a mob vigilantism to arise within the student body, this could happen. Worse, certain students could get singled out or targeted unfairly, or certain groups within the school become the unjustifiable victims of a restless search. This kind of treatment might engender the very ostracism that community-building struggles to discourage; or might simply be unreasonably deplorable.

Hence, searches must be applied equally to all, by an outside force, presumably a police force. They must be explained to the students as a system for enforcing the peace deserved by all.

Analysis of Essay

When you approach the topic of the *Sample Question Prompt,* your job is to adopt a position toward it. Your position is your point of view on the matter presented to you in the *Question Stem.* You cannot simply repeat the fact contained within the stem; you must assert an opinion that is reasonable and comes naturally to you on the matter under consideration. Be sure to stick with the topic raised by the *Question Stem,* which the testing people have provided to stimulate a response they can compare in all of their test-takers, who will all respond to the same *prompt.*

In the example above, it is the opinion of our author that searches are a good idea. But he does not stop at that. A more accurate statement of the author's position would be: "Searches are a good idea because they promote and restore school community."

One way we can test this restatement of the author's position is by looking at how he suggests the searches be conducted and at the problems he concedes might arise with searches. All of these points have to do with potential conflict and division in the community, teacher against student or student against student. The author wants searches to strengthen, not weaken, school community.

When you choose a position, and make your point known by strongly asserting it, go beyond just saying what you think: say why you think your viewpoint would turn things around for the better.

It is especially convincing for the reader to see the bright light at the end of the tunnel. If you can suggest the illumination you envision in detail, readers will want to go your way!

Most of all, write with confidence and conviction, and let one thought lead to another. Remember to include your assertion and two to three reasons that support your idea. Also remember to integrate a concession to the other side. Wrap up strongly by reasserting the merit of your idea.

Constructed Response Structure Summary

1. Assert your thesis

2. Support your argument with two or three reasons

3. Make a concession to the "other side"

4. Wrap up strongly with a thesis reassertion

Interested in dual certification?

XAMonline offers over 20+ FTCE study guides which are aligned to current standards and provide a comprehensive review of the core test content. Want certification success on your first exam? Trust XAMonline's study guides to help you succeed!

FTCE Series:

- **Educational Media Specialist PK-12**
  978-1-58197-578-9
- **Middle Grades General Science 5-9**
  978-1-60787-008-1
- **Middle Grades Social Science 5-9**
  978-1-60787-010-4
- **Exceptional Education Ed. K-12**
  978-1-60787-473-7
- **Guidance and Counseling PK-12**
  978-1-58197-586-4
- **Prekindergarten/Primary PK-3**
  978-1-60787-386-0
- **FELE Florida Education Leadership**
  978-1-60787-001-2
- **Elementary Education K–6**
  978-1-60787-506-2
- **Middle Grades English 5-9**
  978-1-58197-597-0
- **Middle Grades Math 5-9**
  978-1-60787-464-5
- **Physical Education K-12**
  978-1-58197-616-8

- **General Knowledge Test**
  978-1-60787-533-8
- **Mathematics 6–12**
  978-1-60787-383-9
- **Professional Education**
  978-1-60787-474-4
- **Social Science 6–12**
  978-1-60787-381-5
- **English 6-12**
  978-1-60787-463-8
- **ESOL K–12**
  978-1-60787-530-7
- **Biology 6-12**
  978-1-58197-689-2
- **Chemistry 6-12**
  978-1-58197-046-3
- **Physics 6-12**
  978-1-58197-044-9
- **Reading K-12**
  978-1-58197-659-5
- **FTCE Spanish K-12**
  978-1-60787-093-7

Don't see your test? Visit our website: www.xamonline.com

CPSIA information can be obtained
at www.ICGtesting.com
Printed in the USA
BVOW07s2026010218
506931BV00043B/345/P